STUDIES IN PLAY AND GAMES

A CHILDREN'S GAMES ANTHOLOGY

Studies in Folklore and Anthropology

Brian Sutton-Smith, Editor

ARNO PRESS

A New York Times Company

New York — 1976

GN
454
C45

Editorial Supervision: SHEILA MEHLMAN

——◆——

Reprint Edition 1976 by Arno Press Inc.

Copyright © 1976 by Arno Press Inc.

STUDIES IN PLAY AND GAMES
ISBN for complete set: 0-405-07912-5
See last pages of this volume for titles.

Manufactured in the United States of America

Publisher's Note: This book has been reproduced
from the best available copies.

——◆——

Library of Congress Cataloging in Publication Data
Main entry under title:

A Children's games anthology.

    (Studies in play and games)
    Includes bibliographical references.
    1. Games, Primitive—Addresses, essays, lectures.
2. Play—Addresses, essays, lectures. I. Sutton-Smith,
Brian. II. Series.
GN454.C45   398'.355   75-35080
ISBN 0-405-07928-1

ACKNOWLEDGEMENTS

Aufenanger, H., A CHILDREN'S ARROW-THROWER IN THE CENTRAL HIGHLANDS OF NEW GUINEA in *Anthropos,* Vol. 56, 1961 (p. 633) is reprinted by permission of *Anthropos.*
Aufenanger, H., CHILDREN'S GAMES AND ENTERTAINMENTS AMONG THE KUMNGO TRIBE IN CENTRAL NEW GUINEA in *Anthropos,* Vol. 53, 1958 (pp. 575-584) is reprinted by permission of *Anthropos.*

SOME ABORIGINAL CHILDREN'S GAMES by R. M. Berndt and SOME CHILDREN'S GAMES FROM TANNA, NEW HEBRIDES by W. Watt are reprinted by permission of *Mankind.*

PASTIMES OF MAORI CHILDREN by Elsdon Best in the *New Zealand Journal of Science and Technology,* Vol. 5, No. 5, 1922 is reprinted by permission of the Science Information Division of the Department of Scientific and Industrial Research, Wellington, New Zealand.

FOUR GAMES OF TAG FROM INDIA by Paul G. Brewster and BALL BOUNCING CUSTOMS AND RHYMES IN AUSTRALIA by Dorothy Howard are reprinted by permission of the Folklore Institute, Indiana University.

JOHNNY ON THE PONY by Paul G. Brewster is reprinted by permission of the New York Folklore Society, The Farmers' Museum, Cooperstown, New York.

SOME UNUSUAL FORMS OF "HOPSCOTCH" by Paul G. Brewster and THE JUGOSLAV CHILDREN'S GAME *MOST* by Jelena Milojković-Djurić are reprinted by permission of *Southern Folklore Quarterly.*

SOME GAMES OF ARIKARA CHILDREN by Melvin R. Gilmore is reprinted by permission of the Museum of the American Indian.

GOOD FRIDAY SKIPPING by Stanley Godman and MARBLE GAMES OF AUSTRALIAN CHILDREN by Dorothy Howard are reprinted by permission of *Folklore.*

AUSTRALIAN CHILDREN'S GAMES by Alfred C. Haddon is reprinted by permission of *Nature.*

BABIES' RATTLES FROM 2600 B.C. by Richard A. Martin is reprinted by permission of the Field Museum of Natural History.

CONTENTS

Culin, Stewart
STREET GAMES OF BOYS IN BROOKLYN, N. Y. (Reprinted from
Journal of American Folk-Lore, Vol. IV, 1891, pp. 221-237). Boston, 1891

De La Cruz, Beato A.
AKLAN SUPERSTITIONS ABOUT TOYS (Reprinted from *Philippine
Magazine,* Vol. 30, June, 1933, p. 30). Manila, 1933

Dorsey, J. Owen
GAMES OF TETON DAKOTA CHILDREN (Reprinted from *American
Anthropologist,* Vol. IV, No. 4, October, 1891, pp. 329-345). Washington, D.C.,
1891

Gilmore, Melvin R.
SOME GAMES OF ARIKARA CHILDREN (Reprinted from *Indian Notes,*
Vol. III, No. 1, January, 1926, pp. 9-12). New York, 1926

Godman, Stanley
GOOD FRIDAY SKIPPING (Reprinted from *Folklore,* Vol. 67, No. 3, 1956
(pp. 171-174). London, 1956

[Haddon, Alfred C.]
AUSTRALIAN CHILDREN'S GAMES (Reprinted from *Nature,* Vol. LXVI,
August 14, 1902, pp. 380-381). London, 1902

[Haddon, Alfred C.]
GAMES AND TOYS (Reprinted from *Reports of the Cambridge Anthropological
Expedition To Torres Straits, Vol. IV: Arts and Crafts,* pp. 312-314). Cambridge,
England, 1912

Howard, Dorothy
BALL BOUNCING CUSTOMS AND RHYMES IN AUSTRALIA (Reprinted
from *Midwest Folklore,* Vol. IX, No. 2, 1959, pp. 77-87). Bloomington, Indiana,
1959

Howard, Dorothy
MARBLE GAMES OF AUSTRALIAN CHILDREN (Reprinted from *Folklore,*
Vol. 71, 1960, pp. 165-179). London, 1960

Im Thurn, E. F., editor
INDIAN CHILDREN'S GAMES (Reprinted from *Timehri,* Vol. 3, 1884,
pp. 147-148). Demerara, British Guiana, 1884

Lambert, H. E.
A NOTE ON CHILDREN'S PASTIMES (Reprinted from *Swahili,* Vol. 30,
1959 (pp. 74-78). Arusha, Tanganyika, 1959

Martin, Richard A.
BABIES' RATTLES FROM 2600 B.C. AND OTHER ANCIENT TOYS
(Reprinted from *Field Museum News,* Vol. 8, No. 8, August, 1937, p. 5).
Chicago, 1937

Milojković-Djurić, Jelena
THE JUGOSLAV CHILDREN'S GAME *MOST* AND SOME SCANDINAVIAN
PARALLELS (Reprinted from *Southern Folklore Quarterly,* Vol. 24, No. 3,
1960, pp. 226-234). Gainesville, Florida, 1960

Mishra, Dinesh
RECREATION OF BAIGA CHILDREN (Reprinted from *Vanyajati,* Vol. 6,
No. 2, 1958, pp. 70-73). New Delhi, 1958

Mistry, Dhan K.
THE INDIAN CHILD AND HIS PLAY [Parts I and II] (Reprinted from
Sociological Bulletin, Vol. 8, No. 1, 1959, pp. 86-96 and Vol. 9, No. 2, 1960,
pp. 48-55). Delhi, India, 1959-1960

Monroe, Will Seymour
COUNTING-OUT RHYMES OF CHILDREN (Reprinted from *American
Anthropologist,* New Series, Vol. 6, 1904, pp. 46-50). Washington, D.C., 1904

Sutton-Smith, Brian
THE GAME RHYMES OF NEW ZEALAND CHILDREN (Reprinted from
Western Folklore, Vol. XII, 1953, pp. 14-24). Berkeley, 1953

Sutton-Smith, Brian
THE MEETING OF MAORI AND EUROPEAN CULTURES AND ITS
EFFECTS UPON THE UNORGANIZED GAMES OF MAORI CHILDREN
(Reprinted from *Journal of the Polynesian Society,* Vol. 60, 1951, pp. 93-107).
Wellington, New Zealand, 1951

Sutton-Smith, Brian
PSYCHOLOGY OF CHILDLORE: The Triviality Barrier (Reprinted from
Western Folklore, Vol. XXIX, No. 1, January, 1970, pp. 1-8). Berkeley, 1970

Watt, W.
SOME CHILDREN'S GAMES FROM TANNA, NEW HEBRIDES, edited by
A. Capell (Reprinted from *Mankind,* Vol. 3, No. 9, July, 1946, pp. 261-264).
Sydney, Australia, 1946

A CHILDREN'S ARROW-THROWER
IN THE
CENTRAL HIGHLANDS
OF NEW GUINEA

H[enry] Aufenanger

A Children's Arrow-thrower in the Central Highlands of New Guinea. – The children of different tribes in the Highlands (of the Vaugla, the Kulxkane etc.) divert themselves by catapulting toy arrows which consist of the thick middle *indaun* grass rib. The children, usually young boys, break off the upper part of a grass blade, and throw it away. The remaining lower part of the blade is now about 8 inches long. The two halves are severed from the bottom part of the middle rib on both sides of the latter almost half the length of the rib. There the two halves of the blade are still connected with the middle rib and the blade. Now the two loose ends of the blade are wound around the index finger of the left hand. They are kept in position by pressing the middle finger of the left hand against the index. The naked part of the middle rib lies on the left hand index, while the thumb of the same hand rests lightly on the remaining blade. Then the boy inserts his right hand index underneath the blade and behind the left hand index. Fast pressure with the right hand index tears the arrow, i. e. the middle rib, from the remaining parts of the blade and sends it towards its aim or just into the air. The boys shoot at one another with these toy arrows or at things. Since there is any amount of *indaun* grass available, this game may be continued for a long time.

Another way of catapulting an *indaun* grass rib is the following : The two halves of the blade are torn from the middle rib as described above, but the two ends of the blade are not wound around the index. They are knotted together and the thumb of the right hand is laid in the loop thus formed. At the same time the tip of the right hand index rests on the end point of the middle rib. Now the boy jerks his arm forwards into the air, releasing at the same moment his index from the rib, which flies away, tearing off those parts of the blade which were still connected with the rib.

This children's device seems very simple and unimportant, but could not this or another similar gadget have given the clue for the manufacturing of the first spear-thrower?

H. AUFENANGER.

CHILDREN'S GAMES AND ENTERTAINMENTS AMONG THE KUMNGO TRIBE IN CENTRAL NEW GUINEA

Heinrich Aufenanger

Children's Games and Entertainments among the Kumngo Tribe in Central New Guinea

By Heinrich Aufenanger *

Contents:

Introduction: habitat, origin, and division of the Kumngo tribe

The Kumngo people, who speak a dialect of the Nondugl-Banz language[1], live on the right side of the Wahgi River. About five hours' walk in a westerly direction, on the same side of the river, lies the Government station and Catholic mission of Minj. Towards the east, across the river, we find Kondiu, where the Catholic mission conducts a standard school and a catechist school. The area where the Kumngo live is known as Kup.

The story of how the Kumngo tribe came into existence goes as follows:

Komuna vei kin Kumump[2] tendagl vondin.   *Ndanden peng*
At first true we at Kumump we came into existence. Our father's head

yiglamp pam. Mene kamber pam. Embe pange, ambigl ende vo, kam.
human it was. Below snake it was. So as it was, girl one coming, she saw.

Kanmbe, tau tu ngom. Nom. Ngo pagilmbe, kegl
Seeing banana bringing she gave. He ate. Giving when she had put, removing

pum. Pambe, ala vom. Tau[3] ende tsi tum.
she went. When she had slept, again she came. Banana one taking she brought.

---

* The author is grateful to J. E. Mertz for revising the English form of the article.

[1] See H. Aufenanger, Vokabular und Grammatik der Nondugl-Sprache in Zentral-Neuguinea. MBA Vol. 5, Posieux (Freiburg), Schweiz 1953. — L. J. Luzbetak, The Middle Wahgi Dialects. Vol. I, Banz Grammar. Banz 1954.

[2] Kumump is a grassy stretch of land near the Wahgi river, to the north of Kup.

[3] *Tau* is the name for a banana. In Nondugl and Banz it is called *kamp*.

Embe tsi   tumbe,   kam,   kamber na pam. Ngagl mom. Ye ngagl
So   taking when she brought, she saw, snake   not was.   Child it was. Male child

pam. To   kon   to tsi   pim [4]. *Tsi   Nggagul* [5] *pum.   Pa   van*
was. Filling netbag in taking she went. Taking Nggage ugl she went. Lying walking

mondil.   Yiglamp ku   nggandip.   Ougl   mbalnambigl
the two of them were. Men   stones they heated. Leaves the two of them were

ngang ambigl pundil.   Ambigl ngang ka   kam.
going to break off, boy   girl   the two of them went. Girl   boy   good she saw.

Punal   ni   pim.   Elep   ougl   mbarndil.
I shall go saying she knew. The two of them leaves the two of them broke off.

Ndam   mam: "Nim kamber punal   ni   pizin?"   pa nindil.
Her father her mother: "You snake   I shall go saying do you know?" the two of

"Na punal ni   pis,"   pa nim. Kegl   ya   vondil.
them said. "I   shall go saying I know", she said. Removing hither the two of them

Ya   vo,   Kumump vondil.   "Na malnan tseim, kegl
came. Hither coming, to Kumump the two came. "My land my it lies, removing we

punambigl,"   pa nim. Embe ninge,   kegl   vondil.   Kumump
two shall go", he said. So   when he had said, removing the two came. At Kumump

vo   mondil.   Ngagl kangindil.
arriving the two remained. Children the two begot.

Free translation: In the very beginning we originated at Kumump. The head
of our first ancestor was that of a man; the rest of his body was that of a snake. A girl
came and saw him. She offered him a big banana which he ate. She went away then, but
the next morning she came back and gave him another banana. Now she saw that the
snake-man had turned into a small boy. She put him into her netbag and took him to
Gage ugl. There they lived together. Once the people were heating stones for an earth
oven. The boy and the girl went to gather banana leaves. The girl fell in love with the
boy and wished to marry him. Her parents did not like it and they asked her: "Why?
Do you really want to marry that snake?" "Yes", she replied, "I do want to marry
him". So the two came to this side of the river and stayed at Kumump, which was the
property of the snake-man. Here they begot several children.

The name of this first ancestor of the Kumngo is not known. The six clans
of the Kumngo are called after the names of his six sons: *Mandekup; Nggelbi
ngaglim; Vive kanem; Korikup; Paua kanem; Kokup.*

1. Social Games

a) Hide and seek [6].

This game is called *ogil cre pandip,* i. e., they (the children) lie down
and hide. One of them kneels on the ground with both knees and covers his
face with both hands. Sometimes he lies flat on his stomach. The other children

---

[4] *Pim* here stands for *pum; i* and *u* may be interchanged.

[5] In the Chimbu language *Nggagul* is called *Gage ugl.* It lies opposite Kup.

[6] This game is played at Banz and at Bundi, and probably in other areas of
the Highlands as well.

withdraw from sight in the neighbouring grass, shrubs, etc. Then one of them sings out: *Ku!* Whereupon the seeker goes about searching the probable hiding places. While doing this he says: *Ku pā, ku pā. Ngunts kogl punum mo? Komil kogl punum mo?"* — *Ku* means stone, but in this connection *ku pā* has hardly any meaning. *Ngunts kogl punum mo* means: Did the *ngunts* lizard perhaps go thither? *Komil*, etc. means: Did the *komil* lizard perhaps go thither? When the seeker finds one of the hiding children he sings out: *Pā!* And thus he continues until all are found. After that the game is finished and another child may be assigned as the seeker.

b) *Anger kupan kondip*, "Clenching fists", is a guessing game. Two groups of players sit facing each other. A member of one group holds a small stone between his fingers and slaps his fist into the opened hand of each member of the opposite group in turn, leaving the small stone in the hand of one of them. The fists are always clenched again as soon as the players have gone through their motions, so that no one can see whether the stone has been transferred or not. Now one member of the first group must guess in whose hand the little stone is hidden. If he guesses correctly he has won the round and receives the stone, and the game begins again. If he guesses wrong, he must try again. To avoid cheating, the others have to open their hands also. Sometimes two children play this game. In that case one of them puts his right fist into the palm of his left hand, either transferring the stone or pretending to do so. Now the other child must point to the hand where he thinks the stone is hidden. If he guesses correctly a point is counted in his favor and he receives the stone for a new round. If not, a point is counted against him and he must guess again until he guesses correctly.

c) *Tsimp ambigl kegl pundip*, "Hopping on one leg" The children, usually boys, raise one foot and hold it with one hand. One of the children is appointed as watcher. The ones who join in the game say to him: *"Na tsimp ambigl vonal. Nim kan moglo."* "I shall hold my foot and come. You watch."

d) *Kai tontspa tondip*, "Snake running'. A number of children hold one another by the hand, forming a long chain. The one at one end of the chain stands still while the others run around him in a circle, wrapping themselves around him until the whole chain is wound on him as on a spool. Then they run around in the opposite direction, unwinding themselves again.

e) *Tugu tege ni pundip*. The children climb to the top of a little hill, and, half-standing, half-sitting, they slide down the slope. Sometimes this is done on flat ground as well.

f) *Ents peng gi bondip*, "Standing on one's head". The children clasp their hands over their heads, get down on the ground, and try to stand on their heads. Some of the children are able to bend their legs and straighten them again, or shake both feet in the air, etc.

g) *Bugl tunigtung pundip*, "Walking backwards". The faster and the farther a child is able to walk thus, the more credit he receives and the more laughter he arouses.

h) *Dugl kuvil pundip*, "Walking with eyes shut". Boys and girls try to walk towards a certain object or along a certain path, keeping their eyes closed. As with most of these games, rules are seldom known or observed strictly. The children will open their eyes to see whether they are still going in the right direction. They also like to show off by stretching out their arms and making strange movements with their arms and body.

i) Kiam tondip, "Making faces and grimaces". This game is played by both boys and girls. Eyes, ears, mouth, tongue, nose and hands are all brought into play to make their playmates laugh.

j) Gent bogl ga ezim, "Pretending to be beaten, and crying". One of the children pretends that he is being beaten by the other children and starts to cry. Thereupon the "parents" of the child come running with sticks and shout : *"Ye na vo na ngagl tonom?"* i. e., "who has beaten my child ?" The "culprits" run away and the "parents" take their child home. Sometimes the children just pretend to cry. They cover their faces with their hands, but look through their fingers and laugh.

k) Bere kare nindip, "They roll themselves about". The children choose a grassy slope where they lie flat on the ground and roll downhill.

l) Kegl pu, tau agl mondip, tau ugu nim, "Sled-riding on a slippery banana stalk". The children carry banana stalks to the top of a steep hill. There they sit or lie on them and slide downhill. Since the stalks are round, they roll over and buck the riders off, which only makes the fun all the greater.

m) Kirkova nim, "They tickle one another". While the children stand looking about and talking to one another, one will sneak around and seize another suddenly by the waist. The one thus surprised jumps and laughs. Later he will try to play the same trick on somebody else, or on the one who played the trick on him.

n) Tsimp nggagl vagizim, "They tickle the feet of the children". Boys and girls tickle one another without warning on the soles of the feet, using their fingers, a little stick, etc. All the others watch and enjoy the victim's reaction.

o) Moi kaikir nim. The children extend their arms at either side of them and turn round and round until they are giddy. Sometimes they hold a stick out horizontally in one hand to give themselves an additional swing.

p) Nogl minman kandip. The children look at themselves and their playmates reflected in a pool of water, and they have great fun especially when the reflection is distorted by small waves,. etc.

q) Nogl tu ndazim. Damming up a little stream is another source of entertainment for the children. They do not have to worry about how dirty they get. When there is enough water in the "weir", they tear down their dam and watch with great interest as the water rushes out.

r) Ngagl kembis tagl el nomin nguntse kangigl, aiyu vanmbigl. Little children hug one another and walk along this way. Boys do this with boys and girls with other girls, but one never sees a little boy embracing a little girl.

2. Fighting Games

a) *Nonts kapil bondip*, "Fighting with nettles". This game is very exciting and rather rough. The children (men and women too sometimes) form two opposing groups and strike one another with nettles, which are called *nonts*. Since the natives wear so little clothing, the game calls for a good deal of courage and endurance. After the fight the big blisters on their bodies tell the story vividly enough. Since the *nonts* nettles are regarded as very good medicine for all kinds of ailments, the children do not seem to care a great deal how much they suffer from the nettle strokes.

b) *Kuglang tondip*, "Spear-throwing". Boys enjoy throwing spears at such targets as trees, ferns, leaves, etc. One sometimes sees a tree trunk or branch with a number of spears sticking in it. These "spears" are usually just pointed sticks or reeds. When the latter are used, the game is called *ngamp kuglang ezim*.

c) *Kanagl ezim*, "Dancing with a spear". This is always a sight the natives enjoy immensely. The spear-dancer kicks his feet very rapidly backwards and upwards, almost touching his buttocks, but without advancing forward. Sometimes he runs forward a few steps, brandishing his spear continuously as though about to throw it. Then again he stands still, his whole body trembling and the spear quivering.

d) The following is a sort of *kuglang tondip* or spear game. Two boys sit about five feet apart facing each other. Each has a sweet potato lying on the ground in front of him. They take turns throwing at their opponent's potato with pointed sticks or bamboos, about two feet long or less. Whoever hits the other's potato wins a point for himself.

e) *Opo tondip*, "Shooting with bow and arrows". Even very small children like to shoot arrows, using toy bows. Older boys shoot at birds, rats or other objects, just as it strikes their fancy. The game often turns into a competition, the one who hits a certain target scoring a point for himself. In their games they usually use sticks or reeds for arrows, but when hunting they use pronged arrows or other arrows of good workmanship.

f) *Taglpa bondip*, "Foot-fight". This is a very rough game. Two opposing groups of boys kick one another, each side trying to make their opponents fall down. Sometimes several members of one side concentrate on one member of the opposite party, in which case his mates will rush to the rescue. Tears often flow, but nobody wants to miss the excitement of the game.

g) *Minmagl bondip*, "Fighting with sticks". This game does not seem to have any rules at all. The term is used for fighting with sticks between members of the same tribe.

h) *Nogl ndaglpa bondip*, "Water-fight". After a heavy rain, when puddles of water are left standing about, the children splash water on one another, using their feet for this purpose. After a water battle of this kind the youngsters are sometimes almost unrecognizable, being literally covered with mud. Boys and girls both play the game. The girls often draw the lower part of their little string dress through their legs and fasten it to their waist girdle at the back.

3. Hunting Games

Such activities as shooting birds, snaring and digging out rats, catching marsupials, looking for honey, robbing birds' nests and collecting bugs and caterpillars are always considered as much forms of play as of hunting. Moonlit nights are a favourite time for hunting games.

a) Kong tsimbil ezim, "Wild-pig hunt". One of the boys hides in a patch of grass or shrubbery. The others take their "spears" and go in search of the "wild pig". When they approach the spot where the "wild boar" is hiding, he jumps out and charges them, imitating the angry grunt of a pig. The hunters throw down their spears and run for their lives. When the "wild pig" has returned to his hiding place, the hunters will come back and attack in the same manner as before. After doing this several times they catch hold of the exhausted "pig" and carry it off to the fire. There they give it to one of the boys, saying: "*Nim kong*," "your pig".

b) Mboglngamp tondip, "Catching cockchafers". This is a real chase and there is much fun connected with it. These insects fly about in the evening during certain months. The children catch them while they fly low or when they land on the lower branches of trees and shrubs or in the grass. After being caught the insects are held captive in a bamboo or in the hand until roasted alive over a fire and eaten as a delicacy. To make the cockchafers come down where they can catch them, the children sing: "*Tsivil tsivil tagl*", or: "*Tsivil tsivil, tsivil tsivil.*" [7] "*Tsivil kogl pandil*" means: The two are mating. When they mate they can easily be caught.

c) Valpe tondip, "Bat-hunt". This again is a make-believe hunt in which other boys represent the bats. Two boys hold their hands together in such a way as to leave a space between them as a "bat trap". The other boys run around the trap, flapping their hands at their sides as though flying. From time to time one of the bats tries to fly through the trap, but the two boys lower their hands and the bat is caught. Thus, one bat after another is trapped and "killed". Then the two trappers, using the edge of their open hand as a knife, go through the motions of carving up the bats, saying meanwhile: "*El ye ende ngont, el ye ende ngont.*" "This one I give to one man, this one to another man." Then they distribute the heads of the bats, saying: "*Nim peng na nont*", "I eat your head." Suddenly one of the "dead bats" jumps up and shouts: "*Ye na na peng nonom?*" "Who is going to eat my head?" Then he beats his captors till they take to their heels and flee into the bush.

4. Athletic Contests

a) Ont mong konts tondip, "Batting the *konts* ball". There are two teams. A boy from one team throws the very hard fruit of the *kaui konts* tree towards the boys of the opposing team. These try to hit the "ball" with a piece of wood. If the first boy misses it, the second tries, then the third, etc. If they

---

[7] The children at Banz say: *til tal, til tal*, which seems to have the same meaning. *Tal* or *tar* means "two".

all miss it, the "ball" must be picked up and thrown (not hit) back to the other team. The other boys, in their turn, try to bat it back. The game may go on for hours.

b) The *konts* fruit is also used as a soccer ball. The children of one team try to kick it through the goal defended by the other team. The goal is simply two sticks stuck into the ground. There are scarcely any rules, but the goals are carefully counted.

c) *Nogl pandip*, "Swimming and bathing". This is a sport of quite recent origin. When we missionaries passed through here in 1934, not one native of the Highlands knew how to swim. Now quite a number of the younger ones swim, even the strong currents of the Wahgi River.

d) Two or more boys often race against each other. Frequently they choose different routes which meet at a certain point. The boy who arrives first usually teases the other because he *embiglim enim*, i. e., he was strong. Sometimes it is agreed that they will walk, not run. But when they are hidden from each other's view by trees, etc., they often cheat by running along that part of the road. The loser will tell the winner : "Well, you won because you ran."

e) *Ku kapil ezim*, "Throwing stones". The children enjoy throwing stones at almost any sort of target, even when they are tired of other games. Sometimes they simply throw without counting the hits, but on other occasions the one that hits the target scores a point and a competition is on.

5. Various Pastimes

a) *Tsimp tur tsindip*. In this game boys and girls plant their heels firmly on the ground and turn around in a complete circle so that their big toe describes a circle on the ground.

b) *Kon ezim*, "Making a netbag". This is a girls' game. Often it is only *kon gent ezim*, i. e. "pretending to make a netbag", especially with the younger children. The real knitting of netbags is enjoyed, however, by the girls. The children also make *kipan* (armlets) and *kopung* (leg bands), these mainly for the menfolk. The girls also make girdles, *kumagl ambizim*. These are long thin strings into which marsupial hair is interwoven.

c) *Magl mon*, "Drawing on the ground". With a sharp stick the children, especially the girls, trace out the figure of a pig, rat, etc., on the ground. The favourite subject is a slaughtered pig, which the children pretend to carve and distribute, saying : "This piece I give to my father, this one to my mother, etc."

d) Cat's cradle is also a very popular game, played mostly by girls but sometimes by boys as well. Several different figures are used. With the Kumngo cat's cradle is simply a game ; there is no magical significance to it. The ordinary term for this game is *taimagl kan ndazim*.

e) The playing of musical instruments sometimes helps to pass the time. The jews'-harp, used by boys and girls, is called *tambagl*. These harps are usually decorated with poker-work.

f) Whistling through the lips is a poorly developed art with these people, since they have only a few tunes. Children, especially boys, do enjoy it, however. It is called *kumbag tondip*.

g) More to their liking is the playing of a thin bamboo flute with four tone-holes. Playing this instrument is known as *pup ming tondip*. The *pup ming* is open at both ends and is held in a vertical position. Young boys play it but it is mainly a man's art.

h) Mengagl tal tsi tal tsi pup tondip. This is a name which the Kumngo apply to a little, organlike instrument, a sort of aeolian harp. It consists of four small bamboo pipes tied together. One blows into the upper end of it. It does not seem to be very popular, however, with the Kumngo people.

i) Upigl apigl is an instrument made from the fruit of a pumpkinlike plant. The fruit is rather small and cone-shaped. There is a hole in the middle of the upper end, and two smaller holes in the walls on either side of it. The children blow into the larger hole, opening and closing the small holes with the tips of their index fingers. The Kumngo do not seem to make these ocarinalike instruments out of clay, as their neighbours the Chimbu people do [8] Sometimes the children bore a small hole in the neck of the *upigl apigl* and fasten a string to it. When they hold the end of the string and swing the fruit around on it it makes a peculiar sound.

j) The Kumngo have one diversion which they describe as: *Magl koning tsi, ambigl ndang to, magl agl tondip, mbulo nim*, "Taking wet clay, kneading it, they hit it on the ground, whereupon it sounds". So far as I know this has never been mentioned before. They mould the wet clay into the form of a ball, use their elbow to press a round hole into it and fashion it into a sort of bowl. Then they turn it upside down and bring it down hard on the flat earth. The escaping air makes an unusual sound.

6. Games with Certain Gadgets

a) Tomong gilang bogl tondip is played with one or more singing tops. These are made of large acorns, pierced by a thin stick. The bottom of the stick extends out just a little but the upper part is much longer. A small hole is burnt in the shell of the acorn around the middle. Two or more children (grown men sometimes also) sit on the ground facing one another about two yards apart or less. Each side has its own "field", separated from the other's by a line scratched on the ground with a pointed stick. Each side sticks about ten small pieces of wood into its own "field", spacing them at short but irregular intervals. Then they spin the stick of the humming top between their palms and release it in the opponent's "field". If the spinning top hits one of the latter's sticks, it is removed and laid flat on the ground. Now the other side has its turn and the game continues until all the little sticks have been hit. After that a new game may start.

---

[8] See H. AUFENANGER, Irdene Gefäßflöten bei den Kuman im Wahgi-Tal (Zentral-Neuguinea), Anthropos 1946-49, pp. 877-880.

b) Nogl ndrr ni bondip. In this game the children use a home-made syringe to squirt water at their playmates. The syringe is a section of thick-walled bamboo fitted with a stick that passes snugly through the opening.

c) Wusil mong to mbulo nim, "Playing with a popgun". The popgun is made from bamboo, much like the syringe. Two small fruits of the *wusil* tree are inserted, one at either end of the tube. When the one is pushed forward the other flies away with a pop. The *wusil* tree bears bunches of these small fruits along the entire length of the trunk, each bunch consisting of hundreds of fruits.

d) Ku tsivil mengagl pagile tondip. The children fasten a rope to the end of a flexible stick. They fashion a loop at the end of the rope and place a small stone in it, holding it with their right hand. By tightening the string then suddenly releasing it like a slingshot they project the stone into the air or at some target.

7. Children Imitating their Elders

a) Gol gent ezim, is a game in which the children try to imitate the dancing of their elders. These dances are usually performed in honour of deceased ancestors. Sometimes one sees very small children imitating the dancing movements. The natives, tall and small, watch these performances of the little ones with great interest.

b) Nggar gent taundip. This is a boys' game, in which they build a tiny house, perhaps a foot high. They try to imitate as well as they can the manner in which their elders build a real house.

c) Mogine gent to koim is a game in which the girls make a small hole in the ground, to represent an earth oven. Small stones are placed in it and grass is used as a substitute for vegetables.

d) The following is really a girls' game, although small boys may occasionally join in it. The girls take the seeds of a pumpkin or a banana, wrap them in leaves, and put them in their little netbags. They hang the end of the bag over their head, the bag resting on their back. In this way they carry their "children" about, and call the banana or the pumpkinseeds *na ngalna,* "my child". If the "child cries" they take it out and give it their breasts. When it "dies", they perform the funeral rites. The *apap,* the mother's brother, will come along and bring a "pig" with him (represented by a stone). This is called *peng endin to tunum.* He may bring another stone with him also, representing a mother-of-pearl shell. They will kill a "pig" (really an insect). Sometimes the *apap* may start a mock fight of revenge, hitting the "parents of the deceased child". The mourning, weeping and singing are very closely imitated.

e) The making of a play garden. The boys pretend to fell trees, burn them, make fences, and plant bananas, i. e., they plant little sticks, grass, etc. The girls pile up little heaps of gravel or earth and plant sweet potatoes in them.

f) Boys often take part in the spirit-acting of the grown-ups, but sometimes they do it on their own. Spirit-acting is called *kipe ndazim.* The actors smear mud all over themselves, put moss, leaves, etc. on their heads, and run around, singly or in groups, behaving like madmen. Some use fantastic masks made from the shell of the *ndip* fruit. The *ndip* is a kind of pumpkin, the shell of which becomes very hard when it is ripe. The seeds are roasted in a fire or steamed in an earth oven and can be eaten that way. When young the whole fruit is edible. If the *ndip* fruit is to be kept, water is poured into it, and after three or four days the seeds and the pulp can be removed. Then the fruit is dried over a fire and can be used for various purposes, especially as a container for pig grease. The boys use one half of such a shell as a mask. Holes are cut out for the eyes and mouth, and after a little painting the ghost, *kipe*, comes out of his hiding place. Men, women and children enjoy this spirit-acting immensely.

I do not regard this short description of children's games among the Kumngo as exhaustive, but most of the games are here recorded.

GAMES OF WASHINGTON CHILDREN

W. H. Babcock

GAMES OF WASHINGTON CHILDREN.*

BY W. H. BABCOCK.

These games and the songs that go with them have been collected, with very few exceptions, from the children themselves.   My method has been to wander through promising neighborhoods in the twilight of summer evenings or lie in wait in my study and sally out when anything novel in the way of child music was borne in through the windows, hurried notes being taken in either case, often under great difficulties.   Often, too, my young friends would organize entertainments for my benefit, clearing up doubtful matters by practical illustration.   I had juvenile reporters out also, who brought me novelties with great enthusiasm.   Their accounts were compared and tested as opportunity offered.   The few instances in which my own recollections or those of other adults have been made use of will be sufficiently indicated.

In classification I have adopted form as a criterion chiefly because it is obvious and easy of practical application.   Sentiment must always be a confusing test.   My divisions are Ring Games, *Vis à Vis* Games, Archway Games, etc., as will appear hereafter.   A few of them have been subdivided, falling naturally into groups.   Of course there are a few marginal cases which might be shifted about with no great violence to the arrangement.   In all there are about a hundred games reported, excluding those which have no literary element nor much interest to the student of folk-lore.

Of course the field is by no means exhausted.   About fifty additional games collected elsewhere by Mr. Newell, Miss Courtney, Mr. Halliwell, and others, on both sides of the Atlantic, may reasonably be looked for in this District, which has a cosmopolitan population. Some of them must be here, though I have not found them.   On the other hand, my list includes more than a dozen which are unrecorded, so far as I know, and many of the others are well-marked variants.

RING GAMES.—These are great favorites, involving, as they do, continuous action of limb and voice of nearly every player and hav-

---

* See Lippincott's Magazine, March and September, 1886.

ing to do with the great perennial themes, death and love and the delightfulness of living. Here is one which claims kindred with the lyke-wake songs of the Celtic people and such as are still in use in the Greek islands.

THE LILY-WHITE DAISIES.

One of the party stands at first in the center. Before or during the chanting of the fifth stanza he lies down as if dead. Those forming the ring move around hand in hand, singing:

> Johnny is his first name,
>   His first name, his first name,
> Johnny is his first name,
>   Among the lily-white daisies.

> (*Surname*) is his second name,
>   His second name, his second name,
> (*Surname*) is his second name,
>   Among the lily-white daisies.

> Emma is her first name,
>   Her first name, her first name,
> Emma is her first name,
>   Among the lily-white daisies.

> (*Surname*) is her second name,
>   Her second name, her second name,
> (*Surname*) is her second name,
>   Among the lily-white daisies.

> And now poor Johnny's dead and gone,
>   Dead and gone, dead and gone,
> And now poor Johnny's dead and gone,
>   Among the lily-white daisies.

SWEET GRAVEL.

Here is another ring-ditty on the same lugubrious topic, but with an opening hard to account for:

> Sweet Gravel, sweet Gravel,
>   Your true love is dead;
> He wrote you a letter
>   To turn back your head.

One in the ring turns her head over her shoulder. Then the lines are sung again and another turns likewise. This continues until all have turned.

which she does with the usual result.   This game has been reported from several parts of England and the United States, with some changes of words, but none of sentiment.   It is the only one, I think, to mention Waters and sand.

Two games, having very little in common except the manner of playing, pass by the name of

GREEN GROWS THE WILLOW TREE* *a.*

In the first, which has, I fancy, the better right to the title, the children in the ring go round a girl in the middle, singing:

> Green grows the willow tree,
> Green grows the willow tree,
> Come, my love, where *are* you been?
> Come and sit beside of me.
> O, how she blushes so!
> Kiss her sweet and let her go,
> And don't you let her mother know.

There is not in my collection a more engaging bit of arch and absolute simplicity, notwithstanding that dangerous conclusion.

The second form looks like a graft on this stock of Mr. Newell's "Rose in the garden," yet one cannot be certain.

GREEN GROWS THE WILLOW TREE *b.*

The song this time is:

> Green grows the willow tree,
> Green grows the willow tree,
> Green grows the willow tree;
> Up steps a lady with a rose in her hand.

A girl steps into the middle, thus far vacant, and sings:

> Bargain, bargain, you young man;
> You promised to marry me long ago;
> You promised to marry me, you shan't say no.

All in chorus:

> Up steps a lady with a rose in her hand.

All stoop down.   The last one to stoop has to name her "beau" as a forfeit.

---

* See "Green grow the rushes O," No. 7, Newell.

LILY, LILY, WHITE FLOWERS

gives one the same feeling of sweet bells that were not always jangled
in tune:

> Lily, lily, white flowers,
>   Growing up so high;
> We are all young ladies,
>   And we are sure to die.

These pretty verses recall Spenser's

> Maidens, lily white,
> All ranged in a ring and dancing for delight,

but the lines appended to them are an odd fragmentary jumble:

> Clap your hands, tiddy-bo-teague;
> Who comes in is a nice young man,
> With a rose in his bosom.
> To-morrow, to-morrow is a very good day,
> To-morrow, to-morrow is a very good day.

This is nearly meaningless until we compare it with the following
variant:

> Walters, Walters, wild flowers,
>   Growing up so high;
> We are all young ladies,
>   And we are sure to die.

> To-morrow, to-morrow is the wedding day.
>   I think Johnny Thompson is a nice young man,
> And they shall get married to-morrow.
> To-morrow, to-morrow the wedding will begin
>   In an old tin-pan.

ROCKING CHAIR,

in its present shape, is direct and business-like, if not very poetical.
The method of it is much like Little Sally Waters. All sing:

> I went to Mr. Johnson's
>   To buy a rocking chair,
> And who should I see there
>   But Willie and his dear!
> He kisses her, he hugs her,
>   He calls her his dear;
> He makes her a present
>   Of a handsome rocking chair.

The furniture would indicate an American origin ; but some of the lines are nearly identical with a courtship rhyme in Chambers' Popular Rhymes of Scotland.

ROLY-BOLL

has a distinct plot rather dramatically stated.   A girl being in the center the rest sing to her :

> Roly-boll, roly-boll, let your beau's name.

She gives that of some boy.   Then all sing together, using his name and hers :

> Mr. Blank is handsome,
>   Mrs. Dash is handsome as he,
> And they will get married,
>   As they wish to be:
>
> O, dear doctor, can you tell
> What will make this lady well ?
> A sword and pistol by his side,
> And that's what makes the lady cry.
>
> Sword and pistol by his side,
>   The wedding day is over ;
> Sword and pistol by his side,
>   The wedding day is over.*

During the singing (by the ring) the bride stands in the middle weeping.

I LIKE COFFEE AND I LIKE TEA

contains a naïve confession of feminine strategy :

> I like coffee and I like tea ;
> I like boys and the boys like me.
> *I'll tell my mother when I get home*
> *The boys wont let the girls alone.*
> O sweet beans and barley grows,
> O sweet beans and barley grows,
> Nor you nor I nor nobody knows
> How O sweet beans and barley grows.

---

* See section 3 of " Marriage ; " also, " Uncle John," No. 16 of Mr. Newell's Songs and Games.

We're waiting for a partner,
We're waiting for a partner,
      So open the ring
    And choose your queen
  And kiss her when you get her in.

The fifth and all succeeding lines, as well as those which follow, are borrowed from a common game of imitation, in which the same curious misleading of sense by sound is the rule, at least with us.

"O sweet beans and barley grows" is a title warranted by right of usage. As in the game last mentioned, the ring whirls and sings around one in the center, but mimicry is added at the appropriate words:

O sweet beans and barley grows,
'Tis O sweet beans and barley grows;
You nor I nor nobody knows,
But O sweet beans and barley grows.

'Tis the way the farmer does,
'Tis the way the farmer does:
Stamps his foot and claps his hands,
And turns around to view the lands.

We're waiting for a partner,
We're waiting for a partner;
Open the ring and choose her in
And kiss her when you get her in.

It will be quite evident that these two games (leaving out the satirical introduction to the first) are rather distorted outgrowths of the widely-disseminated May Day song, which Mr. Newell supposes to be "of romance descent."

THERE WAS A YOUNG LADY WHO SAT DOWN TO SLEEP

is sung to the same tune as Humpsy and acted out in the same way. Here we have the bare bones of that wonder tale which had charmed the fancies of men before Sigurd awoke Brunehild from her enchanted slumber.

A girl seated in the middle of the ring pretends to sleep, while the song goes on:

There was a young lady who sat down to sleep,
Sat down to sleep, sat down to sleep,
There was a young lady who sat down to sleep,
      HiO′,   HiO′,   HiO′.

She wants a young gentleman to keep her awake,
To keep her awake, to keep her awake,
She wants a young gentleman to keep her awake,
HiO′,   HiO′,   HiO′.

Write down his name and tell it to me,
And tell it to me, and tell it to me,
Write down his name and tell it to me,
HiO′,   HiO′,   HiO′.

The elected one enters the ring and awakens her by a kiss. He then takes her place as the sleeping beauty.

RING AROUND A ROSY

has certainly been played in Washington within a few years, but my little informants could only remember the first two lines:

Ring around a rosy,
Pocket full of posies.

TAILOR BOY

is fairly popular. He stands in the middle. The others do the singing:

Here comes a jolly, jolly tailor boy,
   Just lately come from town;
He makes his work in a very pretty way,
   As we go marching round,
As we go marching round and round,
   As we go marching round.
He takes his partner in a very pretty way,
   And kisses her on the ground.

Thereupon he selects one and kisses her.

More often he is a "sailor boy." As played by a sea-shore party of children from Washington, Baltimore, and certain Maryland villages, it began as a *vis-à-vis* game, the sailor boy facing the others. Then they sang:

Here comes a jolly, jolly sailor boy,
   Just lately come on shore;
He spends his time in a merry, merry way,
   Just as he did before.
He fell in love with a very pretty girl,
   And kissed her kneeling down.
Swing around and around and around,
   Swing around and around.

At the fifth line he selected one of the girls from the line ; at the sixth, knelt and kissed her ; then rose.   At the word "swing" the pair took hold of hands and swung around.   Then the girl selected another from the line in the same way, forming a ring of three, and so on, with repetitions of the song, until all were circling together. I am inclined to think this the more correct version.

I first heard

THE MAN IN THE CELL

(Mr. Newell's "The farmer in the dell") sung by colored children, perhaps more familiar with the phenomena of station-houses than with those of the hill country.   Afterwards white children, still retaining the cell, gave it to me in more complete form, the final four lines being added by a nurse :

> The man in the cell,
> The man in the cell,
>   High O ! Cherry O !
> The man in the cell.
>
> The man rings the bell,
> The man rings the bell,
>   High O ! Cherry O !
> The man rings the bell.
>
> The man takes a wife,
> The man takes a wife,
>   High O ! Cherry O !
> The man takes a wife.
>
> The wife takes the child,
> The wife takes the child,
>   High O ! Cherry O !
> The wife takes the child.
>
> The child takes the nurse,
> The child takes the nurse,
>   High O ! Cherry O !
> The child takes the nurse.
>
> The nurse takes the dog,
> The nurse takes the dog,
>   High O ! Cherry O !
> The nurse takes the dog.

The dog takes the cat,
The dog takes the cat,
  High O! Cherry O!
The dog takes the cat.

The cat takes the rat,
The cat takes the rat,
  High O! Cherry O!
The cat takes the rat.

So we'll all stand still,
And we'll all clap hands,
  High O! Cherry O!
We'll all clap hands.

This reads like a satire on the cumulative consequences of matrimony. Its refrain may very probably have been Heigh-ho, Cheery O. Mr. Newell gives Rowley instead of cheery or cherry.

QUAKERS

is a ring game in a different sense. The players are seated in a ring. Each in succession asks her neighbor on one side :

" Neighbor, neighbor, how art thee ? "
" Very well, I thank thee."
" How is neighbor next to thee ? "
" I don't know, but I'll go see."

ROUND AND ROUND THE VALLEY

is a pretty and spirited game, full of the pleasure of motion. The hero of the piece is at first outside of the ring, which circles, singing :

Go round and round the valley,
Go round and round the valley,
Go round and round the valley,
  As we are all so gay!

The ring then halts and they sing :

Go in and out the window,
Go in and out the window,
Go in and out the window,
  As we are all so gay!

During this second verse the leading player enters the ring under the clasped hands of two ring-members, then passes out again though the next " window" of the same sort, and thus back and forth around the circle. At last he stops on the inside and indicates his choice. Then the song becomes:

> Go in and face your lover,
> Go in and face your lover,
> Go in and face your lover,
> As we are all so gay!

The chosen one enters during this stave and take up the burden, addressing the first player:

> I'm in because I love you,
> I'm in because I love you,
> I'm in because I love you,
> As we are all so gay!

The reply is:

> What love have I to show you?
> What love have I to show you?
> What love have I to show you?
> As we are all so gay!

SUGAR LUMP

begins with one in the middle:

> Bounce around, my sugar lump,
> Bounce around, my sugar lump,
> Bounce around, my sugar lump,
> Bounce around too.
>
> Lower the window, my sugar lump (*all stoop*),
> Lower the window, my sugar lump,
> Lower the window, my sugar lump,
> Lower the window too.
>
> Hoist the window, my sugar lump (*they rise*),
> Hoist the window, my sugar lump,
> Hoist the window, my sugar lump,
> Hoist the window too.
>
> Don't miss a window, my sugar lump (*she runs in and out*),
> Don't miss a window, my sugar lump,
> Don't miss a window, my sugar lump,
> Don't miss a window too.

This game is played like "Go round" and "Round the valley." It seems to continue until a window is missed.

AS WE GO ROUND THE MULBERRY BUSH

is played here, and probably as much as elsewhere, with a versicle for the work of every day, but I have not seen it, and the reports are too incomplete to be worth giving.

BLIND FROG.

While the members of the ring shout these words the blindfolded one in the middle hops about and tries to catch one.

LOST.

There is a single player outside of the ring.   He or she marches around it, striking each member of it successively with a handkerchief and crying:

> I lost my handkerchief Saturday night
> And found it Sunday morning.
> Lost, lost, lost!

Finally she drops the article at the foot of one of them and runs, with him or her in hot pursuit.

Another form of the chant is

LUCY LOCKET.

> Lucy Locket lost her pocket,
> Katy Gray found it.
> Lost, lost, lost!

And yet another:

> Lady Locket lost her pocket,
> Lady Fisher found it,
> And every night she went to bed
> And dreamed her cows were drowned.
> Lost, lost, lost!

Lucy Locket and Kitty Fisher are said to abide in the Beggars' Opera, with most of that quatrain.

33

VIS-À-VIS GAMES.

No one ring game is, perhaps, quite so frequently heard or seen as

HERE COME THREE DUKES A RIDING.

The children are all in line, except one, who dances up to them and back again, singing:

Here comes one duke a riding,
A riding, a riding,
Here comes one duke a riding,
Sir Ransom Tansom Tiddy Bo Teek.

The last line is sung during his return. He then stands still, while the line in like manner dances up to him and back, singing, in like manner:

I'm riding here to get married,
Married, married,
I'm riding here to get married,
Sir Ransom Tansom Tiddy Bo Teek.

They answer, dancing with great show of derision:

You're too black and dirty,
Dirty, dirty,
You're too black and dirty,
Sir Ransom Tansom Tiddy Bo Teek.

He replies defiantly, the backward and forward movement being always the same:

I look as good as you do,
You do, you do,
I look as good as you do,
Sir Ransom Tansom Tiddy Bo Teek.

They respond:

Well, who do you think will have you,
Have you, have you?
Well, who do you think will have you?
Sir Ransom Tansom Tiddy Bo Teek.

He returns:

I think Miss Lucy will have me,
Have me, have me,
I think Miss Lucy will have me,
Sir Ransom Tansom Tiddy Bo Teek.

The supposition usually proves correct, and the lady of his choice becomes strangely metamorphosed into a second duke. Then the game takes a new start, with " Here come two dukes a riding," and proceeds as before.   In other places the refrain takes other forms ; for example, "ransy dansy dukes," "ransom dansom dee, "ransy tansy tee," and even "dilsy dulsy officer."

In spite of the peculiar style of compliment, this game is a spirited and pleasing spectacle.

THREE KINGS.

I have never witnessed this game, but give the following account of it as I get it from children.

Three suitors approach a mother and daughter and say :

> Here come three sweeps,
> And at your door
> They bend their knees (*doing so*).
> May we have lodgings here, O here,
> May we have lodgings here ?

The mother replies, "No." The suitors recede and then approach again, saying :

> Here come three bakers,
> And at your door
> They bend their knees.
> May we have lodgings here, O here,
> May we have lodgings here?

The mother replies, " No." They recede a second time and again approach, saying:

> Here come three kings,
> And at your door
> They bend their knees.
> May we have lodgings here, O here,
> May we have lodgings here ?

The mother relents and answers :

> Yes; here is my daughter all safe and sound,
> And in her pocket a thousand pound,
> And on her finger a Guinea-gold ring,
> And she's quite fit to walk with the king.

She hands over the daughter, for whom the suitors pretend to search.   Then they bring her back to the mother and say:

> Here is your daughter, safe and sound,
> And in her pocket no thousand pound,
> And on her finger no Guinea-gold ring ;
> She's *not* fit to walk with the king.

They run and the mother runs after them.   If she catches one, the latter becomes the mother for the next game.

I have not found "Knights of Spain," an elder brother of these two games, unless we ascribe to it the following fragment, recited in the same vibratory fashion as the Three Dukes:

THE ONE THAT'S FAIREST IN YOUR SIGHT.

> The fairest one that here I see
> Is Julia (some name) to walk with me.

THE OLD WOMAN FROM BARBARY

is very frequently seen on our streets.   She advances with her daughters on each side of her, all dancing, in line, toward a husband-elect, who stands by himself.   The mother sings, the children sometimes joining, I believe:

> Here comes an old woman from Barbary,
>   Barbary, Barbary, '
> Here comes an old woman from Barbary;
> Oh, who'll take one of my daughters?
> One can bake and one can spin
> And one can make a lily-white cake;
> Oh, who'll take one of my daughters?

He chooses and retains one, and the line dances back, singing:

> Now poor Nell has gone away,
>   Gone away, gone away;
> In her pocket a thousand dollars,
> On her hand a solid gold ring.
>   Good-bye, Nell, good-bye.

This is repeated until all have been chosen but one, who assumes the character of husband, and the child who filled that _rôle_ before now becomes the old woman from Barbary in turn until all the "daughters" have been traded off again.

SWING OVER THE GATE, VOLINSEY,

has come into Washington from down the river, perhaps only for a time.   Two players, hand in hand, march towards two others, linked similarly, all vociferating, "Bow-wow-wow!"   Then they take hands all round and whirl about, singing:

> Swing over the gate, Volinsey.

What it means, if anything, and who Volinsey is or was may be as worthy of study as the identity of Sir Ransom Tansom, the North-African nationality of our thrifty widow, or the very odd refrain of

BLACKBERRY WINE.

Two girls, hand in hand, face two others.   The first pair, dancing forward and backward, sing :

> Have you got any blackberry wine,
>   Blackberry wine, blackberry wine ?
> Have you got any blackberry wine,
>   Mizzouri and Mizzauri ?

The first three lines are sung as they advance, the last one as they recede.   The other pair then advance and retire, singing likewise :

> Yes, we have some blackberry wine,
>   Blackberry wine, blackberry wine ;
> Yes, we have some blackberry wine,
>   Mizzouri and Mizzauri.

The song proceeds in this manner, the couples taking it up alternately :

> Will you lend me a pint of it,
>   Pint of it, pint of it ?
> Will you lend me a pint of it,
>   Mizzouri and Mizzauri ?
>
> No, I wont lend you a pint of it,
>   Pint of it, pint of it ;
> No, I wont lend you a pint of it,
>   Mizzouri and Mizzauri.
>
> Then I'll break your dishes up,
>   Dishes up, dishes up ;
> Then I'll break your dishes up,
>   Mizzouri and Mizzauri.
>
> Then I'll break your tumblers up,
>   Tumblers up, tumblers up ;
> Then I'll break your tumblers up,
>   Mizzouri and Mizzauri.
>
> Then I'll send for the red-coat men,
>   Red-coat men, red-coat men ;
> Then I'll send for the red-coat men,
>   Mizzouri and Mizzauri.

What care I for the red-coat men,
  Red-coat men, red-coat men !
      (*With great flaunting of defiance*)
  What care I for the red-coat men,
      Mizzouri and Mizzauri !

Then I'll send for the blue-coat men,
  Blue-coat men, blue-coat men (*as before*).
  What care I for the blue-coat men,
      Mizzouri and Mizzauri !

Well, are you ready for a fight, fight, fight,
  For a fight, fight, fight, for a fight, fight, fight ?
Well, are you ready for a fight, fight, fight,
  Mizzouri and Mizzauri ?

Yes, I'm ready for a fight, fight, fight,
  For a fight, fight, fight, for a fight, fight, fight ;
Yes, I'm ready for a fight, fight, fight,
  Mizzouri and Mizzauri.

All four roll up their sleeves and make pretense of a furious onset.

ARCHWAY GAMES.

The feature which gives name to this little group will sufficiently appear from a description of

LONDON BRIDGE,

which has held its own in the favor of children and the memory of adults for many generations.

Two children agree on two articles—for example, a gold thimble and a gold ear-ring—as badges and shibboleths of their respective parties. Then they join hands and raise them to form an arch, representing the bridge.

Then they drop their hands and catch one of the line passing through, whom they carry away, singing :

You stole my watch and broke my chain,
  Broke my chain, broke my chain,
You stole my watch and broke my chain,
  So fare you well, my lady love.

Off to prison you will go,
  You will go, you will go,
Off to prison you will go,
  So fare you well, my lady love.

Then they whisper to their captive, "Which would you rather have, a gold thimble or a gold ring?" According to the choice the prisoner's companions fall into line and pass through, while the pair forming the bridge sing :

> London bridge is falling down,
>   Falling down, falling down,
> London bridge is falling down,
>   So fare you well, my lady love.
>
> What will it take to build it up,
>   Build it up, build it up ?
> What will it take to build it up ?
>   So fare you well, my lady love.
>
> Lime and water will build it up,
>   Build it up, build it up,
> Lime and water will build it up,
>   So fare you well, my lady love.

A new bridge is formed and the marching and singing are resumed, with the same result as before. By this procedure, repeated again and again, all the children are finally arranged in two lines, with their leaders facing each other. The latter take hold of hands, and the two parties pull to see which is the stronger. The sport usually ends in a general downfall.

It should be mentioned that the little girls in passing through the archway often catch hold of each other by the gown behind, forming a marching ring, if they are numerous enough ; but this is only a temporary, and probably accidental, element.

The same may be true of two interpolated stanzas which I once heard :

> Here comes a hatchet to cut off your head,
>   To cut off your head, to cut off your head,
> Here comes a hatchet to cut off your head,
>   So fare you well, my lady love.
>
> Here comes a wheelbarrow to roll over you,
>   To roll over you, to roll over you,
> Here comes a wheelbarrow to roll over you,
>   So fare you well, my lady love.

Nevertheless they fit in rather oddly with Mr. Newell's theory that the original kernel of the game was the pre-Christian belief in malevolent beings, who destroyed bridges and could be propitiated only by human sacrifice.   The refrain above given takes (invariably, I think) the place among us of the prettier, but less significant, "Dance over my Lady Lee."

Should

OPEN THE GATES AS HIGH AS THE SKY

be regarded as a variety of the foregoing?   I hardly think so. Only the title has reached me of late years, though it is still played ; but I remember very well the second line,

And let King George's men pass by.

Have we not in this rather stately couplet a reminder of that frequent though stirring mediæval picture, the passage of an armed force through a portcullis-guarded gateway.

This leads us naturally to less chivalric

GAMES OF MIMICRY.

Some such have already been given, but I retain for this general heading a group not easily classified by form.

WHEN I WAS A SHOEMAKER

is, perhaps, the most common of these.   The children stand in a row, all imitating successively the motions of each mentioned trade or type of person while singing the words that relate thereto:

> When I was a shoemaker
> A shoemaker was I,
> And this-a way and that-a way
> And this-a way went I.

> When I was a carpenter &c.,

with as long a list of occupations as may be desired, commonly ending with

> When I was a gentleman
> A gentleman was I,
> And this-a way and that-a way
> And this-a way went I.

> When I was a lady
> A lady was I,
> And this-a way and that-a way
> And this-a way went I.

NEW YORK.

The players are divided into two parties, which stand in line facing away from each other, their positions being indicated by lines of chalk or charcoal drawn on the pavement. One line turns around and advances, announcing, "Here we come." The children in the other line also turn and inquire, "Where from?"

"New York."

"What's your trade?"

They imitate in dumb show the motions of any occupation which may have been agreed on. The others guess what it is. If right the imitating party cry, "Yes," and endeavor to escape to their own chalk line or base. The members of the other party pursue, making recruits of all prisoners. The fugitives who reach the base are safe. The pursuers then return and select a trade for mimicry, the *rôles* of the parties being reversed. When the first guess fails additional trials are allowed before the flight and chase. The name of any other place may be substituted for "New York."

This game is a curious instance of grafting one imitation on another, for

PRISONERS' BASE,

which contributes everything except the trade mimicry, is itself a very good representation of primitive warfare as practiced in many parts of the world. The linear arrangement of the combatants, the sallies and "dares," the pursuit by individual champions, even the incorporation of captives in the conquering tribe, will all be readily recognized.

POST OFFICE,

the very barest of kissing games, brings us back to civilization, copying closely (with change of coin) what sometimes occurs at the delivery window over unpaid postage. The "postmaster" announces, "Letters in the post office for you," and the girl indicated has to step out and pay for them in kisses. The extent of the tax is limited only by the requirements that he shall announce the number of letters (and consequently of kisses) in advance. The girls are in line, the postmaster being in front of them.

34

CRACK THE WHIP

is played by a line holding hands, the last player at one end *facing to the rear*. He or she turns half round and runs along behind the row, the others successively joining in this motion as best they can until the player at the other end flies out like the snapping of a whip cord.

MOUSE-TRAP.

Four players take hold of hands to form an enclosure. A fifth creeps about within it, pretending to nibble. The first four sing:

O mousie dear, O mousie dear,
Take my advice and run away.

JUMPING GAMES.

The simplest of these is known as

MAMMY DADDY.

The children try who can longest continue jumping from one foot to the other, singing:

Mammy Daddy jumped the gutter,
Loaf of bread and a pound of butter.

BAKING BREAD

requires a rope with two to turn it. The performer holds in one hand a stone (representing a loaf of bread, I suppose) while she jumps three times. Then she puts the stone down and jumps three times without it. This alternation continues till she comes in contact with the rope and has to change places with one of the turners.

ROCKING THE CRADLE.

The rope is oscillated three times, then turned three times, this alternation being continued until a miss occurs, with the same result as before.

FOX AND GOOSE.

The players (except those who are turning) form in line one behind another, usually beginning with the eldest and ending with the youngest, and run under the rope successively. Then they form similarly in line on the other side and skip "back door" over the rope; then a line and one jump for each; then a line and a skip; then a line and two jumps, etc.   The penalty of missing is as before.

PILE OF BRICKS.

In this the rope is raised after every jump, every such elevation being counted as a brick.   At last the pile gets too high for some player and she misses.

SKIPPING-ROPE PROPHETS.

Little girls are constantly practicing augury with the skipping-rope.   Most of these deliverances take for their topic the incidents or consequences of wedlock.   "Silk, satin, velvet, calico, rags!"—they cry, keeping time to the words, and the one which marks a failure in leaping foretells the nuptial apparel of the girl who fails. The same test is applied to equipage, social position, and even the tint of the children.

But the most interesting game of the rope is what we may call

MARRIAGE BY THE KNIFE.

While the rope is turning two girls run in and jump side by side, all singing vigorously:

> By the holy and religerally law
> I marry this Indian to this squaw;
> By the point of my jack-knife
> I pronounce you man and wife.

A friend gives the following as the first line:

> By the Holy Evangels of the Lord.

From New England comes another form:

> By the old Levitical law;

or, in a fourth version, "Leviticus law."   Virginia makes it

> The Bible is a holy and visible law.

Divers endings have been reported to me from remote parts of the country as taking the place of the liturgical cold steel.   Two are borrowed from Marriage as reported by Mr. Newell, viz.:

> You must be kind, you must be good,
> And split up all her oven wood.

And

> You must be kind, you must be true,
> And kiss the bride, and she'll kiss you.

Only one is in proper aboriginal keeping :

> Sober live and sober proceed,
> And so bring up your Indian breed.

There is a very active tendency to lay on good advice and spare not in all the forms which are traceable directly or indirectly to New England—that is to say, in every version which has reached me, except the two in this District and the one still employed by Virginia negroes.

Even more crude if not equally savage is

CHARLIE BUCK,

not precisely a jumping game, but nearly akin. It often may be heard attending the motion of a swing or hammock, as a metrical measurement of fun and dizziness :

> Charlie Buck
> Had money enough
> To lock himself in the store-room ;
> So when he dies
> He shuts his eyes,
> And never see Charlie no more.
> High swing,
> Low swing,
> Die away Charlie, this day.

The swinging dies away with the words and the occupant must make way for a successor. I know nothing whatever of the meaning or history of this jargon beyond what appears in the words themselves; but it seems to be in exclusive possession of its particular field.

There is a more sensible

RHYME FOR JACKS.

In this game a set of oddly shaped bits of metal are picked up by the fingers, alternating in divers ways with the motion of a ball tossed upward. The various figures, as they may be called, of this play bear the names of Oneses, Twoses, Threeses, Sweeping the Stairs, Apple Barrel, Milking the Cow, and Putting Horses in the Stable. There are others, but few players are so proficient as to get beyond a very few of those which are best known. The jingle which gives regularity to the movements, however rapid, is

Jack was nimble, Jack was quick,
Jack jumped over the candlestick;
The candlestick was made of brass,
So, Jack, I've caught you now at last.

Sometimes the first two lines are in the present imperative.

A MARCH.

I have met a formidable array of small children shouting in high
glee—

Here we go, two by two,
My little sister jinktum joo,
　　Hither, hither,
Because she's afraid of the bugaboo.

I learn that the unintelligible final sounds of the second line
should be "lost her shoe." The "bugaboo," whether permanent
or not, has a mythological value. "Hither," an unfamiliar word
among little people, seems to mark my version as authentic, besides calling for some such timorous explanation. Nevertheless
this pendant is not found with Mr. Newell's New York form nor in
a slightly more complete one reported from Baltimore:

Here we go, two by two,
Dressed in yellow, pink, and blue,
Poor old maids.

RIGMAROLES AND JINGLES,

traditional among children, but not properly belonging to any
game, are rather plentiful. Their uses are as various as their origin.
Some accompany dancing and serve to time the steps. Thus:

PUT YOUR FOOT DOWN.

Put your foot down,
Put your foot down,
Put your foot down
　　Just so.

Again:

MOBILE BUCK.

Give me the sign of the Móbile, Móbile,
Give me the sign of the Móbile buck.
Here comes Jennie with the Móbile, Móbile,
Here comes Jennie with the Móbile buck;
And all the birds of the Móbile, Móbile,
And all the birds of the Móbile buck.

There is a piece of music having the same name, but without words. Nevertheless those given above may be the remnant of some comparatively recent street song with more meaning in it than they have now.

Others are used for purposes of divination ; for example:

STAR, STAR THAT SHINES SO BRIGHT.

> Star, star that shines so bright,
> The first star I've seen to-night,
> I hope, I wish, I hope I may,
> I hope my wish may come true
> To-morrow night.

HALLOWE'EN CHARM.

> I shape my shoes in the shape of a T,
> Hoping my true love for to see,
> The color of his eyes and the color of his hair,
> And the color of the clothes that he every day wears.

The magical practices which go with the words are, perhaps, forgotten among us, but they were in use jestingly not very many miles from this city a few years ago.

Others are relics of conjuration :

> Lady bug, lady bug, fly away to your home,
> Your house is on fire and your children will burn.
>
> Rain, rain, go away ;
> Come back on my mother's washing day.
>
> Two little blackbirds sitting on a hill,
> One named Jack and the other named Jill ;
> Fly away Jack, fly away Jill ;
> Come back Jack, come back Jill.

This last invocation accompanies a pretty set of motions. Two fingers (one of each hand), being slightly moistened, take up two slips of paper. The player raps on the table, tosses up the fingers, pretends to make the birds fly, then changes fingers to hide the slips, and finally exhibits them as having returned.

This brings our magic very close to the

CATCHES AND RIDDLES.

Of these are

> Twenty-nine and one?
>   Thirty.
> Your face is dirty.

> April's gone, summer's come;
> You're a fool and I'm none.

> A flock of white sheep
>   On a red hill,
> Here they go, there they go,
>   Now they stand still.

The teeth and lips.

> Tell story?
>   Who?
> My old shoe,
>   Dressed in blue,
> That came walking down the avenue.

Sometimes the jingles are mere bits of derision:

> Red-headed sinner,
> Come down to your dinner.

> Red-headed fox,
> Stole your mother's pigeon-box.

> Reddy in the woods
> Can't catch a butterfly.

Sometimes they are aphorisms or wise queries:

> Over latch, under latch,
> It takes good kisses to make a match.

> Where was little Moses when the light went out,
> What was he adoing and what was he about?

One is a dialogue recited as a monologue, for no reason that is apparent except wit:

> I climbed up the apple tree
> And all the apples fell on me.
> Make a pudding, make a pie.
> Did you ever tell a lie?
> Yes, you did, you know you did,
> You stole your mother's teapot lid.

Another I at first attributed to the plantation, on account of its "Master Fox" and witchlike aspect:

> Riddledy, riddledy, riddledy right,
> Where were you last Saturday night ?
> The wind did blow, my heart did quake,
> The great old hole Master Fox did make !

But in an Oxfordshire folk-tale reported by Mr. Halliwell it occurs (approximately) with a context which gives it meaning :

> One moonshiny night as I sat high,
> Waiting for one to come by,
> The boughs did bend, my heart did ache
> To see what a hole the fox did make.

The fox being a treacherous and murderous lover who was digging a grave for the woman he expected to kill. Through another channel I learn also of the entire tale as having existed in this country not many years ago. No doubt the prose part slipped away from the memories of the children in some places, and the four rhyming lines were converted into a puzzle. In its transition the first line may have been "Riddle my riddle, O riddle aright."

Two or three others are bits of childish sentiment.

BOBBY SHAFTON.

> Bobby Shafton's gone to sea,
>   Gone to sea,
> With silver buckles on his knee,
>   On his knee ;
> He's going to come back and marry me,
>   Marry me.
>
> I wish I were a china cup,
>   In which they all drink tea,
> Because the one that drank it up
>   Would give a kiss to me.

That might have come out of Mr. Stevenson's A Child's Garden of Verses.

Others are used for counting :

> One, two, buckle my shoe ;
> Three, four, shut the door ;
> Five, six, pick up sticks ;
> Seven, eight, lay them straight ;
> Nine, ten, a good fat hen ;
> Eleven, twelve, in the well ;

Thirteen, fourteen, boys acourtin';
Fifteen, sixteen, maids in the kitchen;
Seventeen, eighteen, maids awaitin';
Nineteen, twenty, your plate's empty.

Sometimes ending with

* * * twenty-four,
Mary's at the cottage door,
Eating grapes upon a plate,
Five, six, seven, eight.

But the oddest rigmarole is

A MAN OF WORDS AND NOT OF DEEDS.

Its origin is unknown, though in the Harleian MSS. there is one form of the time of James I. Afterward it seems to have been applied to purposes of indecent wit and political burlesque, the latter on the battle of Culloden. Mr. Halliwell gives this last version, which begins with

Double dee, double day,

and ends with

Like our Geordie's bloody battle.

Many of the intervening lines are almost or quite identical with those now used by Washington children. These have brought it back to what may have been its first intention, the mere sport of thought chasing words instead of leading them:

Deed'n deed'n double deed,
I sowed my garden full of seed.
When the seed began to grow,
Like a garden full of snow;
When the snow began to melt,
Like a garden full of hemp;
When the hemp began to peel,
Like a garden full of steel;
When the steel began to rust,
Like a garden full of dust;
When the dust began to fly,
Like an eagle in the sky;
When the sky began to roar,
Like a lion at my door;
When the door began to crack,
Like a hickory at my back;

When my back began to smart,
Like a penknife at my heart ;
When my heart began to bleed,
'Deed, indeed, I was dead indeed.

COUNTING-OUT RHYMES.

These, perhaps, belong rather to folk numeration than to the children's games, in which they are employed as a convenient means of selecting the "old man" or other invidious and laborious character, generally by a process of successive elimination.   A few of those employing recognizable English words may be welcome :

Hayfoot, strawfoot,
    Specklefoot, crawfoot!
Some flew east, some flew west,
Some flew over the cuckoo's nest.

One, two, three,
    Nannie caught a flea ;
The flea died, Nannie cried,
    Out goes she.

One, two, three, four, five, six, seven,
All good children go to heaven.

Enee, menee, tipsy-toe,
Catch a nigger by the toe ;
If he hollers let him go.
        O-u-t
Spells out goes he,
Right in the center of the dark-blue sea.

Rather suggestive, that, of the middle passage :

As I went up the golden lake
I met a little rattlesnake,
Who ate so much of jelly-cake
It made his little belly ache.

Doctor Franklin whipped his scholars
Out of Scotland into Spain
And then back again.

This is our only legacy from the legend of Dr. Faustus.

COUNTING PAPERS.

In this, elimination by numbers becomes almost the entire game. A circle is formed with bits of paper, one piece, larger than the rest, being called the Boss.   Beginning with any of them, seven are counted, and the one then reached is thrown away. The player begins again with the next, counts as before, and again throws away. This continues until the Boss is hit, when the game ends. The Dutch word above given may hint a New York origin, though it is common enough everywhere now. The magical number seven might, of course, come from anywhere.

GAMES OF HANDS AND FEET.

Two of these are played by clapping the palms together, and alternating with this movement a similar clapping against the knees or face. The scheme of motion varies with the words, the latter being used for keeping time. They are as follows:

PEASE PORRIDGE HOT.

Pease porridge hot,
　Pease porridge cold,
Pease porridge in the pot
　Nine days old.

MISSY MASSY.

Missy Massy gone away,
Wont come back till Saturday.

The first is common in many places. The second may be of negro origin.

THIS IS THE CHURCH.

The fingers of one hand are passed through, from behind, toward the wrist, between those of the other hand, and the palms are brought toward each other; the index fingers are raised and made to converge; the combination is then inverted or the thumbs are preferably thrown apart, showing the finger-tips in bowing rows within. Every motion is timed to the appropriate words:

This is the church,
　And this is the steeple;
Open the door
And see all the people.

THIS LITTLE PIG WENT TO MARKET,

a game with infants, is played by older children as well as adults. The player touches or lightly takes hold of the baby's toes, one after the other, singing:

> *This* little pig went to market;
> *This* little pig staid at home;
> *This* little pig had roast beef to eat;
> *This* little pig got none;
> *This* little pig said " We, we, we,
>   I wish I had some."

CAT'S CRADLE

is played with an endless cord, which slips from one form to another on the fingers, each form having a traditional name and sequence. Captain Porter, during the cruise of the Essex three-quarters of a century ago, found the unclad Happah belles very expert in this amusement, and gives a glowing account of the exhibition.

GAMES WITH TOYS.

It would be neither profitable nor practicable to go into the details of all these or even to name them; but certain odd or suggestive terms and practices may be touched on in passing. Thus, mumblety peg, played with a knife (a savage survival) thrown at a target from the eyes, nose, and mouth; the use of "fen" in the old sense of defend, for prohibiting certain actions in playing at marbles; "conjure roots," pronounced while drawing a magic circle about one's own "alley" to baffle the enemy's aim; "duck on the rock," wherein a stone has life given it; the ancient and honorable game of quoits, wherein the discus keeps flying still; the "one old cat" and "two old cats" which dwell in the ball ground; the "bandy," whose crippling tactics may explain "bandy-legged;" the winter "coasting;" the the Easter egg-picking and egg-rolling; and, leaving toys behind, the "horse heaven" and "cow heaven" of liberal Hopscotch.

DOG LATIN AND CAT LATIN

conversations occupy the time of the more erudite. The former are concocted by adding "us" to most words; the latter, by the similar addition of liga to syllables ending with a vowel and oliga, aliga, or iliga to those ending with a consonant. From such speech to

SILENCE

is not far. The word tells the whole story. Who speaks first loses. It may be the remnant of some belief in a spell, an imitation of "Quaker meeting," a commonplace test of endurance, or an invention of higher powers for promoting rest and quiet occasionally.

GAMES OF TRANSPOSITION.

The most familiar of these is

PUSSY WANTS A CORNER.

Its players outnumber the corners by one and scramble for them, the child left unprovided for being Pussy. She approaches one of the others and announces, "Pussy wants a corner." "Ask my neighbor," is the reply. As Pussy passes on to repeat the petition before the next, the girl just left tries to exchange places with her other neighbor, and Pussy hurries back to slip into one of the temporarily vacant corners if she can. This is repeated until the latter effort is successful. The girl or boy left out thereby becomes Pussy in her stead.

FRUIT BASKET

is more elaborate. Fourteen chairs (for example) are ranged in two parallel lines, facing one another. Fifteen girls play, all seated but one. The odd girl, standing in the space between, says "currants" (for instance) to one of the others, who must cry "currants, currants, currants," before the first speaker can repeat the word. Another and another of the seated girls is tried in the same way, a new and, as far as possible, unexpected fruit-name being chosen each time. As soon as one fails to deliver the triple utterance quickly enough, the children of the two rows rush to exchange places, and in the confusion the girl who has been standing gets a seat if she can. Of course one of the fifteen is left on her feet and the game begins again.

GUESSING GAMES.

BUTTONS

offers an excellent chance for a mind-reader. The "buttoner" holds a "deem" over the head of the guesser and asks, "Fine or superfine?"—*i. e.*, a boy's or a girl's, the article being obtained from one of the players. If the reply be correct, the next question is, "What shall the owner do?" The guesser then states a forfeit, which the owner must pay or perform to redeem the pledge. If the first guesser makes a mistake another is tried in like manner. The game continues until every one has had a turn at redemption.

In
THIS AND THAT

all the players go out of the room except one, who touches an article in their absence and then calls them in, bidding them do likewise. As she does not name it they must guess. If they touch the wrong thing, she says, "This;" if the right thing, "That."

GAMES OF SEARCH.

Under this head we must class the common infantile diversion of "Peek-a-boo," as well as the ancient open-air games of "Hide and seek," "I spy," and their modifications, in all which a person sought and discovered is the central idea. Here also we put

HIDE THE THIMBLE,

similar to "This and that," but unlike in its problem. Instead of guessing the identity of something unknown but visible, the players are to find something hidden but known. They are called by the couplet

Hot bread and butter,
Please come to supper.

While they search, the one who has hidden the article aids them by suggesting "Freezing," "Cold," "Hot," or "Burning," according to degrees of proximity.

STILL POND.

One player is blindfolded and searches for the others, who are given a certain "start" to hide themselves.

BLIND MAN'S BUFF.

As before, one is blindfolded. The rest of the party say to him, "Pick up some pins." The blind man stoops and pretends to try, answering : "I can't do it."

"Pick up some needles," they command. He goes through the same motion as before and again replies : "I can't do it."

They demand : "What kind of a coat does your father wear?" "Gray," he answers.

"Catch whom you may," they cry, and the groping pursuit begins. It is naturally a search rather than a chase, being usually played indoors and kept at a low rate of speed by his infirmity.

GAMES OF CHASE.

TAG, CROSS-TAG, HAND CHASE, AND RED LINE

are the most rudimentary. The first is a chase and touch; the second compels the pursuit to be diverted when a second of the escaping party crosses the trail; the third makes a recruit of each one caught, so that there is a continually increasing line of pursuers, hand in hand; the fourth is the running of the gauntlet, the one caught taking the place of him who has lain in wait.

BULL-DOG

goes a step further. One girl says to the others, "Let us put on our clothes," and they pretend to dress for church. Then they start out in Sunday procession. This meets another child, the "bull-dog." They dance at him and from him, crying, " Bull-dog, bull-dog," till, in one of his rushes, he makes a capture. The prisoner becomes "bull-dog" in turn. Most likely this quadruped was something else at first, or why the hostility to religion?

ROTTEN EGG.

A mother sends her children, one after the other, to find out whether the bread is done. Each reports affirmatively. She replies, "I don't believe it;" then pretends to go and see for herself. She declares, "It isn't done;" then pretends to beat them, swinging the child, each one successively with her left hand while she plies the switch with the right. Then every child of this parent is made to take a squatting posture, with hands clasped under the thighs. The mother and an assistant lift the child by the arms from the ground. If the clasped hands give way the child is placed on one side and said to go into "the apple barrel;" if not, she is set on the other side and said to go into "the sugar barrel."

The ending of this has gone sadly astray, no doubt, as will appear by comparison with its probable parent,

THE DEVIL IN THE BANDBOX.

One child, assuming the *rôle* of the devil, hides himself. The "mother" sends her sons and daughters toward him successively, with the command, "Get me ——" (any article which may come to mind). The messenger pretends to make a frightful discovery, and rushes back, crying, "The Devil's in the bandbox." The mother replies, "I don't believe you" and sends another. At last she goes in person, with all her tribe. Catching sight of the Devil, she cries, "Oh, sure enough, he is!" and they all run. The Devil springs out in pursuit and the one caught becomes Devil in turn.

This seems to be nearer to the idea of the German original mentioned by Mr. Newell than his "Ghost in the cellar" or Miss Courtney's Cornish "Ghost in the well" (Folk Lore Journal, January to March, 1887). I believe, though, that the Devil sometimes becomes a ghost with us.

OLD MAMMY TIPSY TOE.

A mother gives her children sticks for needles and sets them a task, then walks off to get a switch. They follow, singing irreverently:

> Old Mammy Tipsy Toe,
> I've broke my needle
> And I cannot sew.

She turns and asks, "Are these my children?" They reply, "No." The question is twice repeated; the third answer being "Yes." She pursues. If she catches one the latter becomes Old Mammy for next time.

Each of the disobedient children holds up her apron with both hands. The mother strikes it three times. If the "child" lets go, she must pretend to go into the house and complete the task.

MARLYBRIGHT.

Two players face each other. One is "the witch," presumably in disguise. The other seems to be a traveller. The dialogue proceeds:

> How far from here to Marlybright?
> Three score miles and ten.
> Can I get there by candle-light?
> Yes, and back again,
> If the old witch doesn't get you.

Thereupon she springs out and the chase begins.

This is a game of peculiar interest, being a descendant or collateral relative of the stately Barley Bridge, a favorite at court in Queen

Elizabeth's day.   But our "*three score* miles *and ten*," with the un-known one lurking by the way, hint a deeper thought than anything in the chivalric Scotch variant which Mr. Newell thinks may give us an idea of that older form.

In

BIRDS

the occult knowledge of supernatural beings would seem to be the germ of the play.   There are a row of "birds," a namer, and an angel.   The namer, unheard by the angel, whispers a special name, such as "blue bird," "red bird," or "yellow bird," to each one of the birds, then stands in front facing them.   The angel comes up and touches her on the back:

> *Namer.*   " Who is that? "
> *Angel.*   " It's *me*."
> *Namer.*   " What do you want? "
> *Angel.*   " I want some birds."
> *Namer.*   " What color? "
> *Angel.*   " Blue " (for example).
> *Namer.*   " Run, blue! "

the angel having guessed the color chosen for one of them.   A chase ensues.   If the angel touches blue bird before the latter reaches a certain spot, blue bird becomes an angel and the angel becomes a bird.   If the blue bird gains this asylum she goes back to her place in the row and the angel must try again.   If the angel does not guess the color of any bird, the namer answers, "I haven't got any."   If this occurs three times the namer exclaims irrever-ently: "Go back and learn your A B C's!"   The angel then withdraws to her original post, but soon comes forward to try again.   This continues till she has guessed correctly and caught a bird.

RIBBONS

is played like the latter, with this change of name for the row, except that there is a devil as well as an angel, and they alternate in their guessing.   These games are notable for the mediæval lack of cere-mony in dealing with heaven and hell.   I suppose that they prob-ably once ended like Mr. Newell's "Colors," with a visible strife between the two.

CHILD-STEALING GAMES.

The mythical and savage elements in these are very manifest. They seem to be related, and many intermediate or proximate forms are found in this country and Europe. They are known to be very old and are believed to be relics of an earlier drama or tale now utterly lost.

GIPSY

preserves a memory of magic and (perhaps) cannibalism. A mother and child go to sleep. The gipsy enters and steals the child, who opens her eyes and goes with her captor to the latter's home. There she is named "blackberry pie" or after some other edible. The mother raps on the gipsy's back, as a door:

> *Gipsy.* " Who's there ? "
> *Mother.* " Jack Frost."
> *Gipsy.* " What do you want ? "
> *Mother* (for example). " Raspberry tart."
> *Gipsy.* " It's in the oven baking,"

this guess being an approximation.

> *Mother.* " Then custard pie."
> *Gipsy.* " We haven't got any."
> *Mother.* " Blackberry pie."
> *Gipsy.* " Here she is."
> *Mother.* " Let me taste it."

(Touches the child with a stick and puts the latter to her mouth.)

" Why, that tastes like my Julia" (or whatever the child's name may be). " What brought you here ? "

> *Child.* " My big toe."
> *Mother.* " Well, take your big toe and march yourself home ;"

which is done.

This game passes under the name of "Old witch" in Cornwall. Another nearly related goes in many places by the same name. I think the name "Old man" is more commonly used in Washington, though he is also spoken of as a witch, recalling the days when that word was used for both sexes.

OLD MAN.

A mother having children for all the days of the week cautions Sunday, the eldest, to "take care of Monday and all the rest and

don't let them get hurt.   If you do, you know what I'll give you."
After the mother has gone the witch comes in and says: "Little girl,
please go (pointing) and get me a match for my pipe.   There's a
bull-dog over there and I am afraid to go."   She goes for the
match.   He snatches up Monday and makes off.   The mother returns.

> *Mother.* "Where has my Monday gone?"
> *Sunday.* "The old witch has got her."
> *Mother.* "Do you know what I told you?   I am going to beat you."

She makes a pretense of doing so.

This programme is repeated until all the children are stolen except Sunday.   At the next visit the witch says: "Little girl, little
girl, come with me, and I'll give you some candy."   She goes with
him.   All the children are shut up in a room.   During the absence
of the witch the mother breaks into it and rescues them.

CHICKAMY CRAMERY CROW.

Witch discovered making a fire.   Enter mother, with children
behind her in single file, each grasping the clothes of the one next
in front.   This line marches around, singing:

> Chickamy, chickamy, cramery crow,
> I went to the well to wash my toe,
> When I came back my chicken was gone.

Pausing before the fire-builder, the mother asks, in continuation
of the song, "What time is it, old witch?"   The witch replies,
"One o'clock."   The march and song are resumed.   On coming
around again, the question is repeated and the answer is "Two
o'clock."   This is continued, with ascending numerals, until the
twelfth round.   After the answer "twelve o'clock" this conversation begins:

> *Mother.* "What are you doing there?"
> *Witch.* "Making a fire."
> *Mother.* "What are you making a fire for?"
> *Witch.* "To roast chickens."
> *Mother.* "Whose chickens?"
> *Witch (fiercely).* "Those of your flock."

She springs out at them and they scatter.
I have found no other forms of the game in Washington (beyond
trivial variations and repetitions), but on the Eastern Shore of
Maryland the mother fights for the chickens.   In Salem, Mass., the

chant represents the chickens as "pecking brown bread," and there
are many other modifications.

The substance of the above paper was read before the society at
its 104th regular meeting, February 2, 1886, under title of "Song
Games and Myth Dances in Washington."

SOME ABORIGINAL CHILDREN'S GAMES

R. M. Berndt

Australia : Social Anthropology. Berndt.

Some Aboriginal Children's Games. *By R. M. Berndt, Honorary Assistant in Ethnology, South Australian Museum.*

INTRODUCTION.

The following observations on several native children's games were made during an expedition to Ooldea, south-western South Australia, in August, 1939. The expedition was conducted under the auspices of the Board for Anthropological Research of the University of Adelaide.

Work was carried out at the Ooldea Soak (*Juldi*), which is four miles to the north of Ooldea siding on the east-west railway line.

The local natives are members of the 'Anta'kirinja tribe, although representatives of the Pitjandara, Murunitja and Wirangu tribes are to be found in this neighbourhood, having congregated here on the fringe of white occupation and away from their own tribal lands. They all speak dialects of Pitjandjara, the language of the Great Victoria or Western Desert.

The two photographs[1] on Plate AC will serve to show the type of native child at Juldi. Left, a boy ; right, a girl, both of the 'Anta'kirinja tribe.

GAMES.

Dr. Haddon[2] states that the games played by children have a most varied origin, and a similarly unequal value to the student. Before we consider the games played by Aboriginal children, it is desirable to glance at those played by other primitive boys and girls. In an earlier issue of this journal Mr. Bell[3] has considered some Melanesian games which, although

---

[1] Photographs by courtesy of the South Australian Museum. Taken at Ooldea, August, 1939. Nos. O.69 and 76.

[2] Haddon, A. C., *Study of Man*, pp. 219-24.

[3] Bell, F. L. S., " Play Life of the Tanga," *Mankind*, Vol. 2, No. 3, pp. 56-61 ; No. 4 pp. 83-86.

imitative, in many cases, of the activities of adults, vary considerably in form from those of the Australian aboriginal child.

IMITATIVE GAMES.

Much of the play life of the children at Juldi is imitative of adult activities, as for example play about hunting exploits or play about ceremonies.

Great benefit is obtained from participation in these games, especially by the boys who, when they reach manhood, are already partially proficient in the use of the thrower and the spear, the boomerang and the club. They also gain knowledge from playing these games as to the procedure of the chanters around the camp fires at ceremonies, although they have no deep understanding of ceremonial life until it has been revealed to them as adults.

These imitative hunting games and " sing-songs " are greatly enjoyed by all children, and are taken seriously because they are playing at being grown-up. Such behaviour is common among children the world over. Play of this type is encouraged by parents, who take pleasure in watching their own children and, if needs be, advise them when a difficulty arises.

Hunting games are only indulged in by boys. After watching one of their elders making a spear-thrower (*meru*), three or four boys will set to

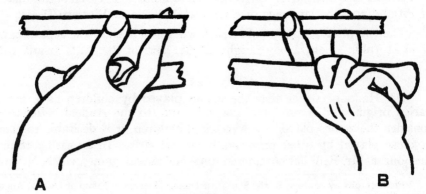

Text Figure 1.

A. and *B.* *The right hand, showing the position in which spear and spear-thrower are held.*

work and endeavour to shape one for themselves. Before the thrower is eventually produced, several attempts may be made, often taking three or four days. The boys do not tire, but industriously labour until the weapon closely resembles that of their elders. A stone-knife or flake mounted on the haft of a spear-thrower (*'kandi-'tjurna*) was formerly used in shaping the *meru*, but in latter days a chisel or an axe serves the same purpose. When finished, the *meru* is about two and one half feet in length, but is not decorated (or incised) as are those of the adults.

Spears (*'katji*) are also made by the children, but more often than not they are borrowed from the parents, as are the spear-throwers.

In using the thrower and spear, the boys hold them, as do their elders (see Text-fig. I, A and B), in the right hand, in such a way that the spear shaft passes, and is held, between the thumb and the forefinger, the remaining fingers holding the handle of the thrower. The arm is then flexed backwards ready to throw. As the arm is brought forwards, the thumb and the forefinger are released and the spear careers through the air, the accuracy of its flight largely depending on its manufacture.

The sandhills surrounding the soak or a camp dog offer excellent targets for these youthful marksmen.

Hours are spent in this amusement, which is accompanied with much shouting and singing. Imaginary animals are tracked and ambushed with great care. Quite often they actually spear or trap a small animal or bird. The trophy of the chase is then brought back to camp (*'ŋura*) and cooked in the embers of the fire and eaten by all the children who took part in its capture.

Boomerangs (*kali*) of a small type and clubs (*tjurtiŋba*) are also used.

Spears, made from long sticks obtained from a creeper (*'orutjanba*) and hardened by drying in the fire, are used by the children.

In the evenings boys and girls up to about nine years of age have their own camp fires around which they sit and boil billy-tea and eat damper prepared by their parents. When their meal is finished they begin to sing, to the accompaniment of rhythmic beating, with wooden batons, upon the sand at the fire's edge. The songs, in this case, consist of one word continually repeated. The intonation of the voices of the singers varies.

At a little distance away older boys, their ages ranging from nine to sixteen years, also have their camp fire. Some are marked with bands of white lime (*'tjinki*) and red ochre (*'turtu*) upon the chest (*'ŋaruka*), arms and legs (*tunta*). At intervals these boys dance (*'walputi*), while others chant to the beat of the wooden baton, in the same manner as described above.

It can all be very effective, especially when the intonation of the voices of the singers varies from a whisper to comparative loudness. The simplest songs consist of one or two words indefinitely repeated. Others are of three or four words, the rhythm of the beat changing to each song. It is very difficult to obtain a correct transcription of these songs, as the pronunciation of a word may vary, stress sometimes being placed on certain syllables which distort the original word. Also, the interpretation of the words is made difficult, as the older informants consider it beneath their dignity to be present.

Examples of three chants are here given :

    (*a*) *'manta 'okeri 'ŋaranja*.
        ground/fresh-leaves/lay down (or spread).

    (*b*) *tali ma-war:u kapi*.
        spit[4]/along-fire/water.

    (*c*) *'juwa 'mako-'ilkoara ŋulgo*.
        give-me/witchetty-grub/eat.

The above seem to have little meaning beyond their lay value. Thus, (*a*) refers to fresh leaves being spread on the ground, whilst in (*b*) spitting (into) fire is (likened unto) water, and (*c*) is a request for a witchetty-grub. They are probably made up by the children as they sing.

Great amusement is derived from such an evening's entertainment, there being much laughing, chattering and bantering, which unfortunately one cannot follow.

These " sing-songs " are not to be confused with those performed by older uninitiated boys and initiated young men. These latter are known as " play-about ceremonies " (*'inma-'inkanji*). Quite often the younger children endeavour to imitate the performers in the *'inma-'inkanji*, making the head pads or head-dresses (*'inma-tali*) which are used by the older boys.

SUMMARY OF OTHER GAMES PLAYED.

Other games played by the children are :

(*a*) Shadows on the ground. A few only appear to be known. One of a rabbit was recorded.

(*b*) String-games are played by both the boys and girls, but such are simple in construction.

---

4 *tali*=spit, also a sandhill. *'Inma-tali*=head-dress worn during *'inma-'inkanji*.

(*c*) Sand drawing is common. The child either uses its fingers or a twig. The motif, more than often, is " Europeanized," although Aboriginal conventionalized drawing is frequently carried out.

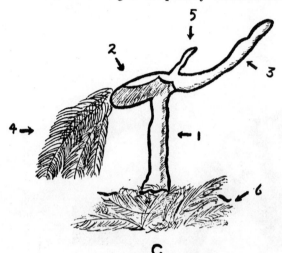

Text Figure 1.
C. Sketch of a child's hobby-horse or emu, at Juldi.

(*d*) In Text-fig. I, C, is reproduced a drawing of a child's " hobby-horse " or, in this case, an emu ('*kulaja*), upon which the little boys have much enjoyment. It is prepared by them from a strong young tree (C1) which will withstand the child's weight, at the same time giving slightly so that it sways. All projecting branches are removed, except that representing the '*kulaja* neck (C3) and a short stump (C5) used as a handle to hold on to. Fresh branches are left at one side (C4), representing a (much accentuated) emu's tail. At the centre, towards the top of the tree-trunk, a pad (C2) of leaves or bagging is placed to act as a seat. Branches and leaves are then strewn at the foot of the tree (C6) to break a fall if one should occur.

The whole is a realistic representation of an emu.

CONCLUSION.

For the student of primitive life the chief interest in the imitative play of native children lies in its obvious educational value. The primitive child's school is its playground, and his playground is everywhere.

R. M. BERNDT.

ABORIGINAL CHILDREN'S GAMES.

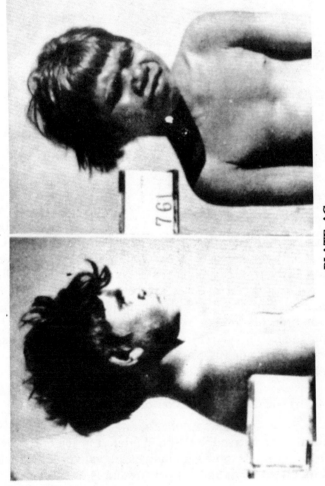

PLATE AC.

Two native children of the 'Anta'kirinja tribe, at Juldi.   Left : A boy.   Right : A girl.

By courtesy of the South Australian Museum.

PASTIMES OF MAORI CHILDREN

Elsdon Best

play, competition, two sides, rules, and criteria for determining a winner, we simply ignored most of the games of young children which have rules but are somewhat diffuse with respect to rules, competition, and winning (as, for example, Farmer in the Dell and Red Rover). I suspect that the road ahead in children lies in a series of such narrowly concentrated efforts from which there can be considerable yields of empirical data.

First, with respect to games of strategy in general. Our cross-cultural studies had indicated at first that there were some cultures with no games, that rich cultures had more, and that more games of physical skill were relatively simpler cultures. But, by contrast, cultures which already had games of chance or games of strategy were much more com-

PASTIMES OF MAORI CHILDREN.

By Elsdon Best, Dominion Museum.

With illustrations by J. McDonald.

Upokotiti.

The illustration shows the first action in this childish pastime, as described in Volume 31 of the *Transactions of the New Zealand Institute*, page 52. In a paper, "Games, Sports, and Amusements of the Northern Queensland Aboriginals," by Walter E. Roth, B.A., M.R.C.S., published twenty years ago,[*] was given an illustration showing native children of that region performing the same action, their hands in the same position. It was to illustrate a native pastime.

The Maori Game of *Upokotiti*.

Hapi Tawa.

This picture illustrates the second act in the pastime of *hapi tawa*, in which children dart their fingers into the cupped hands of one who strives to catch the swiftly moving hands.

The Maori Game of *Hapi Tawa*.

[*] Report of the Australasian Association for the Advancement of Science, Hobart, 1902, page 493.

FOUR GAMES OF TAG
FROM INDIA

Paul G. Brewster

Four Games of Tag from India

By Paul G. Brewster

Games in which chasing is the central element have always been, and still are, high in favor with children of all parts of the world. The thrill of pursuit and eventual capture is as old as the human race. There is in such games a challenge not only to the pursuer's fleetness of foot and to the quickness of his muscular reflexes but also to the rapidity of his mental reactions in the anticipating of his quarry's next move. Nor is the pleasure wholly on the side of the pursuer. Just as there is an atavistic thrill in chasing and seizing, so is there also in fleeing and eluding. In fact it would be difficult, if not impossible, to tell which is the greater.

The very large number of games of chase recoverable from widely separated parts of the world bears eloquent testimony to their continuing popularity. Sometimes it is one player who chases another; sometimes he chases a group of players. In some games all the members of one group pursue all those of another; in others the members of a group go in pursuit of an individual player. In many instances there is the added element of hiding, but even here it is not the cleverness of concealment but the outcome of the race following discovery that decides the winner.

In India, as in most other countries, games of chase are high in favor with children of both sexes. Four of the most popular of these games played by Indian children are Uthali, Limbdi-Pipali, Tadki Chanyadi, and Langadi, all of them forms of Tag.[1] Interesting in their own right, they become more so when compared with games of the same type found in countries far from India and among peoples widely different in language and cultural background.

Uthali (*Utha*=get up) is a variant of the game which American youngsters know as Squat Tag. After the player who is to be the chaser or "It" has been chosen by the drawing of straws, the reciting of a counting-out rhyme, or some other method, he starts in pursuit of the others participating in the game. As long as they are able to do so, they escape his grasp by running. However, if a player is becoming exhausted or is a slower runner than the one who is chasing him, he can save himself by sitting down before the other has been able to touch him. He is permitted to rise and re-enter the game only after

---

[1] For information regarding the playing of these games I am indebted to the kindness of Dr. Kalpalata Munshi, of Andheri.

having been tapped by a comrade, who calls out, "Uthali!" This form of Tag is found also in Italy, in Spain, in Greece, in Korea, and elsewhere.[2]

Escape from capture in Limbdi-Pipali is effected in a different manner. This game is always played in a large open space with trees round about, and players who are particularly hard-pressed by the chaser can avoid being tagged by climbing either the Limbdi (the Neem tree) or the Pipali (the Pipal). In the absence of these, they are permitted to climb any other large tree available. In the game of Hang Tag, the American equivalent, a player may not be tagged by the pursuer so long as his feet are not touching the ground, so the usual method of escape is that of grasping a tree branch and then swinging clear of the ground. The same is true also of the Greek game of Tree Toad.[3]

Players participating in a game of Tadki Chanyadi can escape only by standing in the shade. So long as they are in the sun, they must continue running in order to avoid being tagged.

Perhaps the most interesting of all Indian forms of Tag is that called Langadi (Lame). One of the players, chosen by lot, is termed the Langadi, or when girls alone are playing the game, is called the Langadi doshi (Lame old woman). The field of play is divided into two parts of unequal size. Approximately one-fourth of the entire area is the old lame woman's house; the rest is for the other players to run in. The Langadi, hopping on one foot, chases the others. Those whom she succeeds in touching have to go with her to her house and aid her in catching the rest.[4] Players may enter her house and tease her if they are daring enough. But they have to make their escape

---

[2] See Mason and Mitchell, p. 247; Bernoni, p. 62; Kyvernetakis, p. 125; Maspons y Labros, p. 81; Culin, p. 51. In the Greek form of the game that is termed kathistos gunegetos there is apparently no limit to the number of times a player is allowed to squat during the course of the game. However, a definite number is usually decided upon before a game begins. In Korea the player who is "It" is known as *Syoun-ra* (watchman). Those pursued can avoid capture by sitting down and saying *"taik-kok."* The first player to be caught becomes "It" for the following game. Gomme (II, 291ff.) describes English forms in which the player avoids capture by squatting and calling out "a barla," then calls "Ma barla oot" when he rises and rejoins the others in the game. No assistance on the part of his comrades is required.

[3] See Hunt and Cain, p. 123; Boyd, p. 18.

[4] Cf. Link Tag, Press Gang, Fish Net, and similar forms in which the captured players must aid the captor. See, for example, Acker, p. 97; Maclagan, p. 208; Boyd, p. 16. A good example of the type is the Czechoslovak game of Fisherman. In this game one of the players is the fisherman and the rest are fish. The fisherman calls out, "The fisherman is coming!" and starts in pursuit of the others. Those who are caught by him become fishermen. They must now join their captor and hold each other's hands in order to form a "net" for the capturing of the remaining players.

before her return, as she is permitted to use both legs inside her house. The player who is last to be caught becomes the Langadi for the next game.[5]

It would be interesting to know whether among the Indian games of Tag there is one similar to the Swedish *haller i Guds grona jord,* particularly in view of Dr. P. K. Gode's recent research. In the Swedish game just mentioned, a player escapes capture or tagging by bending over and grasping a handful of grass. Working on a quite different problem, the antiquity of a popular saying, Dr. Gode has discovered numerous allusions to the ancient practice of holding grass *in the mouth* in token of surrender or submission. He has treated the subject in *Gurukula-patrika* (July, 1950), 21-24, in a volume of *Indian Culture* commemorating Dr. B. M. Barua, and more recently, in his "Antiquity of the Custom of Holding Grass in the Mouth as a sign of surrender in the light of a reference to it in the *Mahabharata.*" The *Mahabharata* reference—

> One should not kill (on the battlefield) an old man, a child, a woman, a brahmin and a person, who with his *mouth full of grass* says: "I am yours"

makes it clear that the practice goes back to near the beginning of the Christian Era. Dr. Gode points out further that the practice was early prevalent in Europe, citing a reference to it by Pliny (23-79 A.D.).

Since in very early times the performing of this act saved the vanquished from further molestation, may not children have incorporated it into their play, thus saving themselves, at least temporarily, from *their* enemy, the tagger? If we accept this hypothesis, then we may assume that originally the player held grass *in his mouth* and that the Swedish game represents a form intermediate between the original and such degenerate variants as Squat Tag, in which the role of the grass has been entirely forgotten and the player merely squats or crouches on the ground.

Henderson State Teachers College   *Arkadelphia, Arkansas*

---

[5] Hall (p. 61) describes a similar Syrian game in which the player who is "It" has to hop, while the others may run. A Greek form in which the chaser, who is blindfolded, must hop throughout has been recovered from Pont Euxin. See also Boyd, p. 31 (Lame Fox) ; Hunt and Cain, p. 41.

JOHNNY ON THE PONY

A New York State Game

Paul G. Brewster

JOHNNY ON THE PONY

A NEW YORK STATE GAME

By PAUL G. BREWSTER

JOHNNY on the Pony was described to me by a New York student of mine at the University of Missouri in 1940. Johnny on the Pony is played by two teams, both having the same number of players. One team is designated as "Johnny," the other as the "Pony." The Pony team selects one of its members to act as "pillow." This player stands upright with his back braced against any convenient building, tree, or other strong support. Another on the same team bends over and places his head between the thighs of the "pillow," at the same time grasping the latter's legs in order to brace himself. The rest of the Pony team then assume a similar position in a line formed behind these two lead men.

When the Pony team is ready, the first man on the Johnny team backs off far enough to give himself a good running start. He runs toward the Pony, and without stopping places his hands on the back of the hindmost man for leverage and vaults as far as possible, coming down in a sitting position on the back of one of the group. The same procedure is followed by the rest of the Johnny team. As soon as the last man alights, the members of the Pony team begin to chant "Johnny on the pony, one, two, three." If they can repeat this three times while supporting the others on their backs, the two teams exchange roles. If, on the other hand, they collapse under the weight before they can repeat it three times, the Johnny team jumps again. Should any player on the latter fall off or even touch one foot to the ground, his becomes the Pony team.

Since, naturally, the object of any Johnny team is to bring about the collapse of the other, the members of the former try to concentrate as much weight as possible un one player, previously singled out as a weak link in the human chain.

[Cf. Alice Bertha Merck Gomme, *The Traditional Games of England, Scotland, and Ireland*, I, 52–53 (illustration on page 52), and G. F. Northall, *Folk Rhymes....*, p. 401. See also my article, "Some African Variants of 'Bucca, Bucca'" (*Classical Journal*, XXXIX, 293–295).]

#

SOME UNUSUAL FORMS
OF "HOPSCOTCH"

Paul G. Brewster

SOME UNUSUAL FORMS OF "HOPSCOTCH"

by

Paul G. Brewster

The playing methods to be described in the following pages were noted down from information furnished by the writer's students at the University of Missouri in 1940. One, the last was supplied by a New York boy; the rest are from Missouri students.

1. The player hops into each square with the same foot, and goes through the whole diagram and back again without putting the other down. If he is successful in so doing, he puts his initials in any square he chooses. The next player then hops as did the first, but must not alight in the square containing the first player's initials. Any number may play, but ordinarily there are not more than three or four players.

21	16	15	6	5
22	17	14	7	4
23	18	13	8	3
24	19	12	9	2
25	20	11	10	1

2. This form is played in the same way as that above, except that each player may "rest" at "Home" before returning to the starting-point.

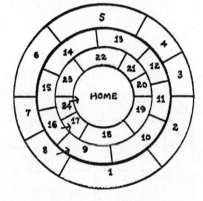

3. Any number of players may participate. Each throws his pebble into 1, hops into 1, picks up the pebble, and hops out. Then he throws the pebble into 2, hops first into 1 and then into 2, picks up the pebble, hops back into 1, and hops out. So he proceeds, first tossing the pebble into each square in succession, then hopping after

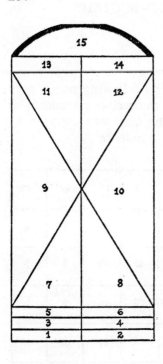

it and hopping out with it. If he fails to throw it into the right square or steps over the line, he is out and another player takes his turn. His pebble remains in the place where it was last thrown and the next player is allowed to step into the square in which it lies, but must hop over it. Playing is sometimes varied as follows: on the first round the player alights on both feet in each square, then goes through on the right foot and then on the left. Next, he puts the pebble on his shoe and tries to walk through the squares in rotation without its falling off. Then he pitches the pebble with his eyes blindfolded, and tries to take it through the squares. Finally, he walks the field with the pebble on his forehead.

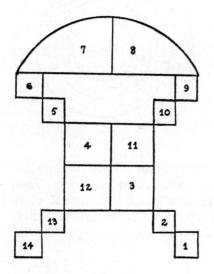

4. This is much like the usual form except that each player goes through the whole field before picking up the pebble. He hops over the square in which it lies as he goes forward, and hops into the square and picks up the pebble when he makes the return trip.

5. A player standing on the baseline tosses a small wooden block into 1, hops in, works the block around with his foot until he can kick it out at the baseline, then hops out after it. Then he does the second "bedroom" in the same way, but must hop through 1 on the way in and out. Numbers 3 and 6, the "pick-ups," are like 1 and 2 except that the block is picked up and carried in the hand as the player hops back through the preceding spaces. Squares 4 and 5 are played like 1 and 2, and so are the "pies," 7, 8, 9, and 10. The "moon," at the top, is the climax of the game. The block is thrown in as before, worked toward the curved side of the "moon," and kicked out backward. Then the player hops out after it, picks it up, places it under his knee and holds it in the angle of the raised leg while he hops back through all the squares in reverse order. An error of any kind ends

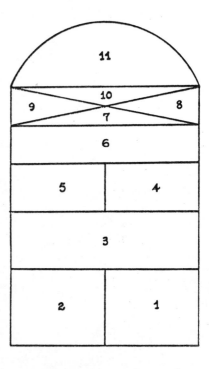

1, 2, 4, 5 are "bedrooms"
3 and 6 are "pickups"
7, 8, 9, 10 are "pies"
11 is "the moon"

player's turn, and he must begin his next turn with the square into which he last threw his block. A player must hop through each square in 1, 2, 3 order to the one where he is due, and must come back in reverse order. He must not step on a line at any time. The block must not stop on a line or be dropped into any square except that for which it is intended.

STREET GAMES OF NEW YORK CITY

John H. Chase

STREET GAMES OF NEW YORK CITY.

By John H. Chase,
Head Worker, Maxwell House, Brooklyn, N. Y.

Children have been asked what games they liked the best, and from these lists the most popular games have been tabulated. Such lists have been made for Brooklyn children, and for Worcester children.

The trouble with this method is that the most recent games played are apt to be recorded by children as the best, gambling games—like craps—are rarely mentioned, and finally children often record games which they enjoy, but rarely play.

Realizing these defects, and desiring to obtain an accurate list of the most popular out-door games of New York City, I followed the plan, for two years, of walking through the crowded tenement house streets and tabulating (1) the different games being played, (2) the number of children playing each, (3) the amount of seeming interest, (4) the date. The same streets were generally covered each day, but this was varied occasionally to see if different regions were doing the same thing. As a rule, with some variations, the great mass of tenement house children played the same games at the same time the city over. And the ten most popular games during the season when I could watch them, were:

I. Playing with fire—bonfires, fires in buckets, etc.

II. Craps—a gambling game with dice.

III. Marbles—always "for keeps," and a simpler game than in the country; several simple varieties.

IV. Potsie—a primitive kind of hop scotch.

V. Leap frog—over milk cans and fire pumps, as well as over boys. Commonest contest to see who can leap the farthest before clearing the obstacle. Many varieties—"head and footer," Spanish fly, etc.

VI. Jumping rope.

VII. Baseball. Probably should be nearer head of the list, but my observations did not include the summer.

VIII. Cat. It is probably also played in the summer. A short stick is pointed at one end and placed on the street. The point is tapped with a longer stick or bat. When the short stick bounds into the air it is hit down the street, and the other boy throws it back as near the starting point as possible.

9

There are three ways of scoring, according to which variety of game is being played.

IX. Buttons. Boys throw, or slide, buttons in turn, from street curb toward a wall. The boy coming the nearest throws all the buttons up into the air. They fall in a shower and the ones which land "heads up" are his. Then the boy who came second closest throws the rest up, and keeps those that land "heads up," etc. The same game is played for other things. Cigarette pictures are played for in this way during January; pennies and almost anything flat at different seasons.

X. Tops. They are generally put in a ring, and the game is to split your opponent's top. You may have a poor top for splitting purposes and a good one for spinning.

The dates for different games are as follows :

	Oct.	Nov.	Dec.	Jan.	Feb.	Mar.	April.	May.
(1)	Leap frog.	Leap frog.	Potsie.	Potsie.	Snow balling.	Cat.	Base ball.	Base ball.
(2)	Craps.	Craps.	Craps.	Craps.		Tops.		
(3)	Buttons.	Buttons.		Cig. Pic.				Cat.
(4)	Fire.	Fire.	Fire.	Fire.	Tops.	Marbles.	Marbles.	Marbles.

CONCLUSION.

1. These ten games are unlike any lists made from the answers of children.

2. The table shows the fire instinct to be very strong.

3. The gambling instinct is very strong.

4. Three popular games are generally going on at the same time.

5. The running games such as tag, prisoner's base, etc., are replaced by cramped games such as leap frog, hop scotch, etc.

HISTORY OF THE GAME
OF HOP-SCOTCH

J. W. Crombie

The following paper was read by the author :—

History *of the* Game *of* Hop-Scotch.
By J. W. Crombie, Esq., M.A.

[With Plate XVI.]

It is a notorious fact that children's games are often imitations of the more serious occupations of the grown-up people they see around them, and that a game once introduced is handed down from generation to generation of children long after its original has ceased to exist. Thus children continue to play with bows and arrows though their parents have long ago discarded those weapons ; and many innocent-looking children's games conceal strange survivals of past ages and pagan times.

The game of Hop-Scotch[1] is one of considerable antiquity. As it is mentioned in Poor Robin's Almanac for 1667 it must have been a prominent game in England for several centuries ; and it has spread over the whole of Europe, appearing under numerous *aliases* in England, Scotland, Ireland, France, Spain, Italy, Sweden, Finland, and other places.

The main features of the game are too familiar to need description. An enclosure is marked off on the ground and

---

[1] Probably a corruption of *Hop-score.*—Halliwell.

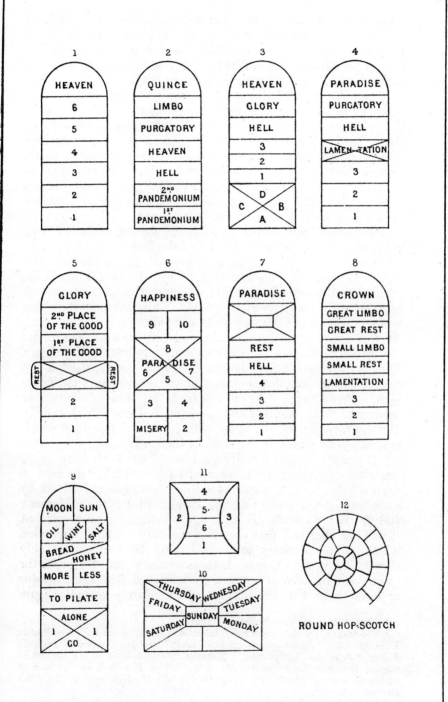

FIGURES OF THE GAME OF HOP-SCOTCH

divided into several courts.   Through those the player, hopping on one foot, successively kicks a piece of stone, taking care not to touch with his foot any of the division lines, and avoiding certain prescribed courts, till the last one is reached, when he turns and kicks it out again in the same way.

Signor Pitré attributes a solar origin to Hop-Scotch.   The stone, he thinks, originally represented the sun, which is kicked through the courts as that luminary passes through the signs of the Zodiac.[1]   While Signor Pitré's opinion is entitled to high respect, his theory appears to me quite untenable; for it would require the number of courts into which the figure is divided to be twelve, whereas in no place where the game is played are there twelve main divisions, and very seldom can this number be made up even if subdivisions be reckoned.

After examining a large number of figures collected from different parts of Europe,[2] I find that the form of most frequent occurrence, and the one from which all the other varieties appear to have developed, is that of figs. 1 and 2, Plate XVI, where a rectangle is divided into six compartments and crowned by a seventh, and almost invariably semicircular court.   This figure is still in use in many parts of Spain, Italy, and Portugal. As they acquired skill, children would very soon wish to render the game a little more difficult by complicating the figure. Thus we find at Venice, though the seven courts of fig. 1 are retained, a vertical line is drawn down the centre of the figure bisecting each court.   Again, one court is often split into four by diagonals, as at Fregenal, Spain (fig. 3, Plate XVI), and La Marca, Italy (fig. 4).   A figure with seven courts, one of which is split by diagonals, is also used in England.[3]

"When we wanted a really good game," an Irish lady writes me, after describing the figure used in her youth, "we used to draw all the lines double so as to make more courts."   It is by some such process that fig. 8, Plate XVI (used in Mazzara, Italy), has been evolved.   This figure contains nine courts, but it will be observed that the names of two courts occur twice, which points strongly to there having been originally only seven.   So in fig. 7, used both in France and England, the extra court introduced between that marked *Rest* and *Paradise* appears to be the embodiment of an entirely separate figure

---

[1] Pitré, "Guiocchi Franchuilleschi," xxxvii.

[2] The Italian, Spanish, and French varieties of the game are fully described in Pitré, *loc. cit.*; "Bibliotheca de las Tradiciones Populares Españolas," tom. iii; Belèze, "Jeux des Adolescents."   For the information as to the method of playing the game in different parts of the British Islands I am indebted to numerous correspondents, especially to Mr. G. H. Kinahan, of the Irish Geological Survey.

[3] "Loy's Handy Book of Games" (Ward, Lock & Co.), p. 12.

g. 10, Plate XVI), which will be spoken of presently. On the other hand, we find many variations of the original figure which have gone in the direction of simplification, one or more of the seven courts being omitted. In Llerena, Spain (fig. 5, Plate XVI), there are only six courts, but the analogy of the nomenclature of a number of other Spanish figures points to the third court having been omitted. Similar omissions have produced fig. 6, Plate XVI, used in county Antrim, Ireland, and a number of others in various places. There is thus a considerable body of evidence to show that seven was the original number of courts in the figure. Even the children themselves seem to have been struck by this characteristic, for in several parts of Italy, Spain, and France they have given to the seven courts the names of the seven days of the week, and sometimes called the game itself "the week."

But even in the places where this is done, those names always co-exist with others which are widespread, and evidently very ancient. Although in this country the names of the courts have almost entirely disappeared, we still find the top court called *Paradise*. Now *Paradise, Heaven, Glory, Happiness,* or some such name, is applied to this court with the most striking frequency in every country in which the game is played, the few exceptions being where it has been supplanted by a name alluding to its shape, such as *Quince, Calderon,* &c., and even then *Paradise* is generally found in the name of one of the lower courts. In Sicily this court is called *Death.* *Purgatory* or *Hell* occurs almost as frequently as a name for one of the lower courts, and it the player has to scrupulously avoid alighting in. In Limerick the next to the last court is called *Caol,* meaning *Narrow,* or *Hell;* and *Narrow* occurs as a name of one of the courts in several parts of Spain and Italy. *Rest* is also a common name for one of the lower courts, and in it the player has the privilege of reposing for a moment and putting both feet on the ground.[1] *Misery, Lamentation,* &c., are found as names for the lower courts in many places, while *Limbo* also occurs with frequency. Let us now trace the course of the player on some of these figures. In England and France (fig. 7, Plate XVI), after traversing four nameless courts and *Rest,* he has to avoid *Hell,* pass through the four triangles (called *Culottes* in France), when at last he reaches *Paradise.* In La Marca, Italy (fig. 4), his course lies through 1st, 2nd, 3rd, when he enters *Lamentation,* and has to pass through *Hell* and *Purgatory,* after which he ends his wanderings in *Paradise.* In

---

[1] In some parts of Ireland the player, when he reaches the cross courts (fig. 8, Plate XVI), has to stand on one leg till he counts "seven times seven."

Fregenal, Spain (fig. 3), he passes through 1st, 2nd, 3rd *Hell*, and *Glory*, and he finds himself in *Heaven*. In Mazzara, Italy (fig. 8, Plate XVI), 1st, 2nd, 3rd, *Lamentation*, two *Limboes*, and two places of *Rest* have to be traversed before the *Crown* awards his completed labours. But in some places he gets off easier. In Villafranca, Spain, he reaches *Heaven* by passing through 1st, 2nd, 3rd, the *Place of Rest*, and the *Place of Asses*. In Llerena, Spain (fig. 5), it is even smoother sailing. There he enters successively 1st, 2nd, and the *Places of Rest*, then he passes through the *first* and *second quarters of the good*, and he soars into *Glory*. Let us now take the Seville figure (fig. 2, Plate XVI) as an example of a confusion of names. The top court has changed its name to *Quince (Gamboa)*, and the central court is called *Heaven*. This alteration makes the player's course far less satisfactory, for after passing through 1*st Pandemonium*, 2*nd Pandemonium*, and *Hell*, he suddenly finds himself in *Heaven*, but only to be hurried out of it into *Purgatory* and *Limbo*, and after all he reaches nothing but a place called by the senseless name of *Quince*. The conclusion to which this curious nomenclature points is self-apparent, and when we add to it the fact of the game being called "Paradise" in Italy, and "the Holies" in Scotland, there can be little doubt that in early Christian times the children who played it, whether from their own inventiveness, or at the inspiration of their teachers, had some rough idea of representing the progress of the soul through the future state, and that they divided their figure into seven courts to represent the seven stages of Heaven, which formed a prominent feature in their eschatological beliefs.

It might be objected to this conclusion that it will not explain many names such as those in fig. 9 (used at Malaha, Spain), which is one of the most corrupted I have met with. But the originals of those names are often apparent corruptions of words which accord with the theory;[1] and, considering that they have been handed down for centuries through generations of

---

[1] I have been careful to select all my illustrations from cases where the meanings of the names were beyond dispute. In fig. 5, Plate XVI, however, there are two further names, *Palajanso* and *Calajanso*, applied to the diagonal courts. My inquiries as to the meaning of those corrupted words have not been successful. The name of the top court in fig. 8 is *Corna* (horn) ; but I think the analogy of several other figures indicates that this is a corruption of *corona* (crown). As an instance of how the names get corrupted I may mention the word *Plato* (silver), occurring at Dos Hermanas, which is evidently a corruption of *Pilato* (Pilate), frequently used in other Spanish figures. In Zafra, Spain, the penultimate court is called *Gato* (cat). I think that this may possibly be a corruption of the word *Purgatorio* (Purgatory), which is so frequently found elsewhere. To Spanish children this latter word would be a little difficult, and they would catch at the familiar syllable *gato*, just as our own do at *cat* in *catechism*. If this be conceded, the Zafra figure is a very perfect example. The seven courts are all simple, and called 1, 2, 3, *Rest*, *Narrow*, *Purgatory*, *Crown*.

children entirely ignorant of their original intent, and even of their meaning, the wonder is not that they are corrupted, but that they remain so perfect as they actually are. Even in the Malaha figure the names *Sun, Moon, Pilate,* and the formula at starting, *I go alone,* are not a little suggestive.

There remains to trace the earlier history of the game. Previous to Christianity it obviously cannot have existed in its present form, but games, in order to be as lasting as this has been, must not be invented, but grow. There is reason to believe that Hop-Scotch developed itself from a combination of several ancient games. Julius Pollux speaks of a game played by the ancients where they counted the number of hops which could be made on one foot, but no scores are spoken of.[1] The penalty of ἐφεδρισμὸς used in connection with an ancient game of marksmanship, and in which the vanquished player had to carry the victor on his back, has also associated itself with Hop-Scotch, and forms part of the game both in Spain and Italy.[2] It would seem, then, that the game of hopping got wedded to some other game consisting of a figure, some recess of which it was the player's object to reach. Whether this union took place before or after Christianity it is difficult to determine, but certain it is that even now Hop-Scotch is played in many places, both at home and abroad, without any hopping at all, so much so that Sr. Ferraro[3] suggests it may be a modification of the ancient game of quoits. We must therefore look for some pre-Christian game with a figure which would supply the remaining features of Hop-Scotch.

Pliny,[4] in his description of the labyrinths, mentions casually a game played by the Roman boys where they drew labyrinthine figures on the ground. Now, labyrinthine figures are still used for Hop-Scotch, though far less frequently than those of the type already described. Fig. 12 is used in France, the inner circle being called *Paradise.* The same figure is found in England,[5] and the game played on it called "Round Hop-Scotch," while a less perfect form of it also occurs in Scotland. Fig. 10 (which is not unlike a rough sketch of the Cretan labyrinth) represents another form the game takes in France, the same figure also being used for the game of Marelle. Fig. 11 is perhaps the transition between the two types. It is used at Villafranca, Spain, but a figure conforming to the ordinary type obtains also in that place. It is therefore not unreasonable to suppose

---

[1] Jul. Poll., "Onomatiscon," ix, 7.
[2] Pitré, "Guiocchi," p. 142; "Tradiciones pop. Espan.," iii, p. 203.
[3] "Archivio per lo studio delle tradizioni populari," p. 246. Palermo, 1882.
[4] Pliny, xxxvi, 13.
[5] Crawley, "Manly Games for Boys," p. 79.

that those labyrinthine figures may be survivals of a form of figure more ancient than those of the ordinary type by which they have now been superseded.

Moreover, we know that among the ancients the tradition of the labyrinths was more or less vaguely associated with the future world, and this might have suggested to the Christian children the eschatological ideas which they introduced into the game, even if the difficulties and wanderings of the labyrinth had not in themselves offered sufficient analogy to the wanderings of the soul in a future state.   But how came the labyrinthine figure to be exchanged for that of the rectangle with the rounded end ?   It is well known that when Christianity replaced a pagan culture, it did not destroy, but assimilate.   It adopted the stones of the old edifice, but it insisted on hewing them into Christian shapes.   I can account for the transition of figure in the game of Hop-Scotch only by suggesting that this principle had been in operation there also.   The Christian children, I believe, not only adopted the general idea of the ancient game, converting it into an allegory of Heaven, with Christian beliefs and Christian names; but they Christianised the figure also. They abandoned the heathen labyrinth, and replaced it by a form far more consistent with their ideas of Heaven and future life, the form of the Basilicon, the early Christian Church, dividing it into seven parts as they believed Heaven to be divided, and placing the inmost sanctum of Heaven in the position of the altar, the inmost sanctum of their earthly church.

Explanation of Plate XVI.

Various figures of the game of Hop-Scotch, as played in different countries of Europe.

Figs. 1 and 2 represent forms frequently used in many parts of Italy, Spain, and Portugal; fig. 3 is found at Fregenal, Spain; fig. 4 at La Marca, Italy; fig. 5 at Llerena, Spain; fig. 6 in co. Antrim, Ireland; fig. 7 in France and England; fig. 8 at Mazzara, Italy; fig. 9 at Malaha, Spain; fig. 10 in France; fig. 11 at Villafranca, Spain; and fig. 12 in France and England.

DISCUSSION.

Dr. E. B. TYLOR thought that the author had made out his case that the various forms of the game, especially in the South of Europe, point back to an original game probably in vogue before the Christian Era.   In that case, for the source of the seven compartments we may perhaps look back beyond the Christian seven heavens to the seven planetary spheres from which these were derived.

STREET GAMES OF BOYS IN BROOKLYN, N.Y.

Stewart Culin

STREET GAMES OF BOYS IN BROOKLYN, N. Y.

THE games of which I shall give an account are all boys' games or games in which both boys and girls participate, and were all described to me by a lad of ten years, residing in the city of Brooklyn, N. Y., as games in which he himself had taken part. They are all games played in the streets, and some of them may be recognized as having been modified to suit the circumstances of city life, where paved streets and iron lamp-posts and telegraph poles take the place of the village common, fringed with forest trees, and Nature, trampled on and suppressed, most vividly reasserts herself in the shouts of the children whose games I shall attempt to describe.

Marbles and tops and kindred sports, which have their set times for advent and disappearance, together with the special amusements of girls, I have left as deserving more extended consideration than can be given them in this article, where I shall confine myself to the outdoor games of boys as played in the city of Brooklyn.

"Who shall be it?" is the first question asked when children assemble to play games. Counting out is the general procedure, but among boys in Brooklyn the method referred to by Mr. Bolton,[1] as conducted by boys in New England under the name of "Handholders," is more in favor. It is the custom in Brooklyn when boys are discussing some game for one to cry out, "Pick her up!" another, "Handholders!" others, "First knock!" "Second knock!" and so on. The first boy picks up a stone and gives it to the one who cried "Handholders!" and goes free. The subsequent procedure is known to everybody. In ball games, and in many games in which sides are chosen, one of the leaders will toss a bat to the other, and they will then grasp it hand over hand until the one who has "last grasp" is adjudged to have won the first choice. "Counting out" is almost the invariable custom among girls in Brooklyn, and the boys, possibly for that reason, affect to think lightly of it, although they do occasionally resort to it. I have made a collection of the current rhymes, but as they are all given by Mr. Bolton, in his admirable work on the subject, I need not make further reference to them.[2]

And now for the games. Many of them have, no doubt, often been described before, and the writer makes no claims to originality

[1] Dr. Carrington Bolton, *The Counting-out Rhymes of Children*, New York, 1888.

[2] A large number of counting-out rhymes, collected by Francis C. Macauley, Esq., have been kindly placed by him in the writer's hands. As many of them, not included by Mr. Bolton, were contributed by French and Irish maidservants, it is probable that a part at least may become incorporated in the lore of American children.

either in his materials or comments. He has only attempted to arrange the games in groups, so that their relations, one to another, may be apparent, and the scientific value of these specimens of child-lore, which has not, even in our highly developed civilization, ceased to be folk-lore, may become somewhat revealed.

I. TAG.

In its simplest form, one player, who is "it," attempts to tag, or touch, one of the other players, and when successful runs away, so as not to be tagged in his turn. The game is sometimes rendered more complicated by certain places which are called "hunks" or "homes" being agreed upon, where the players may find refuge when closely pursued. One of these forms is known as

2. WOOD TAG.

In this game, the one who is "it" tries to tag any player who is not touching wood, any object of wood being regarded as a "home" or "hunk." Otherwise the game is the same as simple tag.

Tag is sometimes varied by increasing the difficulties of the pursuit, as in the two following games : —

3. FRENCH TAG.

In this game bounds are agreed upon, within which are numerous fences, high stoops, etc. Those who are pursued run up the steps and jump the fences to avoid being tagged, and the first caught becomes "it," as in the simplest form of the game. Any one who is seen to go outside the bounds is at once declared to be "it" by the pursuer.

4. FENCE TAG.

Bounds are chosen along a fence. "It" gives the other players a chance to get over the fence, and chases them until he tags one of them, who becomes "it" for the next game. The players jump over the fence and back again, as they are pursued, but are only allowed to cross the fence within the bounds.

5. SQUAT TAG.

This game is played within boundaries, and the one who is "it" may chase any of the other players. When closely pursued, they may escape being tagged by squatting down. This immunity is only granted to each individual a certain number of times, usually ten, as may be agreed upon, and after his "squats" are exhausted he may be tagged as in the ordinary game.

6. CROSS TAG.

The player who is "it" selects one of the others whom he will chase. The pursued is given a short start, and, while both are running, another player will try to cross between them. If successful, he becomes the object of pursuit, and this is continued until one of the players is tagged. He becomes "it," and the game is continued.

7. LAST TAG.

When a company of children are about dispersing to their homes after their play, one will start up the cry of "Last tag," and endeavor to touch one of the others, and retreat into the house. Each will then try to tag and run, until at last there will be two left, and one of them, getting the advantage, will tag the other, and escape to the refuge of his own doorway. From this point of vantage he will exultingly cry, "*Last tag, last tag!*" Whereupon the second boy will reply, and the following colloquy will ensue :—

Second Boy. "Nigger's always last tag!"
First Boy. "Fools always say so!"
Second Boy. "Up a tree and down a tree,
    You're the biggest fool I see."

Children will frequently exclaim, "You can't tag me, for I have my fingers crossed," or "I have my legs crossed," positions which they regard as giving them immunity from the consequences, whatever these may be, of being tagged.

The three following are games of pursuit :—

8. HARE AND HOUNDS.

Two equal sides are chosen, and each player is provided with a piece of chalk. The "hares" are given three minutes' start, and on their way (they can run wherever they like) they must make a straight mark [——] upon the pavement. The "hounds" who follow them must cross the chalk marks made by the "hares." The chase is continued until the "hares" are caught.

9. ARROW CHASE.

On a cold morning, when boys wish to play some game in order to keep warm, "arrow chase" is proposed. Sides are equally chosen, and a large boundary agreed upon. The side that starts first is provided with chalk, with which the players mark arrows upon the pavement, pointing in the direction of their course. The others follow when five minutes have elapsed, tracking the pursued by the arrow-marks until all are caught.

10. RING RELIEVO.

The two best runners "count out" to see which shall have the first choice, and this done, these two alternately choose a boy for his side until all are chosen. A course is then determined on, and one side is given a start, which, if the course is around a city block, is usually a quarter of the way round. The start given, the chase commences, and when one of the pursued is captured, he is brought back to the starting-place, where he is placed within a ring marked with chalk or coal upon the pavement. If he succeeds in pulling in one of his opponents while they are putting him in the ring, he becomes free. Or one of his own men will watch his chance to relieve him by running and putting one foot in the ring. The game continues until all players of the side that had the start are made captives.

11. PRISONER'S BASE.

Two even sides are chosen, and go upon opposite sides of the street. Bounds are agreed upon about two hundred feet apart, between which the game is played. One of the players starts the game by running into the middle of the street, and another from the opposite side will try to capture him. While the first is running back, one from his side will endeavor to capture his pursuer, and this is continued, any player having the right to take those who ran out before him, and being protected from their attack. The prisoners solicit the players on their own side to rescue them, which they may do by touching them, although the rescuers themselves run great chance of being caught. The side wins that makes captives of their opponents.

In the three following games, the one who is "it" tries to catch the others, who, as they are caught, must join "it" in capturing the remainder.

12. BLACK TOM.

The boy who is "it" stands in the middle of the street, and the others on the pavement on one side. When "it" cries, "Black Tom" three times, the other players run across, and may be caught, in which case they must join the one who is "it" in capturing their comrades. "It" may call "Yellow Tom" or "Blue Tom," or whatever he chooses; but if any one makes a false start, he is considered caught, or if one of the captured should cry, "Black Tom" three times, and any player of the other side should start, he is considered caught. The first one caught is "it" for the next game.

13. RED ROVER.

The boy who is "it" is called the "Red Rover," and stands in the middle of the street, while the others form a line on the pavement on one side.   The Red Rover calls any boy he wants by name, and that boy must then run to the opposite sidewalk.   If he is caught as he runs across, he must help the Red Rover to catch the others. When the Red Rover catches a prisoner, he must cry, "Red Rover" three times, or he cannot hold his captive.   Only the Red Rover has authority to call out for the others by name, and if any of the boys start when one of the captives who is aiding the Red Rover calls him, that boy is considered caught.   The game is continued until all are caught, and the one who is first caught is Red Rover for the next game.

14. RED LION.

The players "count out" to see who shall be "Red Lion," who must retreat to his den.   Then the others sing : —

> Red Lion, Red Lion,
> Come out of your den,
> Whoever you catch
> Will be one of your men.

Then the Red Lion catches whom he can, and takes him back to his den.   The others repeat the call, and the two come out together and catch another player, and this is continued until all are caught. The first one caught is Red Lion for the next game.

Another way : One boy is chosen "Red Lion" as before, and the others select one of their number as "chief," who gives certain orders. The chief first cries "Loose!" to the Red Lion, who then runs out and catches any boy he can.   When he catches a boy, he must repeat "Red Lion" three times, and both he and the boy whom he has caught hurry back to the den to escape the blows which the other players shower upon them.   The chief may then call out "Cow catcher," when the Red Lion and the boys he has caught run out of the den with their hands interlocked, and endeavor to catch one of the others by putting their arms over his head.   When they catch a prisoner, they hurry back to the den to escape being hit.   If a boy's hands should break apart in trying to catch another boy, all the boys from the den must run back, as they may be hit.   The chief may call "Tight," when the boys in the den take hold of hands, and try to capture a boy by surrounding him, and so taking him to the den.   The chief may also call "Doubles," when two boys must take hold of hands, or all the boys in the den may go out in twos and try to catch prisoners.   The chief may call out these commands in any order he likes after the first, and repeat them until all the boys are caught.

15. EVERY MAN IN HIS OWN DEN

is similar to the preceding. When a company of boys and girls are standing in a group, discussing what game to play, one of them will suddenly shout, "Every man in his own den." Each will at once select for his den a place not too near that of another. One player will then run out, and a second will try to catch him. The third player out will try to catch the first or second, and so on until the last one out, who may catch any player who is out of his den. When a player is caught, he goes to the aid of the one who catches him. In this way several sides may be formed, and the side that captures all the players wins the game.

I find three games of hiding, as follows : —

16. I SPY, OR HIDE AND SEEK.

A boundary of a block is agreed upon, within which the players may hide, and then they count out to determine who shall be "it" for the first game. A lamp-post or tree is taken as the "home" or "hunk ;" the one who is "it" must stand there with his eyes closed, and count five hundred by fives, crying out each hundred in a loud voice, while the others go hide. At the end of the five hundred, "it" cries : —

> One, two, three !
> Look out for me,
> For my eyes are open,
> And I can see !

and goes in search of those in hiding. They may hide behind stoops, in areas, etc., but are not permitted to go in houses. When "it" discovers a player in hiding, he cries out, "I spy so and so," calling the person by name, and runs to "hunk," for if the one spied should get in to "hunk" first, he would relieve himself. The players run in to the "hunk" when they have a good chance, and cry *relievo!* and if they get in first, they are free. Sometimes the game is so played that, if a boy runs in and relieves himself in this way, he also relieves all the others, and the same one is "it" for the next game. Two players will frequently change hats in hiding, so as to disguise themselves, for if the one who is "it" mistakes one player for another, as often happens through this change of hats, and calls out the wrong name, both boys cry, "False alarm !" and are permitted, according to custom, to come in free. The game is continued until all the players come in, and the first caught becomes "it" for the next game. In "I spy," the one who is "it" is sometimes called the "old man."

17. THROW THE STICK.

One player throws a stick as far as he can, and the one who is "it" must run after it, and put it back in its place. In the mean time the others hide. "It" then looks for those in hiding, and when he spies one of them, he cries out and touches the wicket. The players may run in from hiding, and if they touch the wicket before "it," they are free. The first spied becomes "it" for the next game.

18. RUN A MILE.

The boy who is "it" runs from one street corner to another, and while he runs, the others go hide. The first boy spied is "it," unless he can get in and touch the base before the spy.

Of vaulting games there are four.

19. LEAPFROG.

This game is played by several boys who vault in turn over each others' backs. Thus if four play, the first leans over, and the second vaults over him ; the third then vaults over the first and second, and the fourth over the first, second, and third. Then the first boy vaults over the fourth, third, and second, and thus the game may be continued indefinitely.

20. HEAD AND FOOTER.

Any number of boys can play. When boys are "standing around," one boy will squat down, and cry, "First down for Head and Footer. He becomes the "leader." Then another boy will squat down and cry, "Second down for Head and Footer!" and so on, and the last one down is "it."

A level place is selected, preferably on the grass, but otherwise on the sidewalk, and a straight line is drawn at a right angle across one end of the course, which latter is usually about thirty feet in length. The one who is "it" stands at the cross line with his feet parallel to that line, and stoops over, and the leader, who is always first, places his hands upon his back, and jumps over him. The others follow in turn, and a fresh line is drawn across the course at the point touched by the one who makes the shortest jump. The one who is "it" must then stoop at the new line, while the leader must jump from the line first drawn to where he is stooping, and then over him as before. The others follow in turn, and this is continued, the one who is "it" advancing to a new line at the end of each round. As the latter goes farther from the line first drawn, the leader may take two jumps before leaping over his back, and finally, as the distance increases, three jumps. If one of the players cannot follow the leader, he becomes "it," and the game is recommenced from the beginning. When a player does not jump squarely over the back of the boy who is down, but touches him with his foot or any part of his body except his hands, it is called "spurring," and he has to go down, and the game is begun again. But if the next in turn leaps over the boy who is down, before he gets up after being touched, the one who touched him is relieved of the penalty. When the boy who is down is touched by one of the jumpers and does not know it, the leader or any of the players who may see it, cry, "Something's up," and the boy who is down may guess three times who it was that touched him. If he succeeds, the one who touched him takes his place, but otherwise he must remain "it."

21. PAR.

This game is identical with "Head and Footer" up to the point where all have leaped over the back of the one who is "it." The latter then moves forward a certain distance, which he measures by placing one foot lengthwise beside the base line and the other foot in the hollow of the ankle at right angles to the first. This distance, amounting to the length of the boy's foot plus the width at the instep, is called a "par." The boys then leap over as before, and this is continued until the distance is so great that some one fails to make the leap, or the one who is "it" is "spurred." The game is then started again from the original line, the one failing to go over, or "spurring," becomes "it."

22. SPANISH FLY.

This game is similar to "Head and Footer" and "Par," except that the one who is "it" remains stationary, and the "leader," who vaults first, practises or suggests various feats or tricks, in which the others must follow him. One of these is called "Hats on the Back." The leader, as he jumps, leaves his hat on the back of the boy who is down. The second boy puts his hat on the leader's, and this is continued, the players piling up their hats, until one of them lurches over the pile, and becomes "it."

23. STUNT MASTER, OR FOLLOW THE LEADER,

is a game in which the leader endeavors to *stunt* the others; that is, perform some feat in which they are unable to follow him. One boy is chosen *stunt master* or *leader*, and the others arrange themselves in order behind him. The leader may vault fences, jump, run, etc., and the others must follow him. Three chances are given to them, and those that fail on the last trial are sent down to the end of the line.

The largest number of games which may be classed together are those in which some object, usually a ball, is either thrown, kicked, or struck with a bat. Of these there is an interesting group, the precursors of our national game of base ball, which are played by the boys in Brooklyn under the following names : —

Kick the Wicket, Kick the Can, Kick the Ball, Hit the Stick, One o' Cat, and *One, Two, Three.*

I find but one hopping game : —

24. HOP SCOTCH.

Two distinct ways of playing this game exist among the children of Brooklyn : one common among boys and girls, called " Kick the stone out," and another, said to be played exclusively by girls, called " Pick the stone up." I shall first describe the former : —

KICK THE STONE OUT.

A diagram, as shown in the figure, is drawn upon the sidewalk, where five flagstones, as nearly of a size as possible, are selected, of which the second and fourth are divided in halves by a line drawn vertically through the centre. The compartment formed by the entire surface of the first stone is marked 1 ; the two compartments on the next stone, 2 and 3 ; the third stone is marked 4 ; the fourth stone, 5 and 6 ; and the fifth and last stone, " home." The diagram may be enlarged, and the numbers continued up to 10, which makes the game longer and more difficult. Each player finds a stone of convenient size, one about an inch thick being usually selected.

The first player stands without the diagram, and throws his stone into the compartment marked 1. If it falls fairly within that compartment, he hops on one foot into the same place and kicks the stone out, taking care not to put down his other foot or to step on a dividing line, as either would lose him his turn. If he succeeds in kicking the stone out and hopping out himself, he throws the stone into number 2, and then hops into number 1, and from that into number 2, kicks the stone out, and hops back as before. This is continued until " home " is reached, and the one arriving there first wins the game.

PICK THE STONE UP.

This is played in the same manner as " Kick the stone out," except that the players pick the stone up instead of kicking it out.

25. KICK THE WICKET.

A lamp-post or a tree is chosen as " home," and several bases are agreed upon, usually four, around which the players run. The boy who is " it " places the wicket, which is sometimes made of wood, and sometimes of a piece of old rubber hose, against the tree or post chosen as home, and then stations himself at some distance from it, ready to catch it when it is kicked by the other players. They take turns in kicking the wicket. If it is caught by the boy who is " it," the kicker becomes " it." If the boy who is " it " does not catch the wicket, he runs after it and puts it in place, and any boy whom he catches running between the bases, when the wicket is up, becomes "it." The players run around the bases as they kick the wicket, and when they make the circuit, and touch home, they form in line, ready to kick the wicket again, each in his turn. If all the boys have kicked the wicket, and are on the bases, the one nearest home becomes "it," and must run in and touch the wicket, as all must do when they become " it."

26. KICK THE CAN.

This game is identical with " kick the wicket," except that an empty tin can, usually a tomato can, mounted on a rock, is substituted for the wicket.

27. KICK THE BALL.

Bases are marked out as in playing base ball, that is, first, second, and third base and home plate, and equal sides are chosen. A small rubber ball or a base ball is used. The boys of one side arrange themselves around the bases, and one of them a little to one side of the home plate. Then a boy from the opposite side, who stands at the home plate, kicks the ball in the direction of the bases, and immediately runs to the first base, thence to the second, and so on to the third base and back home. This is counted as one run. But if the ball is stopped by one of the players on the other side, and thrown to the boy near the home plate before the one who runs has reached one of the bases, he is out, and another player on the same side takes his place, and again kicks the ball. If the runner is touching a base when the ball is thrown home, he remains there, and waits until the ball is kicked again to run towards home. If one of the players in the field catches the ball when it is kicked, the one who kicked it is out. If a player on a base runs when the kicker attempts to kick the ball, and misses it, he is out. Kicking the ball and running around the bases is continued until three of the boys from the one side are put out. Then the side in the field comes in and has its turn. These together constitute what is called one inning.

Four innings are usually played, and the side that scores highest wins.

28. HIT THE STICK.

Equal sides are chosen, and bases are determined upon, usually at the intersection of two streets, where the curb at one corner is fixed upon as the "home plate," and the other corners designated as first, second, and third base. This game is identical with the preceding, except that, instead of kicking a ball, a small wooden wicket is knocked in the air. The players of one side arrange themselves around the bases, with one boy near the "home plate." One player from the oppo-

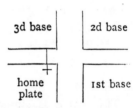

site side also takes his position at the home plate, where he balances a stick, about three inches long by one wide, across the inner end of another stick some ten inches in length, which is laid so as to extend about three fourths of its length beyond the edge of the curb. He then strikes the projecting end a sharp blow with another stick about three feet in length, which he holds in his hands, so that the smallest stick is tossed into the air. The batsman at once runs to the first base, and so to home, which constitutes one run. The boys on the opposite side try to catch the flying stick, however, and if they are successful (they may use their hats for the purpose) the batsman is put out; or, if they should succeed in throwing it to the boy on their side at the home plate, while the batsman is off a base, he is out. The first player is succeeded by another until three men on the side are put out, when the others go in and have their inning. A player on a base may run to another at any time during the game, but he may be declared out by the opposite side, if he is observed, unless the stick has been knocked into the air.

The terms used in this game, as in "Kick the Ball," are the same as those of the game of base ball.

29. ONE O' CAT.[1]

One boy will cry out "Inner!" another will in turn cry "Catcher!" one "Pitcher!" one "First base," and one or two "Fielder!" A home place with a base some feet distant is then agreed upon, and the players take their respective positions. The "inner" takes the bat and stands at the home place between the "pitcher" and "catcher," and strikes at the ball as it is thrown by the "pitcher." If the batter makes three strikes at the ball without hitting it, or if

[1] Dr. Edward Eggleston pointed out, at the Annual Meeting of the American Folk-Lore Society in New York in 1889, that this was originally "one *hole* cat," "two *hole* cat," etc.

he hits it and it is caught by any of the players he is "out," and takes the position of "fielder," while the others move up in order, the catcher becoming batter, the "pitcher" "catcher," and the first base "pitcher," and so on.   If the "batter" strikes the ball, and is not caught "out," he immediately runs to the base and from there "home."   If he reaches that point before the ball, which is at once thrown to the catcher and put on the "home plate," he is considered to have made one "run," and takes his place at the bat again.   The boy who makes the most runs, wins the game.   An ordinary baseball bat is used.

30. ONE, TWO, THREE!

This game is similar to "One o' Cat," except that the players call out numbers, "one, two, three, four," etc., instead of the names of their positions. Those crying "one!" and "two!" become first and second "batsmen;" "three" is "catcher;" "four," "pitcher;" "five," "baseman;" "six," "seven," "eight," "fielders."

```
              ● 3 catcher
              ● 1              ● 2
           1st batsman    2d batsman
              ● 5
           baseman
              ● 4 pitcher
              ● 6 ⎫
              ● 7 ⎬ fielders
              ● 8 ⎭
```

Simpler than the foregoing is the game of

31. HAND BALL.

Only two can play.   A boundary about twenty feet long and as many wide, with a wall or fence at one end, is chosen, and a tennis ball or ordinary rubber ball is used.   One player throws the ball against the wall, and, as it rebounds, the other player strikes it with the palm of his hand back again against the wall.   Then, as it rebounds, the first player strikes it, and so on.   If a player misses the ball, the other player counts one.   The player who thus first counts twenty-five wins the game.   If the ball goes outside the boundary, the miss is not counted.

32. FUNGO.

This game is played on a vacant lot, or in the middle of a wide street.   One boy is chosen for batsman, and the others stand around at some distance from him.   A base ball is used, and the batsman throws it in the air, and then bats it out to the fielders, who endeavor to catch the ball "on the fly."   The one who first catches the ball, a certain number of times that has been agreed upon, takes the batsman's place for another game.

33. SHINNEY.

Sides are chosen, and goals, one for each side, are agreed upon. The latter consist of two lines about three hundred feet apart, which are drawn across the street. The implements of the game consist of sticks with a crook at one end, with which each of the players are provided, and a wooden ball or a block of wood about two or three inches in length, which is placed in the middle of the street, midway between the goals. The sides form two lines facing each other, up and down the street, with a distance of about two feet between them. The two boys on opposite sides of the ball, which occupies the centre of this alley, will strike it at the cry of "Ready;" and each side then endeavors to drive it to its own goal, which constitutes the game. It is not permitted to touch the ball with the hands; and if a player crosses to the side opposite to the one to which he belongs, he is greeted with the cry of "Shinney on your own side!" and liable to a blow on the shins.

34. CAT.[1]

A circle of about four feet in diameter, with a straight line at right angles about twelve feet distant, is drawn upon the sidewalk. The "cat" is whittled from a piece of wood, and is usually about six inches in length by an inch in diameter, with sharp-pointed ends. The players are the "batter," who stands a little to one side of the circle; the "pitcher," who stands at the line; and the "fielders," who are numbered in rotation, and stand about the ring. The pitcher throws the cat towards the circle, and the batter, who stands ready with his bat, a stick about two feet long, hits it or not, as he thinks best. If the cat falls within the circle, the batter is out, and the pitcher takes his place, and all the other players move up one place, while the batter becomes the last of the fielders. If the cat falls without the circle, the batter hits it on one end as it lays on the ground, and as it rises into the air strikes it again. The other boys try to catch the cat in their hats or with their hands as it falls; and if they succeed, the batter is out. If they do not thus catch it, the pitcher endeavors to jump from where it lies into the circle. If it is too far away for the pitcher to cover in one jump, the batter gives him as many jumps as he deems proper. If the pitcher accomplishes the distance in the jumps that have been accorded to him, the batter is out; but if he fails, each jump the batter is allowed counts as one point to his own credit in the game.

[1] The antiquity of this game is well attested by the discovery by Mr. Flinders-Petrie of wooden "tip cats" among the remains of Rahun, in the Fayoom, Egypt (cir. 2500 B. C.). Through the courtesy of Mrs. Cornelius Stevenson, Curator of the Egyptian Department of the Museum of Archæology of the University of Pennsylvania, one of these objects is now exhibited in the writer's collection of games in the American Department of the museum.

35. ROLEY POLEY.

A convenient place is selected, and each player digs a hole three or four inches in diameter. If this is impossible, hats are used instead of holes in the ground. A medium-sized rubber ball is used, and one of the players stands at a distance of about twenty feet, and tries to roll it into one of the hats or holes. All the others stand by their holes; and when the ball enters one of them, its owner must throw the ball at the player nearest to him. Meantime, when a boy sees the ball rolling into any near hole, he will run away to escape being hit. The boy who is hit must put a stone into his hole; but if the thrower is unsuccessful in hitting any one, the stone must go into his own hole. The game continues until one of the players gets ten stones in his hole, when he has to stand up with his back against a wall or fence, and let each boy take three shots at him with the rubber ball, the first time with the thrower's eyes closed, and afterwards with them open. When the boy is put up against the fence, the distance at which the players shall stand, when they throw at him, is sometimes determined by letting the victim throw the ball against the fence three times, and a line drawn at the farthest point to which the ball rebounded is taken as the place at which the throwers shall stand.

36. PICTURES.

This game is a recent invention, and is played with the small picture cards which the manufacturers of cigarettes have distributed with their wares for some years past. These pictures, which are nearly uniform in size and embrace a great variety of subjects, are eagerly collected by boys in Brooklyn and the near-by cities, and form an article of traffic among them.

Bounds are marked of about twelve by eight feet, with a wall or stoop at the back. The players stand at the longer distance, and each in turn shoots a card with his fingers, as he would a marble, against the wall or stoop. The one whose card goes nearest that object collects all the cards that have been thrown, and twirls them either singly or together into the air. Those that fall with the picture up belong to him, according to the rules; while those that fall with the reverse side uppermost are handed to the player whose card came next nearest to the wall, and he in turn twirls them, and receives those that fall with the picture side up. The remainder, if any, are taken by the next nearest player, and the game continues until all the cards thrown are divided.

Of "pitching pennies" my informant knew nothing except that there are said to be three different ways of playing the game. It

was regarded among his associates as a vulgar game, and only prac-
tised by bootblacks and boys of the lowest class, such as compose
the "gangs" that are a well-known feature of street life among the
boys of our cities.   There is said to be a prejudice against other
games on account of their associations among certain sets of boys.
Thus, in Philadelphia the game of *leapfrog* is abandoned to the
rougher outside class, who are known as "Micks" by the boys of at
least one of the private schools.

Concerning the "gangs," my young friend in Brooklyn was unable
to give me much information, other than to relate the name of one
of these organizations, the "Jackson Hollow Gang," which is said to
have obtained more than local celebrity.   I am able, however, to give
at least the names of some of the gangs in Philadelphia, obtained by
personal inquiries among the boys along the Schuylkill river front.
They comprise the Dumplingtown Hivers, of Fifteenth and Race
streets; the Gas House Terriers (pronounced tarriers), of Twenty-
third and Filbert streets; the Golden Hours, of Twenty-fifth and
Perot streets; the Corkies, of Seventeenth and Wood streets; the
Dirty Dozen, of Twenty-fifth and Brown streets; the Riverside, of
Twenty-third and Race streets; the Dung Hills, of Twenty-third
and Sansom streets; and the Gut Gang, of Twenty-third and Chest-
nut streets.   These I am able to supplement with a very complete
list of the names of similar organizations that used to exist in Philadelphia, which has been kindly placed in my hands by Mr. Leland
Harrison.   It is as follows: —

Pots, Twelfth and Shippen.
Skinners, Broad and Shippen.
Lions, Seventeenth and Shippen.
Bull Dogs, Eighteenth and Shippen.
Rats, Almond Street Wharf.
Bouncers, Second and Queen.
Fluters, Tenth and Carpenter.
Niggers, Thirteenth and Carpenter.
Cow Towners, Nineteenth and Car-
penter.
Tormentors, Twenty-second and Race.
Hivers, Broad and Race.
Pluckers, Ninth and Vine.
Buffaloes, Twentieth and Pine.
Snappers, Second and Coates.
Murderers, Twenty-third and Filbert.
Ramblers, Beach and George.
Forest Rose, Seventeenth and San-
som.
Prairie Hens, Fifteenth and Brown.
Bed Bugs, Front and Brown.
Pigs, Twentieth and Murray.

Killers, Eighth and Fitzwater.
Lancers, Twentieth and Fitzwater.
Cruisers, Eleventh and South.
Forties, Eighteenth and South.
Wayne Towners, Eleventh and Lom-
bard.
Mountaineers, Twentieth and Lom-
bard.
Bullets, Twenty-first and Lombard.
Ravens, Eighteenth and Lombard.
Darts, Sixteenth and Lombard.
Spigots, Twenty-third and Callowhill.
Bleeders, Fifteenth and Callowhill.
Hawk Towners, Seventeenth and Cal-
lowhill.
Canaries, Eighteenth and Market.
Clippers, Seventeenth and Market.
Rovers, Nineteenth and Market.
Bunker Hills, Fifteenth and Market.
Badgers, Twenty-first and Market.
Haymakers, Twenty-seventh and Mar-
ket.

Blossoms, Broad and Cherry. Didos, Eighteenth and Lombard.
Railroad Roughs, Eighteenth and The "Didos" were a portion of the
   Washington Avenue. "Raven" gang.

These, however, belong not only to Folk-lore, but to the never-to-
be-written history of our city. They had their laws and customs,
their feuds and compacts. The former were more numerous than
the latter, and they fought on every possible occasion.[1] A kind of

[1] An abstract of this article appeared in the *Public Ledger*, Philadelphia, December 9, 1883, and elicited the following letter from the Rev. Henry Frankland,
of Cheltenham, Pa., which is here printed for the first time : —

The Public Ledger.

Your article on "Street Games" in to-day's (Tuesday) issue of the *Ledger* is
so thoroughly interesting, and has awakened so many memories of the past, that
I cannot resist the temptation of writing a few words in addition. I was especially interested in the account given of the Philadelphia "gangs." It carried me
back to the time when I was a "railroad rough." In those days, under the leadership either of regularly appointed or self-constituted "leaders," the various
"gangs," often by previous arrangement, would meet, and "fight it out" for
hours. What boy of twenty years ago who does not recall these famous "stone
fights"? A scar on my own face near the temple — a scar that will never be
effaced — shows how successfully (?) they were fought. The list of these "gangs"
as given by your correspondent — the most complete I have yet seen — is made
still more complete by the addition of the following : "Buena Vistas," near 13th
and Federal ; "Garroters," south of Federal or Wharton and toward old "Bucks"
Road ; "Schuylkill Rangers ;" and the "Glascous," or "Glassgous," near 20th
and Ellsworth. In addition to these, I distinctly recall the "Tigers" and the
"War Dogs," but cannot now locate them. The "Ravens" and the "Railroad
Roughs" were friendly, and would frequently combine against the combined
forces of the "Glascous" and "Lions ;" they also fought against the "Buena
Vistas."

We had great times in those days. The boy who either could not or would not
fight was of no use. Often, through having to pass through the boundaries of a
hostile "gang" on our way to school, we were compelled to fight. For this reason, we frequently went in companies of three or four. In passing through the
territory immediately in the neighborhood of a fire company, a boy would sometimes be "tackled" and asked, "What hose do you go in for?" If he knew his
neighborhood, and was shrewd enough to "go" for their particular hose, he was
usually set free, but sometimes not before his pockets were rifled. If he was unfortunate enough to "go in for" some other company, he was usually set upon by
his enemies, and most unmercifully "lambasted."

Those days, happily, have passed away. How much the volunteer fire companies were responsible for them, I am unable to say, but my impression is, that
the new and better order of things has prevailed since the introduction of the
paid fire department.

Not all the boys of those "by-gone days" have turned out *bad.* Most of them
were fighters, perhaps, but the habit of taking care of themselves, and fighting
their own battles, has been of incalculable service to some, at least. I could mention at least four preachers of the gospel from down town alone, and many others
who have since occupied positions of honor and usefulness in the church and
State. Let some one else contribute to the list of "gangs" until it is complete,
and if they care to tell us what has become of some of the once famous "leaders" and fighters.

half secret organization existed among them, and new members passed through a ceremony called "initiation," which was not confined altogether to the lower classes, from which most of them were recruited. Almost every Philadelphia boy, as late as twenty years ago, went through some sort of ordeal when he first entered into active boyhood. Being triced up by legs and arms, and swung violently against a gate, was usually part of this ceremony, and it no doubt still exists, although I have no particular information, which indeed is rather difficult to obtain, as boys, while they remain boys, are reticent concerning all such matters. I am also unable to tell how far this and similar customs exist among boys in other cities. They were unknown to my young friend in Brooklyn, although he told me that a new boy in a neighborhood had rather a hard time of it before he was finally recognized as a member in good standing in boys' society. And this leads back to the subject of street games. Here are some of the games the new boy is invited to play : —

HIDE THE STRAW. — Bounds are agreed upon, and the new boy is made "it." All close their eyes while he hides the straw, and afterwards they searched for it, apparently with much diligence. At last they go to the boy and say : "I believe you have concealed it about you. Let us search him." Then they ask him to open his mouth, and when he complies they stuff coal and dirt and other objects in it.

LAME SOLDIER. — The new boy is made "doctor," while the rest are "lame soldiers," who have been to the war, and been shot in the leg. The "lame soldiers" have covered the soles of their shoes with tar or mud ; and, as they hobble past the "doctor," and he examines their wounds, he soon finds that his hands are much soiled, and discovers the object of the game.

FIRE is a game in which the new boy is made a fireman, who is sent in search of a fire ; and when he cries out, as he has been instructed, "Fire! fire! fire!" the others come running from their engine-house, and salute him with a shower of stones.

GOLDEN TREASURE resembles *hide the straw*. The new boy is chosen "thief," two other boys "policemen," and one boy "judge," before whom the "thief" is brought. The "thief" is suffered to go and rob a house. The "policemen" capture him, and bring him before the "judge." The case is tried, and it is discovered that the "thief" has robbed a house where gold was hidden. The "judge" orders him to be searched ; but, as nothing is found on his person, the "judge" says sharply : "Let me look in your mouth, and open it wide, for you may have hidden the gold there." As the prisoner opens his mouth, the others, who stand ready, stuff it with handkerchiefs and dirt and coal, as is most convenient.

Stewart Culin.

AKLAN SUPERSTITIONS ABOUT TOYS

Beato A. de la Cruz

Aklan Superstitions About Toys

By Beato A. de la Cruz

IN the Aklan district in Panay there is some superstition connected with almost every native toy that the children play with, and, strangely enough, almost all the various toys, excepting only a few simple home-made play-things, are believed to bring bad luck.

Take *chongka* for instance, played on a boat-shaped board, called *sungkaan*, with a double row of shallow round holes, each filled with a certain number of small sea-shells, which the two players who take part in the game transfer from one hole to the next according to certain rules that are quite complicated. The first player left without shells is said to be *patay*, dead. The belief is that the one who loses the game will have a death in his family or among his friends or that his house will burn down.

Yo-yo, which has become a fad in other parts of the world, is a seasonal toy in the Aklan region, and is, according to the old folks, a cursed trifle, which, when played with, is an unfailing sign of a coming epidemic. Another superstition connected with the yo-yo is derived from the fact that some imperfection in the string will obstruct the upward movement of the small, whirling wooden disk. The belief is that one who always has trouble with his yo-yo string will die a sudden and unnatural death.

For children to walk on stilts is believed to lead to the affliction of the town with all kinds of *salut*, supernatural beings such a tall, scale-covered *capres* or goblins, long-legged, black-robed skeletons, and enormous demon-pigs and goats. Those who see these frightful creatures are driven out of their wits and will die if not assisted; but the worst of it is that if they are cured they may become *salut* themselves.

It is believed to be harmful to the farmers for the children to fly kites during both the planting and the harvesting seasons. Kites are thought to bring wind, and the rice harvest will be mostly chaff. It is useless even to plant rice with this in prospect. Kite flying also stunts and dwarfs other crops, even root-crops and corn.

On the contrary, for children to play with tops from the time the farmer is plowing and harrowing his field to the time the rice is ready for the reaper, is believed to result in a bountiful harvest. Playing with shells is also believed to bring good crops.

Such beliefs are only strengthened by such occasional events as the fire suffered by a friend of mine after losing in a game of chongka, and as the few deaths from cholera at a time when the children were playing with their yo-yos. However, with the spread of public school education, these beliefs are disappearing and will soon be forgotten. Even the older people who were at first very cynical as to the "science" their children talked about and the modern inventions and ways brought into the region, are beginning to find some relief from the fears inspired by their many false beliefs.

GAMES OF TETON DAKOTA CHILDREN

J. Owen Dorsey

GAMES OF TETON DAKOTA CHILDREN.

BY J. OWEN DORSEY.

The material for the present paper was found in the collection of texts written in the Teton dialect of the Dakota language by George Bushotter, a full-blood Dakota. This collection is now in the possession of the Bureau of Ethnology, in Washington. The present writer is responsible for the arrangement of the information now given, besides its translation into English. Of those games in which children take part as well as their elders, there are five. Games played by none but children amount to fifty-seven, according to Bushotter.

Children of one sex seldom play with those of the other. Each game has its special season or seasons, and it is played at no other times of the year. Wherever Bushotter has named the season for a game, it will be mentioned in this paper.

None but girls can play Shkátapi chik'ála, *Playing with small things,* in which they imitate the actions of women, such as carrying dolls, women's work-bags, small tents, small tent-poles, wooden horses, etc., on their backs; they pitch tents, cook, nurse children, invite one another to feasts, etc.

GAMES PLAYED BY GIRLS OR BOYS.

One played in the spring is Wak'in'kichíchiyápi, *They make one another carry packs.* Some boys pretend to be horses and carry packs; packs are also carried by the girls. The children of each sex imitate their elders. When they pretend to dance the sun-dance, the boys cut holes in their shirts instead of their flesh, and through these holes are inserted the thongs which fasten them to the mock sun-pole.

Hóhotéla, *Swinging,* is an autumnal game. The swing is attached to a leaning tree after the leaves have fallen. When four ropes are used, a blanket is laid on them, and several children sit on the blanket and are pushed forward. Those who push say, "Hohote, hohote! Hohotela, hohotela!" as long as they push them. When two ropes are used, only one child at a time sits in the swing.

Chab ónaskiskíta, *Trampling on the beaver*, is played on pleasant evenings; therefore it is hardly a winter game. Each player gathers his blanket in a roll around his neck. The one who acts the beaver reclines with his blanket around him. The rest form a circle around him, and as they pass around they sing thus: "Chab onaskiskita! Chab onaskita!" Whenever there is a break in the singing, the beaver rises suddenly and chases the others, returning to his former place if he fail to catch any one. Each one caught joins the beaver in the middle of the ring, where they recline with their heads covered. Girls sometimes play this game. Not a game of chance.

Coasting is indulged in by boys and girls, but not by youths old enough to go courting. They use different kinds of sleds.

The seasons for the following games have not been ascertained:

1. Wi-ókichíchiyápi, *Courting the women.*—Played by boys and girls after sunset.

2. Hóshishípa.—Those who cannot keep from laughing are not desired in this game. Each player takes the back of the hand of the one next to him by pinching it, and thus there is formed a perpendicular pile of hands. The hands are swung back and forth while all repeat the word Hoshishipa. The first one who lets go is tickled till he laughs heartily. While each player holds the hand of his neighbor with a thumb and one finger, he uses the other fingers for scratching that hand till it gets red. As they swing their hands they lower them till they get near the ground.

3. Wónape kh'ákh'a.—When one sees that his comrades are dull he says, "My friends, I will wake you up." At once he throws an arrow, a stone, a handful of water, or some other thing into the air, making all scramble for it. Resorted to at times by the girls and young men.

4. *Ghost game.*—Played by boys and girls. One erects a lodge at a distance from the village, and at night he comes hooting like an owl and scratching on the exterior of the tent, where other children are seated. Sometimes the ghost whistles just as they imagine that ghosts do. Some ghosts whiten their faces and paint their bodies at random. Others put red paint around their eyes. All this is at night, when their mothers are absent. Occasionally the children leave the village in order to play this game, going in a crowd to the designated place. Some ghosts whiten their bodies all over, painting themselves black between the ribs. When they do not whiten the whole face they cover the head with white paper,

in which they punch eye-holes, around which they make black rings. The one acting the ghost tickles any one whom he catches until the latter laughs very heartily.

5. *Hide and seek.*—Those who hide whistle when they are ready. Each one who is found becomes the servant of the Wawole or Seeker, and has to walk behind him while he seeks for another.   The servants walk in single file behind their master, in the order of their capture, till all have been found.   Sometimes there are several seekers.

6. Iyópsil echun'pi, *Jumping from a high object.*—The players go to a steep bank, below which there is plenty of sand.   They jump down one after another, each trying to jump further than the others. If they cannot find a suitable bank, they look for a stump or a lean-ing tree.   When night comes their limbs pain them, so some proceed as follows: Mixing ashes with water, they paint an ant on each shin-bone, which insures a speedy recovery.   Other sufferers have their limbs rubbed with grease, and so they go to bed, without having the grease rubbed off.   When their parents remove the grease the pain disappears.

7. Wakan' shkátapi, *Mystery game.*—In this they imitate the deeds of the *wakan* men and women.   A small lodge is set up at a distance from the village, and in it is made a mystery feast, after which the *wakan* persons sing and give medicine to a sick person.   Some pretend to be gods (tawáshichúpi); others claim to hear mysterious sounds; some have pebbles, which they say are gods or guardian spirits which aid them in various ways.   Some pretend to conjure with cacti.   Others give love medicines to boys who wish to gain the love of girls, or to girls who wish to administer them to boys.

8. *Playing doctor.*—This needs no explanation.

9. *Tnking captives from one another.*—Played by many boys (or girls) at the middle of the village area.   Two sides are formed. They approach, each party trying to capture their adversaries.   The game continues till all of one side are captured.   The captive must remain where his captors place him; he can take no further part in the game.   Sometimes his garments are torn into rags, and he is subjected to other rough treatment.   But all is done in sport, and no one gets angry.   When a captive is released and ordered to go home, those on the other side, if boys, say, "Gliye! gliye! gliye;" but if they are girls, they say, "Glana! glana! glana!"

10. *String wrapped in and out among the fingers, etc.*—Played for amusement, not for stakes.   Sometimes one ties a cord in a

strange manner, concealing the ends, which he requests some one else to discover. Occasionally he goes to a tree, bare of bark, or with smooth bark, and marks all over a part of it with many lines crossing at various angles, bidding the spectators find the ends of the lines. In winter one runs his finger along the surface of the snow, tracing a succession of turns hard to follow, concealing the ends for others to find. In summer this is done in the dust, or in the sand when they go swimming.

11. Shkátapi tan'ka, *Playing with large objects*, differs from *Going to make a grass lodge* in this respect: In the latter none but boys take part, while in the former there are girls and boys, who imitate their elders in pitching tents, carrying packs, attending to the children, hunting, etc.

12. Okíchiyut'aᵖ'shni shkátapi, *They do not touch one another.*—The players stand in a circle, and they ask who shall be the first one to sit down? He who sits down last becomes "it," and must chase the others without touching them. Those whom he chases blow their breath at him and spit at him, saying that his skin shall become callous. When he is weary he returns to his place and stands there; the others crowd around him and dare him to touch them. Bushotter says that when one has chased all the others, his place is taken by another, but the next is not very explicit.

13. *Old Woman and her Dog*, an evening game for boys or girls.— The children of the camp assemble and one acts the Old Woman, who says that she has a dog. The children come in a crowd to whip her dog. Each sits with his feet stretched out in front of him. The Old Woman approaches the one at the end of the row, saying, "Grandchild, what did you seek when you whipped my dog?" Then he tells why he did it, for should he or any other player fail to tell about his whipping the dog, the Old Woman must stand with both feet on his knees, pressing them hard against the ground. Thus does she punish those who whip the dog. She passes along the line of players and then retraces her steps, but this time she crawls over the knees of all the players till she reaches the first one. When she questions the children each must give a reason for his conduct. He may say, "I beat him because he tore my blanket." The Old Woman remarks, "You seem very fond of your blanket!" Another may reply, "I hit him because he made me lose my moccasins." If so, she kicks him on the feet. She always makes a ridiculous or an abusive comment on each reply to her questions.

14. Mató-kichiyápi, *Grizzly bear game.*—One child, who acts the bear, digs a hole in the ground and reclines therein. The others crowd around the bear, one being selected as leader on account of his bravery. The leader advances toward the bear, the followers stepping back a little now and then. The leader finally seizes a lock of the bear's hair, saying, "Tunkan'shila Mató, péhin wan! *O, grandfather grizzly bear, here is a hair of your head!*" The bear springs up and chases the players as they flee in all directions. When he overtakes one he beats him or else he tickles him till he laughs heartily. The bear never chases the children until one repeats the words "Mato hin wan." As soon as the captive stops laughing the bear desists from tickling him. The bear has some small sticks fastened to his fingers instead of claws. He goes to some plum trees and reclines beneath one of them. When the players go in a crowd to dislodge the fruit by shooting at it, the bear jumps up and chases them again.

BOYS' GAMES PLAYED IN THE SPRING.

1. Makà kichich'un'pi, *Use mud with one another.*—In the spring, when the ground is soft like putty, this game is played. Two sides are formed. Each boy presses a lump of mud around a stick, then, holding to one end of the stick, he hurls the other end forward, flinging the mud through the air toward one of the opposing players. The hole made by the end of the stick allows the air to pass rapidly through the lump of mud, which makes first a moaning sound like that of a nail thrown into the air; then another sound (tc-tc-tc-tc-tc), as if one blew through a tube. The players chase one another as they throw their mud balls.

2. Anàkichitan'pi, *Running toward one another.*—Played in the spring, when the leaves have opened and the small birds are singing in the forests, the meadow larks singing on the open prairie. The boys form two parties and play making war. They kill and scalp their opponents, using wooden knives. As they scalp they shout, "An'ne!" the cry of victory. Some are taken prisoners. Each one tells of his exploits. No one who is quick to take offense is allowed to join in the game.

3. Makà kichin'in'pi, *They hit one another with earth, i. e.,* with frozen earth.—This is regarded as a very dangerous game. It is played in the early spring. The boys form two parties, and then they chase one another, occasionally knocking down some one on

43

each side. Now and then the players stand on opposite sides of a cañon, armed with switches; the small end of each switch has a lump of frozen earth resembling the peculiar formation, ka°ghítamè, found in the Bad Lands, pressed around it. He flings his stick forward and sends the lump of earth whizzing toward an opponent. Once upon a time when this game was played a brave youth advanced to the front in a boasting manner and hastened toward the other party, relying on the shelter of his blanket; but there came a frozen clod which struck the blanket and hit him squarely in the eye, felling him to the ground; so his comrades carried him home. Those on the other side yelled as they hit their mouths and started in pursuit of the others. Different ones have been blinded from playing this game; yet boys do not hesitate to engage in it, as it hardens them and tests their courage.

4. Tahúka changléshka un'pi, *Game with a raw-hide hoop.*—Occasionally in the early spring the people fear a freshet, so they leave the river bank and camp on the level prairie away from the river. The men hunt the deer, and when they return to camp the boys take part of the hides and cut them into narrow strips, which they soak in water; they make a hoop of ash wood, all over which they put the strips of raw hide, which they interweave in such a way as to leave a hole in the middle, which is called the "heart." The players form two sides of equal number, and ti-oshpaye or *gens* usually plays against *gens.* The hoop is thrown by one of the players toward those on the other side. They are provided with sharp-pointed sticks, each of which is forked at the small end. As the hoop rolls they throw at it, in order to thrust one of the sticks through the heart. When one hits the heart he keeps the hoop for his side, and he and his comrades chase their opponents, who flee with their blankets spread out behind them in order to deaden the force of any blow from a pursuer. When the pursuers overtake one of the fugitives they strike him with the hoop as hard as they can; then they abandon the pursuit and return to their former place, while the one hit with the hoop takes it and throws it, making it roll towards the players on the other side. As it rolls he says to them, "Ho, tatanka he gle, *Ho, there is a buffalo returning to you.*" When the stick does not fall out of the heart, they say that the hoop belongs to the player who threw the stick. This is not a game of chance but of skill, which has been played by large boys since the olden times. Bushotter says that it is obsolescent.

5. Maká shun'kawakan' shkátapi, *Sport with mud horses.*—In the spring boys get some mud from the bank of a stream and shape it into horses or some other quadrupeds.   They play the game midway up the bank or in the forest.   Sometimes they play before the images get dry.   They make the images fight, and sometimes they make them dance.   The players trade images or food.   Now and then they make very good imitations of horses, which each owner keeps a long time.   Sometimes they make buffalo.   But whatever they do make, they use just as men use the real animals.   When they make mud men they cause them to dance the sun-dance, and sometimes they make soldiers or policemen, whom they cause to engage in a fight.   When they become tired of playing they destroy their images, unless they are good imitations of the originals.

6. *Flutes, etc.*—When the leaves appear in the spring the boys go to the woods and make what they call ya-pi'-za-pi, *something made to squeak by blowing with the mouth.*   They make flutes of the wazí washtémna hu tan'ka (*the large stock of the sweet-smelling pine*), of small ash trees, of cedar, and of bone.   Sometimes a boy doubles up a leaf and blows through it.   This leaf is called Yapi-zapi hu, *bone which is made to squeak by blowing with the mouth.*

7. *Egg-hunting.*—Boys take their bows and arrows and go toward the interior of the country in search of birds' eggs.   When the mother bird is on the nest she is sometimes shot, and there are occasions when all the eggs in a nest are broken.   Sometimes they take all the eggs to the village.   There the eggs are boiled, each boy eating those which he has brought home.   When a boy hits a bird he makes a gash or notch with his knife on one end of his bow.   Sometimes they boil the birds and eggs together in the same kettle.

8. Pezhi wokéya kakh ipi *Going to make a grass lodge.*—Bushotter and others played this game on one occasion when they were riding far from camp.   It was in the spring, and the boys gathered tall rushes which they made their horses eat.   Thrice each day they took their horses to water.   They made a grass lodge in which all took seats.   Two boiled food for a feast; the others danced, and after the feast they had a horse-race, putting up stakes for the winners.   They engaged in other occupations, just as if they were men.   They pretended to go on a war expedition, they hunted the buffalo and other animals, they danced the sun-dance, etc., etc.   None but boys were present.

9. Tamníyokhpéye kághapi, *Ball of mud made to float is thrown at.*—In the spring the boys go to a deep stream, where they make two hemispheres of mud, each having one side concave, having been pressed against the elbow for that purpose. They join the hemispheres together, making a hollow ball about three inches in diameter. This ball is thrown into the stream as a mark at which they hurl lumps of mud. Sometimes instead of throwing the mud from the hand they press it around one end of a stick, and when the stick is jerked forward, off flies the mud toward the ball. When the ball is hit it is burst open with a loud report.

BOYS' GAMES PLAYED IN SUMMER.

1. Maghákichiyápi, *Goose and her children.*—This is very popular among the boys, but their mothers seek to break it up. However, the boys manage to slip off one by one and reach a stream where the game is to be played. While on the way to the stream they say one to another, "Let us see who shall be the first to reach there." One acts as the hunter, another as the goose, the rest being the ducks. They enter the water and swim about, slapping the water with the palms of their hands. By and by the hunter catches the boy who is goose, holding him by the hair of the head and saying, "Goose, how many children have you?" The goose gives the number, saying, "There are two," or "There are three." Whereupon the hunter pushes the goose's head under the water two or three times, or oftener, according to the number of children named in the goose's reply. Sometimes when the hunter is about to seize the goose the latter manages to escape to the shore, where the hunter cannot catch him. Sometimes the "ducks" dive; at other times they turn somersaults, alighting on the water in a bent attitude (*i. e.,* either with the body perpendicular and the limbs horizontal or *vice versa*).

2. *Throwing chewed leaves into the eyes.*—When the sun-dance is performed, the boys chew leaves and throw them into the eyes of the boys of another side, usually those of another ti-oshpaye or gens. Two sides are chosen by the players, gens playing against gens. They chew the leaves very fine and slippery. Some of the leaves are gray, others being green. They do not hurt any one by so doing, and no one is offended. Sometimes they moisten deer or buffalo sinew by chewing it, and hit one another across the face with the sinew.

3. *Hunting for young birds.*

AUTUMNAL GAMES OF THE BOYS.

1. Míchapécha un' kich'opi, *They wound one another with a grass which has a long sharp beard.*—When this grass is mature, the boys collect on the prairie and form two sides for the game.   They chase one another, trying to stick their adversaries with the michapecha on the neck, ankle-bones, or on any other part of the body.   The michapecha is arranged in bunches, with which the players hit at one another, not hesitating to give painful blows.   The boys, for the most part, are stout-hearted, and they show no signs of flinching.   They pretent to be engaged in real battles.   This is no game of chance, its sole design being to promote the spirit of bravery among the boys of the tribe.

2. Changléshka kakhwóg'yapi, *Hoop that is made to roll by the wind.*—In the fall, when there are frequent breezes, the children play this game.   They make a hoop, and when there is a wind they hold the hoop perpendicular for a short time and then let it go, the wind carrying it along.   They chase it, going very far before they catch it.   The hoop is made thus: A stick is bent with the hands and pack-straps are fastened to it, crossing one another at various angles.   A piece of calico or of some other material is tied to the middle of the hoop.   He who catches the hoop brings it back to the place whence it started.   Not a game of chance.

3. I'pahotun'pi un'pi, *Pop-gun game.*—In the fall, when the wind blows down the leaves, the boys make pop-guns of ash wood.   They load them with bark which they have chewed, or else with wild sage (*Artemisia*), and they shoot at one another.   The one hit suffers much pain.

4. Chun'kshila wanhin'kpe un'pi, *Game with bows and small arrows.*—These arrows are made of green switches, before the leaves fall in the autumn.   The end of each switch-arrow is charred to a point, and when it hits the bare skin it gives pain.   The boys used to shoot these arrows at the dogs when they went for water.

5. *Throwing fire at one another.*—Played cool nights in autumn, as well as in winter.   When the snow is deep the boys go to a sandy place and kindle a fire.   Sides are chosen and a fight begins.   Each player is armed with a firebrand.   When they do not hit with the firebrands they hurl fire at one another.   This is always played

at night. The next day many boys appear with burnt places on their bodies.

BOYS' WINTER GAMES.

1. Ptehéshte un'pi, *Buffalo horn game.*—The boys assemble at the corral, or some other place where the cattle have been slaughtered, and gather the horns which have been thrown away. They kindle a fire and scorch the horns, noticing how far each horn has been burnt. That part of the horn is cut off, as it is brittle, and they make the rest of the horn very smooth by rubbing. They cut off all the small and pliable branches and twigs of a plum tree and insert the root end into a hole in the horn, tightening it by driving in several small wedges around it. At the small end of the plum stock they fasten a feather by wrapping deer sinew round and round it. The pteheste is then thrown along the surface of the snow, or it often goes under the surface, disappearing and reappearing at short intervals. Sometimes they make it glide over the ice. Stakes are frequently put up by or for the players.

2. Chan káwachipi, *Spinning tops.*—Tops are made of ash, cedar, buffalo horn, red catlinite, or of stone. They put a scalp-lock on the upper surface, ornamenting the latter with several colors of paint. They make the top spin by twirling it with the fingers, or by whipping. When they make it spin steadily by whipping they redden the scalp-lock, and as it revolves very rapidly it seems to be driven into the ground. This game is played on the ice or snow; sometimes on ground which has been made firm and smooth by trampling. For a whip each player takes a tender switch, to the small end of which he fastens a lash of deer hide. He braids one-half of the lash, allowing the rest to hang loosely. They place the tops in a row, after putting up stakes, and say, "Let us see who can make his top spin the longest distance."

3. Itázipa kaslóhan iyéya echun'pi, *Making the bow glide by throwing.*—They do not use real bows, but some kind of wood made flat by cutting with an ax, with a horizontal curve at the lowest part, and sharpened on the other side. At the head a snake's head is usually made, or else the head of some other object. At the other end the player grasps it and hurls it, making it glide rapidly over the snow or grass. This is a game of chance, but the "bows" are never staked, as they are too expensive. It takes so long to make one that the owner does not sell it, preferring to keep it as long as possible.

GAMES PLAYED BY BOYS ALONE; NO SEASON SPECIFIED.

1. *Tumbling and somersaults;* Teton name, Tahu-shipa kichûn'pi, *They play neck out of joint.*—Each player tries to stand the longest with his head down. Sometimes they turn backwards as well as forwards.

2. Tachághu yuhá shkátapi, *Game with buffalo lights.*—The boys used to assemble at the place where they killed the buffalo, and one of them would take a strip of green hide, to which the lights were attached, and drag the latter along the ground to serve as a mark for the rest. As he went along, the others shot at the lights. Sometimes the boy stood still, grasping a long withe fastened to the lights, which he swung round and around his head as he passed around the circle of players, who shot at the lights.   Now and then, when a boy sought to recover his arrow, the other boy would strike him on the head with the lights, covering him with blood, after which he would release the player. Sometimes the boy holding the lights would break off all the arrows which were sticking therein, instead of allowing their owners to reclaim them.

3. Pezhí yuskíl'skíl kutépi, *They shoot at grass tied tightly in bunches.* Played by the larger boys. Grass is wrapped around a piece of bark till it assumes an oval shape, both ends of the grass being secured together. The grass ball thus made is thrown into the air, and all shoot at it, trying to hit it before it reaches the ground; when it is hit the arrow generally penetrates the object very far, leaving only a small part of the feather end visible. The one who sends his arrow near the heart or mark on the grass ball has the right to toss the ball up into the air; but he who hits the heart on the ball throws the ball on the ground, and then throws it where he pleases, when all shoot at it. This game is generally played till dark, but there are no stakes put up.

4. Howi! howi!—*Boys assemble and stand in a circle.* Each boy bends his fingers, connecting each hand with that of the next player on either side. Without breaking the ring, all the players skip to the right (a sort of dressing to the right), saying, "Howi! howi!" When they reach the appointed place they move around a circle, then they dress to the left, to the starting place, after which they move again in a circle. When they cease moving, one is placed within the ring, and he either stands or sits, according to circumstances. When the players stop dressing to the right or left they shout in unison, and the one in the ring hits the joined hands, one

after another, trying to escape from the ring. When the players have dressed to the right and left, and have gone around the circle several times, they stand in silence; then the one in the ring passes in and out beneath the arches formed by the joined hands of his companions. Now and then an arch is brought down with a thump on the back of the stooping boy. When the boy has gone through all the arches he resumes his place in the ring, the others dancing around him with hands unclasped. Again do they clasp hands and order him to try his best to break through the ring. Should he succeed, he runs in a zigzag course away from the camp. If any one of the players can grasp him as he breaks forth from the ring, the fugitive must carry that player away on his back, or the others will go to him and each will say, " I claim this marrow as my own." When the fugitive reaches " home," with the other boy on his back, the latter is called the chief, and is obliged to stand in the ring until he can carry off his successor in like manner.

5. Tókeshke un'pi, *How they are brought up.*—(Compare the English game of Follow my Leader.)—Children choose their leader. One says, "I will be next to him." Another agrees to be the third in order. The others select their places, and all go in single file, passing various obstacles. Now and then one misses his footing, from which time he takes no further part in the game. They continue moving till the last player falls. Then they begin the game anew, the last one to fall becoming leader. Sometimes they encounter a fallen tree, which they climb over; sometimes they have to cross deep gulleys; now and then they have to jump or turn somersaults, always doing what the leader does.

6. Unkchela kutépi, *Shooting at the cactus.*—This game is always played for amusement, never for gain. On the appointed day the boys assemble on the prairie. One, who must be a swift runner, takes a cactus root, into which he thrusts a stick to serve as a handle. Grasping the cactus by this handle, he holds it aloft as he runs, and the others shoot at it. During this game the swift runner himself is regarded as having become the cactus; so when one of the boys hits the cactus, they say that it enrages the boy-cactus, who thereupon chases the others. Whenever the boy-cactus overtakes a player he sticks his cactus into him, turns around, and returns to his former place. Again the cactus is held aloft and they shoot at it as before, and again the players are chased. The game is kept up till the players wish to stop it.

7. *Throwing stones at one another.*—In this game there are two parties of players, standing on opposite sides of a gulley. Each boy uses a sling made by fastening a piece of deerskin to a braided pack-strap. They do not hurt one another, nor is there any chasing.

8. Ichápsîl echun'pi, *Making the wood jump by hitting it* (Catty ?)— When the boys play this game an imaginary stream is marked off on the ground, and the players stand on imaginary ice near the shore. They take turns at knocking at a piece of wood in order to send it up into the air. He who fails to send up the piece of wood loses his stakes, and he who succeeds wins the stakes. (Much of this text is not clear to the translator.)

9. Ogléche kutépi, *Shooting at an arrow set up.*—Some boys back their favorites among the players by furnishing them with articles to be put down as stakes. On each side of a hill there is an arrow stuck upright in the ground to serve as a mark. The players on one side shoot at the arrow set up on the other ; the players at the front shoot at the arrow in the rear, and then the players in the rear shoot at the arrow set up at the front. The nearer a player sends his arrow to the mark, the more it counts. Sometimes one of the arrows set up is withdrawn temporarily from its place to be used for shoot-ing at the other arrow. Only arrows are staked.

10. Tákhcha kichiyápi, *Deer game.*—When the boys play this game each player brings his deer bones, and some have ashes or pul-verized earth in their closed hands. Some act as deer, the rest run-ning around them. Those acting as deer use the deer bones, and they are chased and scattered by those having the ashes or pulver-ized earth. The ashes and earth are used for " shooting " at the deer, as well as for scattering on the ground. While they do not hit any one with the ashes or earth, they say that the clouds of dust which arise therefrom are smoke from guns. Some boys act as fawns, others as does. They play this game on a hillside. Some-times a "deer" is said to be wounded, and then the players pre-tend to flay the animal and to carry the hide to their homes; but the "hide" of the "deer" is a blanket.

11. *They kick at one another.*—Not a game of chance. An equal number of players are chosen for each side after the boys as-semble in the middle of the camp circle. When some say "Chu!" the others reply, "Come, let us play kicking at one another." So they rush at one another and kick in every case with great force. They do not grasp their opponents at first, but when any player runs

towards "home" and is overtaken by his pursuers, he is pulled to the ground and with their knees they make his nose bleed, or else they kick him around. This game is resorted to as a test of bravery. He who cries out from pain is deemed fit only for the society of girls.

12. Kichíkshanpi, *Wrestling.*—In this sport they never trip each other, but each seizes his opponent around the waist in trying to throw him down.

13. Owan'ka kichích'ipi, *Snatching places from one another.* (Pussy wants a corner?)—Played by boys in the evening. Stand in the ring, one in the middle. Those in the ring change places constantly, and the one in the middle tries to get the place of some one of them. When he succeeds, the person displaced must stand within the ring until he can displace some one else. Each player rolls up his blanket and stands on it as his owanka or place.

14. Tuwá tokeya yái-la shnika? *Who shall get there first?*—When boys are going somewhere one says suddenly, "Let us see who shall be the first one to reach yonder bush. The last one who gets there shall be compelled to play with girls and wear girls' clothing;" or he may say, "The last one who gets there shall have a son with very large nostrils." As the threatened result is considered very undesirable by the Indians, each boy runs as fast as he can. The unfortunate boy who gets there last is shouted at and derided until he gets angry and gives them bad names.

15. Hóshnanshnan kichun'pi, *Hopping.*—The boys set up an object as a mark or starting place. One of the boys stands there and hops as if he were lame, going as far from the starting point as possible, and returning thither in the same manner. Each succeeding player tries to hop further than his predecessor. When he desires, he can hop on the other foot. This exercise makes them very weary, but it strengthens their limbs. Sometimes they draw a line on the ground with their toes to mark the distance hopped by one of the less fortunate boys. No one can hold his foot with his hand as he hops.

16. Wíkinil-wichákiyápi, *Causing them to scramble for gifts:*—When a boy has plenty of property, such as paslohanpi, arrows, tops, or many small things of different kinds, he invites his companions to a feast, and throws up one thing after another into the air. Whoever catches an object as it falls becomes its owner.

17. Can-shúng'-akan'-yankápi, *Sitting on wooden horses*—They take sticks of green wood, tie cords to them to serve as bridles, and sit astride the sticks; use a switch for a whip; imitate the gaits of

horses. Sometimes two forked sticks are driven upright into the ground, and in the forks of these sticks another stick is laid horizontally, on which is placed a saddle, on which a boy sits. Sometimes a saddle is placed on a fallen tree and a boy rides thus. Occasionally a boy, who acts the horse, holds two sticks for front legs, going on all fours, and another boy mounts him and rides around.

18. Hohú yukhmun'pi, *Making the bone hum by twisting the cord.*—Bone is not the only material used, for the toy is sometimes made of stone or of a circular piece of wood. This toy is made thus: Some deer or buffalo sinews are twisted together, parts of a deer's foot are cooked till soft and strung together on the sinew. To the ends of the sinew are fastened two sticks which serve as handles, one stick at each end, each being at right angles to the sinew. The sinew is twisted, and when pulled taut the toy makes a humming sound.

Another variety is called Chan' kaóbletuntun'pi, *Wood having edges,* not circular, but made thus: A straight piece of wood is prepared with four sides or edges, and is fastened by a strip of hide to another piece of wood which is used as a handle. The boy grasps the handle, whirls it around his head, making the four-cornered piece move rapidly with a whizzing noise. This may be compared with the " bull roarer " of the Australians.

The third variety is made of stones shaped like the bones in a deer's foot. These stones overlap as do the real bones, and when the leather cord is twisted the bones make a peculiar sound, as if a the boys and girls.

19. *Pretending to die.*—When boys imitate the acts of those who wear grass around the waist (the Pezhi mignaka kaghapi), he who intends to feign death sits and acts as if he were a man, bowing his head while the others sing one of the songs peculiar to the game; but when they beat the drum, he rises to his feet and goes to the middle of the circle. He dances in a crouching attitude. Finally he slips and falls, kicking while he lies there. One of his friends dances toward him and tries to raise him; but as the fallen boy seems to be dead, his friend dances back to his former place, dragging the body.

GAME PLAYED BY BOYS AND YOUNG MEN.

In the winter the boys collect the good ribs of animals that are near the village. They make gashes across them, and on one side

of each rib they make a hole, in which they insert two plum sticks.
The small end of each plum stick they insert into the hole of a
quill feather of some bird. The small end of each plum stick is
bent backwards. Just at the fork of the two plum sticks the player
grasps the toy, called "hutanachute," making it glide over the snow
or ice. Stakes are put down when desired, but sometimes they play
just for amusement. Occasionally young men join the boys in this
game.

GAME PLAYED BY CHILDREN OR ADULTS OF EITHER SEX.

Chŭn wíyushnan'pi, *Odd or even*.—Played at any time by two
persons. A like number of green switches must be prepared by each
player. Sumac sticks are generally chosen, as they are not easily
broken by handling; hence one name for sumac stalks is "Count-
ing-stick stalks." One stick is made the odd one, probably distin-
guished by some mark. When they begin, one of the players seizes
all the sticks and mixes them as well as he can. Closing his eyes,
he divides them into two piles, taking about an equal number in
each hand. Then, crossing his hands, he says to the other player,
"Come, take whichever lot you choose." Both players are seated.
The other player makes his choice, and then each one examines
what he has. He who has the odd stick wins the game.

AUTUMNAL GAME OF THE BOYS OR WOMEN.

Paslóhanpi, *They shove it along*.—The boys play this game when the
leaves become a rusty yellow. They go to a place where the smallest
kind of willow abounds, and there they make a fire. They cut down
the straightest of the willows, shaving off the bark with knives.
Some color the willows in stripes. Others change the willows into
what they call "Chan kablaskapi," *i. e.*, wood flattened by beating;
but what these are Bushotter does not explain. Much of this text
is very obscure. Sometimes the young women play the game, at
othertimes the men do; but each sex has its peculiar way of making
the paslohanpi glide along. Sometimes they play for stakes.

GAME PLAYED BY BOYS, YOUNGER MARRIED MEN, OR WOMEN.

Ta-síha un'pi, *Game with the hoofs of a deer*.—They string
several deer hoofs together and throw them suddenly upward. They
jerk them back again by the cord to which they are attached, and
as they fall the player who has a sharp-pointed stick tries to thrust

it through the holes of the hoofs, and if he succeed he counts
the number of hoofs through which his stick has gone.   A
number of small beads of various colors are strung together and
fastened to the smallest hoof at the end of the string.   When a
player adds a bead to those on the string he has another chance to
try his skill in piercing the hoofs.   When one misses the mark he
hands the hoofs, etc., to the next player.   Each one tries to send
the stick through more hoofs than did his predecessor.   Two sides
are chosen by the players.   Each player offers articles as stakes for
the winner.   The season for playing is not specified.

The women, when they play this game, bring their husbands'
goods without the knowledge of the owners, and sometimes lose all
of them.   When the men play, they sometimes stake all of their
wives' property, and occasionally they lose all.   Now and then this
game is played just for amusement, without having any stakes.

SOME GAMES OF ARIKARA CHILDREN

Melvin R. Gilmore

SOME GAMES OF ARIKARA CHILDREN

SLINGS were made by Arikara boys, just as slings have been made the world over. A pliable piece of hide was cut into elliptical shape about the length of the hand, and with a hole in the center. At each end was attached a thong about as long as the arm. The missile was thrown by swinging in a rotary motion and released by letting go one of the

[7] This mask is described and illustrated in colors in *Boletin del Museo Nacional de Arqueologia, Historia y Etnografía*, Mexico, tomo 1, 4ª epoca, núm. 3, Sept. 1922. It contains also a number of "dictamens" by various persons in favor of the genuineness of the mask.

thongs from between the thumb and finger; the other thong was held securely by being wrapped in several turns about the middle finger. Boys amused themselves by throwing pebbles at targets with slings.

Mud-balls.—Boys played at mimic battle with mud-balls, which they threw at their opponents from the end of a resilent wand.

Mud-balls and Fire.—In the fall, at corn-shelling time, when the cobs were burned in the evening, the boys delighted to make mud-balls and attach them to wands as described above, and then dip them into the burning corncobs. The brands adhered to the mud-balls and were hurled through the air. This was a night-time game, the main attraction in it being the spectacle of the flying firebrands. However, added zest was given to this sport in the circumstance of circumventing the watchfulness of the women who were burning the cobs for the purpose of obtaining salt from the ash, and who naturally were exasperated by the boys messing up and destroying their ash-beds.

Willow wands.—Boys made sets of wands of straight young willows. These were peeled and stained with berry juices or other coloring matter, or were marked with fire. This was done by cutting off part of the bark in rings or spirals, and then holding the wands over the fire. After thus being subjected to heat and smoke, the remainder of the bark was removed. This left the wands marked in designs of smoke-brown on white.

The object of this game was to send the wands forward as far as possible from a given stand by propelling from the hand with a glancing stroke upon the ground. The stake was the set of wands, as in the game of marbles among white boys when they play for "keeps". The boy who sent a wand the farthest took all the wands played.

Coasting.—Boys and girls separately or together played at coasting, and in various ways. Sometimes a woman might have a buffalo-hide which had not been dressed, and which required to be worked into pliability and from which she also wished to have the hair removed. She would let the youngsters have it for coasting. They would drag it to a hilltop and crowd on, as many as could find room. Then away they would go sliding down the hill. This action would be repeated until they were tired of the game, or until the hide became too pliable to slide easily. In this way the children enjoyed great sport, while at the same time they were performing a useful service for the woman who owned the hide by depilating it and at the same time making it pliable, which she otherwise would have had to do at the expense of much hard labor.

[11]

Another device for coasting was made of buffalo-ribs joined together with sticks tied across their ends with sinew. Sometimes they attached a head at the front, and tail at the back, with a piece of old buffalo-robe to sit on. A thong attached at the front was used for guiding.

Stilts.—Both boys and girls walked on stilts which they made from poles, leaving a stump of a fork on the side at the height they desired for a foot-rest, which was bound to the trunk piece with a wrapping of thong.

Snaring Ground-squirrels.—In early spring the boys made nooses of horsehair or other material which would slip easily, and with long strings attached they placed the noose over the opening of the burrow of a ground-squirrel, the "flicker-tail," and waited for the animal to appear. When it did so, the watching boy jerked the noose and captured the animal. He killed it and set the noose again, and so continued. After catching as many squirrels as they wished, a group of boys would make a fire, roast their game, and have a hunters' feast. After the wild onions began to grow, the boys no longer engaged in this sport, because the ground-squirrels would feed on the wild onions and their flesh was disagreeable for eating.

MELVIN R. GILMORE

GOOD FRIDAY SKIPPING

Stanley Godman

GOOD FRIDAY SKIPPING

In her Presidential Address delivered before the Folk-Lore Society on March 10th, 1954[1] entitled *England as a Field for Folklore Research*, Dr. Margaret Murray referred to the custom of skipping on Good Friday which survived at the Bartlow Hills " until well into this century " and " still survives in Cambridge Town ". Since Good Friday skipping is still maintained with great enthusiasm in the Sussex village of Alciston and, since 1954, in the village of South Heighton near Newhaven, I was interested to discover more details about the skipping at the Bartlow Hills, especially in view of the association of both places, Bartlow and Alciston, with large burial barrows. The most prolific barrow area on the South Downs is in the vicinity of Alciston.[2] The Alciston skippers do not actually skip over the Downs but a large party from Newhaven walk the five miles across the Downs " with a rest and a chat whenever they feel like it "[3] passing close to the " Five Lords Burgh " and the Long Barrow overlooking Alciston. It seems likely that there is a connection between the burial barrows and the custom of skipping on Good Friday and the fact of their proximity certainly adds point to Dr. Murray's suggestion that Good Friday skipping and games " were brought into this country by the folk who brought the custom of burial in barrows ". In her paper delivered to the British Association last year in Bristol on *Song and Dance in connection with Funerals* Miss Violet Alford commented that " communal skipping on or near barrows ... does seem to be connected with barrows in the minds of the people who do it .... I think we may consider present-day skipping as a far-off descendant of the sports and games played at burials and, because continuity of tradition is almost ineradicable when people wish it to be so, possibly at barrow funerals ".[4]

It is noteworthy, however, that Good Friday skipping formerly had a wide distribution in places associated with fisher-folk : in particular it survived on the forecourt of Brighton Fish Market until the beaches were closed during the 1939 war. According to Mr. Ralph Merrifield[5] " the recent distribution of Good Friday skipping in Sussex would suggest a close association with the fisher-folk ". The fact that the largest party of skippers still comes from Newhaven may also be significant and the revival of the custom from 1954 onwards in South Heighton, just outside Newhaven, is in line with this tradition. For the fisher-folk it would be natural to play their Good Friday games and do their skipping on the beach beside the watery grave of their comrades drowned at sea and the

---

[1] *Folk-Lore*, Vol. LXV, April 1954.

[2] Cf. L. V. Grinsell, *The Ancient Burial-Mounds of England*, 1953, 2nd ed., p. 189. Also H. S. Toms, " Long Barrows in Sussex," *Sussex Arch. Coll.*, Vol. LXIII, 1922, p. 157.

[3] *Sussex Daily News*, April 17, 1954.

[4] I am grateful to Miss Alford for kindly allowing me to study a copy of her paper.

[5] " Magical Games in Sussex," *Sussex County Magazine*, 1952, p. 58.

link between the two sites, the beach and the barrows, seems a natural one. It may be mentioned here that skipping on the foreshore also takes place on Shrove Tuesday in Scarborough. This year (1956) snow and slush had to be cleared away before the skippers could begin.[6] I have been unable to discover how far back the Scarborough skipping can be traced. The local Public Library and antiquarians in Scarborough have no information. It is interesting, however, that the two customs should take place one at each end of the season of Lent.

The association of Good Friday skipping with burial barrows is also confirmed by the games and sports, in particular, " Kiss in the Ring " which used to be played on the large barrow in Hove sited in what is now the garden at the back of No. 13 Palmeira Avenue. " Hundreds of young people used to play Kiss in the Ring and other games "[7] on this Bronze Age barrow until it was destroyed in 1856. Dr. Curwen also states that " it was a common custom in the Middle Ages and later for games to be played on Palm Sunday and Good Friday on barrows ". " Kiss in the Ring " and also skipping were carried on until forty years ago on West Hill, Hastings (again the association with fisher-folk is clear). At the Hastings games " winkles were sold in penny packets complete with pins ".

This reference to winkles brings me back to Dr. Murray's reference to Good Friday skipping at the Bartlow Hills since one of the immediate reactions to my question " Can you remember skipping on Good Friday? " which I put to a number of old inhabitants in Linton and Hildersham (the villages referred to by Dr. Murray) in August 1954 was " No! I can't, but I remember old Morley and his daughters and their winkle stall at Bartlow Hills on Good Friday " (eighty-year-old Mrs. Salmon of Linton). Her brother, now over eighty, could not remember skipping taking place on Good Friday. A seventy-four-year-old man in Hildersham who left the village when he was fourteen told me " I never saw no skipping in my time ". But he could remember the Good Friday Fair and the dancing that followed in " the barn on old Brocklebank's estate ". Alice Kerr of Bartlow told me " we used to have a rare old time skipping on Good Friday " but it turned out she was referring to her childhood in Bow, London. Her invalid aunt of eighty-four could remember " skipping at Bartlow in my mother's time ". In spite of many other local enquiries I have been quite unable to trace any evidence of skipping at Bartlow Hills in the present century. Dr. Murray also mentioned the skipping on Parker's Piece in Cambridge. This did survive until quite recently but Dr. W. H. Thorpe of Jesus College told me (October 23, 1954) that a friend of his whose house overlooks Parker's Piece " has watched in vain for it on the last two Good Fridays ". There is apparently no association with burial barrows in the Cambridge skipping. At one other place where there are still memories of Good Friday skipping, such an association does however seem possible. Mrs.

[6] The *Scarborough Mercury*, February 17, 1956.
[7] E. C. Curwen, *Prehistoric Sussex*, 1930, p. 33 and also *The Archaeology of Sussex*, 1954, p. 152.

G. Jones of Leamington and Mrs. E. E. Llewellyn of Shrewsbury informed me in 1955 that they could remember skipping on Good Friday on Haughmond Hill near Shrewsbury sixty years ago. " Two men used to turn the rope for us and we paid them a halfpenny for a few skips." There are two ancient earthworks on Haughmond Hill. One is Ebury Hill and the other is known as " The Castle Earthwork ", which may be a prehistoric hill-fort, but this has not been proved.[8]

The present skipping on Good Friday at Alciston owes it survival to one family, the Lillywhites of Newhaven, some of whom now come long distances to join in every year. It was started about fifty years ago and has continued without a break except for the Second World War. For some years it was confined to the Lillywhite family and occasionally the party numbered as few as six. Nowadays the party numbers about two hundred. Good Friday or, possibly, Easter Monday skipping in Alciston presumably has a longer history than the last fifty years. Mrs. S. Bridger, formerly of Alciston, has spoken to an old shepherd who remembered skipping there on Easter Monday but she has not stated how far back his memory went. Presumably, earlier than the Lillywhite revival.[9]

On arrival at the Rose Cottage Inn after their leisurely walk across the Downs from Newhaven the party takes refreshment in the Inn and then begin skipping on long ropes outside the Inn, a few at first, then gradually increasing, the older men, in particular Mr. Albert and Mr. Bill Lillywhite, turning the ropes and the women and girls skipping, though later there is mixed skipping and also some all-male skipping (with women turning). The only rhyme used is " All in together, girls, this fine weather girls! " But in the single skipping which also takes place I have heard an extension as follows :

> Put your paint and powder on,
> Tell the boys you'll not be long :
> Shoot, fire, bang!

I heard the same rhyme in the school playground at Westmeston on Easter Saturday 1955 (two girls with a boy turning). In the intervals of skipping some of the party drink and sing lustily in the Inn. In 1955 I heard a disgusting version of " Oh, dear, what can the matter be? " In her above-mentioned paper to the British Association Miss Alford (to whom I had communicated this information) made the point that this indecent song may confirm the renewal-of-life motive in the skipping, since " obscenity is good fertility magic and is frequently so used ".

Mr. Ralph Merrifield has dismissed the commonest " interpretation " of Good Friday skipping which is that the rope symbolized the rope with which Judas hanged himself.[10] He believes that its origins are magical and he finds it significant that the skipping is mainly carried on by women.

[8] I am grateful to Mr. Hobbs, the Shrewsbury Borough Librarian, for this information.

[9] See *Sussex County Magazine*, August 1954.

[10] " Good Friday Customs in Sussex," *Sussex Arch. Coll.* Vol. LXXXIX, 1950.

He compares it with the magical leaping which accompanies the sowing of the seed. Miss Alford also connects it with the spring-time jumping associated with the growth of crops. The gradual increase in the number of skippers also suggests the idea of growth. The male custom on Good Friday is still the game of marbles. In one village, Fulking, the boys and men used to play marbles while the women skipped with clothes lines and neither joined in the others' game. Mr. Merrifield suggests that both games were magical in origin. " The magic of the men, was intended to ensure the successful planting of the seed, whilst the female skipping represents the germination and growth of the crops."

STANLEY GODMAN

AUSTRALIAN CHILDREN'S GAMES

[Alfred C. Haddon]

AUSTRALIAN CHILDREN'S GAMES.[1]

A certain amount of attention has been paid of late years to the subject of the games of primitive peoples, but so far we are only in the preliminary stage of the inquiry; indeed, a vast deal more evidence must be collected before sound generalisations can be made. A few suggestions have been thrown out by various students which must be regarded more as trial hypotheses than as definite conclusions, indeed they should be looked upon rather as "kites."

So few travellers think it worth their while to mention games and toys, especially those played by children, that the record for any country is imperfect, and for most peoples there is no information to hand. When there is any information it is nearly always simply a bare enumeration of the games played or of the toys employed; very rarely is a description given of the method of playing.

We are slowly learning the lesson that many of those activities which appear to be merely trivial have, or have had, an important significance in the evolution of human culture. The physiological, psychological and sociological aspects of playing have been dealt with by Karl Groos in his book "The Play of Man," but it is not yet possible to map the distribution of most of the toys and games, to trace their origin, or to indicate the meaning that in many cases was primitively attached to their exercise.

Thanks to the investigations of Messrs. A. MacFarland Davis, F. Cushing, Stewart Culin, G. A. Dorsey and others, we have some indication concerning the variations, distribution and significance of the principal games of the North American Indians. Some hundred or so of these games are known, which can, however, be reduced to six main groups. These are derived from the employment of the shield and spear, marked arrows, shields on which were painted the four world quarters, and balls. Some of these games may have been originally merely games of skill, others were divinatory, while others, again, were doubtless magical.

In that vague region known as the Far East, the fragmentary evidence points to similar conclusions as the researches, amongst others, of Messrs. Stewart Culin, G. von Schlegel, R. Andree and E. B. Tylor. The same, too, appears to hold good for Oceania.

These general remarks will show how important it is that further evidence should be collected, and will indicate the welcome that will be given to the last of Dr. Walter E. Roth's studies in the ethnography of North Queensland. The following is Dr. Roth's classification of games, sports and amusements:—(1) Imaginative games, such as tales, of which nine are given. (2) Realistic games, playing with pets, playing with plants, making smoke spirals, bathing, &c. (3) Imitative games, objects and phenomena of nature imitated by attitudes, movements and paintings; the author figures seventy-four examples of those ingenious string figures in which so many primitive peoples excel. Very few illustrations of "cat's cradles" have ever been published, so that we cannot at present say how far particular devices are common to different peoples. One at all events (Plate v., Fig. 6), which represents a duck flying (Fig. 1), is similar to a string figure in Torres Straits which is called "throwing the fish spear," but this is a very simple figure to make. In this category are placed all those games in which children imitate their elders. Several round games are described in which "collecting honey," "catching cockatoos" and similar operations are represented; one of them, "playing bean tree" (Fig. 2), resembles a game I have described as played by Papuan children ("Head-Hunters, Black, White and Brown," 1901, chap. xv.). There are other analogies between the games of the aborigines of North Queensland and those of the Papuans. (4) Discriminative games, hide and seek and a guessing game. (5) Disputative games, wrestling, tug-of-war. (6) Propulsive games, ball games, tops, stick-throwing games, &c.; amongst the latter are certain methods of casting petioles of grass blades similar in principle to what is done by certain Papuan children. Of special interest is the hurling of a toy spear by means of a knotted string; a similar device was used by the men of the Southern New Hebrides, New Caledonia and the Loyalty Islands, and the present writer has recorded it as a child's plaything at Delena, Hall Sound, British New Guinea, and now it has turned up amongst the coastal blacks of North Queensland. (7) Exultative games, songs, dances, music. This little memoir, which is illustrated by thirty-nine plates, is full of valuable information, as it opens up a new field to the student. A. C. H.

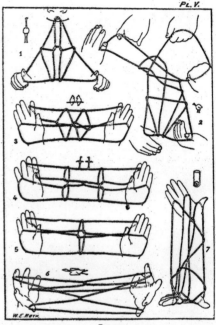

Fig. 1.

Fig. 2.

GAMES AND TOYS

[Alfred C. Haddon]

XVII. GAMES AND TOYS[1]

IT is not an easy matter to classify the games played by the adults and children of various peoples, nor can one draw a hard and fast line between games played without apparatus, those played with objects which may be either actual tools or implements or toy imitations of them, or playing with toys. The following enumeration is not intended as a classification but as a simple method of grouping to facilitate reference.

Game, fun, play is termed *sagul* (W.), *segur* (E.).

1. Games of movement that develop and exercise the bodily powers.

The game that combines agility, endurance, skill and emulation to the greatest degree is that of dancing, but for the sake of convenience dances are dealt with in a special section (pp. 289—293).

Among the games of agility may be mentioned skipping with a rope which is played by children in Mer, where it was stated to be an indigenous pastime. In Mabuiag I heard of young people swinging on the aerial roots of the *kabi* tree, which I believe is a kind of banyan (Ficus) (cf. Holmes, p. 287).

The most energetic of these games is a kind of hockey, shinny or shinty, which is played everywhere. It is called *kokan* in Mabuiag, which is also the name of the ball itself. The ball is made of wood and varies from about 55 to 60 mm. in diameter and $3\frac{1}{2}$ to 4 oz. in weight, the largest being 78 mm. and 10 oz., it is struck with a roughly made bat or club, *bawain, dabi* (W.), which is usually a piece of bamboo, varying from 60 to 85 cm. in length, on which a grip is cut. The game is played over a long stretch of the sand-beach, there are two sides and each player has a stick, but so far as I could discover there were no goals and no rules. The game is very "fast" and causes intense excitement and a tremendous noise; it is not without an element of danger as the heavy ball is hit with extreme vigour. We witnessed in Mabuiag one great match between married and single men (cf. Holmes, p. 282).

[1] In Bulletin No. 4 (1902) of his *North Queensland Ethnography* Dr Walter Roth gives a classification and description of the "Games, Sports and Amusements" of various tribes of North Queensland. Those interested in this subject should consult this valuable paper, and also the following in the *Journ. Roy. Anth. Inst.* XXXVIII. 1908: "Children's Games in British New Guinea," by Capt. F. R. Barton, pp. 259—279; "Introductory Notes on the Toys and Games of Elema, Papuan Gulf," by Rev. J. H. Holmes, pp. 280—288; "Notes on Children's Games in British New Guinea," by A. C. Haddon, pp. 289—297.

2. Games of dexterity and skill.

In the Miriam ball game the players stand in a circle and sing the following *kai wed*, ball song:

Kai tapitari	Ball hit.
Kai tapitari	Ball strike.
Abu kak kai o!	Fall not ball!
Atimed kak kai o!	Throw not ball!

As soon as they begin to sing one player strikes up the ball with his hand towards another player, who in his turn hits up the ball, and so on, keeping time to the rhythm of the music. The song is repeated as long as the game lasts. Should anyone let the ball fall to the ground, he is jeered at. According to one account the game is properly played by two sides.

FIG. 259. Fruit of the *kai* tree used as a ball, 68 mm. long, Mer.

FIG. 260. Palm-leaf ball introduced by South Sea men.

Formerly they used for this game the thick, oval, deep red fruit of the *kai* tree (fig. 259), which is quite light when dry; this fruit, which has a tough rind, varies from about 6—7 cm. (2¼—2¾ in.) in length. At the present time they generally use a hollow cubical ball (fig. 260) made of Pandanus or coco-nut palm leaves. This ball was introduced by South Sea men and is a common Polynesian toy; the names *kokan* (W.) and *kai* (E.) prove that it is a loan object. It varies in size from about 35 to 53 mm. in diameter, an average size being 45 mm.; one oblong example measures 55 × 95 mm. (cf. Roth, p. 17; Holmes, p. 280; and Barton, p. 279, and for a bladder game, p. 264).

Mabuiag children play a catching game called *udai* (*wadai*) or *damadiai*; the former is the red flat bean of a Mucuna, the latter is a hard fruit that comes from New Guinea. Boys and girls go in pairs into the sea, a boy tries to throw a bean to another boy which his partner attempts to intercept; should she succeed she in her turn throws it to another girl and her partner tries to forestall her.

In the north-west season the Miriam men play a game for which I obtained only the name *kolap*. Two mats are laid at a distance of about 15 m. Two men sit behind each mat, those facing each other obliquely being partners. Each man has four *kolap* beans which he tries to throw on to the further mat; a score of twenty finishes the game. I believe there is a similar game in which beans are thrown at a mark on the ground.

Game of hide and seek:—Mr J. Bruce has given me particulars of a game in Mer called *nem deraimer*, "louse searching." It is played by men and women. Two sides are arranged, and they all kneel in a circle on the sand or round a bare spot. One person, who is blindfolded, puts his head down—or if not blindfolded the face is placed so close to the ground that he cannot see what is being done. One of the other side then picks from his hair a louse, which is hidden in the sand in the centre of the circle. All the players begin to sing and beat the ground with their hands, except the man from whose head the louse was taken, whose business it now is to search for it. If he succeeds in finding it, one from the other side has to put his head down and do the searching. Should the man fail to find the louse, one of the other side shows it to him and his side has to remain in until someone has been successful in the search. The one who finds the louse eats it.

A variant of this game is called *pone deraimer*, or "eye searching," the crystalline lens of a fish being hidden in the sand instead of a louse. Roth (p. 17) found this game among several tribes of North Queensland.

Both sexes in Mer play a game by the light of the full moon, in which food is hidden in the bush or gardens for others to find (cf. Holmes, p. 286).

I do not know whether there is a hide and seek game in which players hide themselves, as in New Guinea (cf. Barton, p. 267; Holmes, p. 285).

Dr Macfarlane informed me that they played a guessing game in Mer which consisted of giving two syllables of a name from which the whole had to be guessed, thus: "ia?" "Elia."

Children also play guessing the number of small objects held in the closed hand.

Games with string exhibit great dexterity of the fingers and are distinctly games of skill. For the sake of convenience these will be treated separately at the end of this section.

3. Games of emulation.

Various kinds of spinning tops are to be found in Torres Straits. The most general is a top (fig. 261 A) made of a Queensland bean (Entada scandens)[1]; in Mer both bean and top have the same name *kolap*, but in Mabuiag the top is called *wana* and the bean *kǎlapi* or *kolapi*. The flat, chestnut-coloured bean is perforated and into it inserted a thin stick, *kolap pes* (E.) (usually the mid-rib of the coco-nut leaf), with an average length of about 14—15 cm., the beans averaging about 45 mm. in diameter. In a Mabuiag top the stick was called *tul*, probably because it was made of *tulu* wood; in Mer it is also called *teter*, or leg. The *pewer kolap* of Mer (fig. 261 B) is made from the fruit of the *pewer* which has a diameter of about 20—25 mm., the sticks being 10—12 cm. long. A similar top is made of the dried fruit of the *zom* tree (Thespesia populnea).

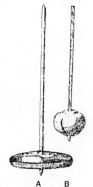

These tops are spun with the fingers and resemble in this respect the tee-totum, but strictly speaking the latter is a four-sided or faceted top used in games of chance. These tops were simple toys for children and never attained the importance of the Miriam stone tops. Small cone-shells are spun by children by twirling them in the usual way between the thumb and finger.

A   B

Fig. 261. Seed tops, Mer; *kolap* and *pewer kolap*.

[1] The plant is called *sirip* or *sireb* and the top is consequently sometimes called *sirip kolap*.

The use of stone tops, *kolap*, is and always has been confined, so far as our knowledge goes, to the Miriam, for it is only in the Murray Islands and to a very limited extent in Erub that the fine-grained volcanic ash occurs of which they are made. The top is shaped like a split pea, the upper surface being occasionally slightly convex. Those in the collection vary from 11 to 19 cm. in diameter, 14—15 cm. being a common measurement; they are generally about 45 mm. thick, and usually weigh about 2 lbs. The top shewn in pl. XXXVII. fig. 4 is 19 cm. in diameter, 5 cm. thick, and weighs 4 lbs.; for further dimensions see figs. 380—385. A top is seen in pl. XXI. fig. 3.

The tops are carefully made and smoothed down, and although not absolute circles they are made as true as possible in order that they may balance when spinning. A hole is drilled through the centre, which is larger above than below, and into this a stick, *kolap pes*, is inserted. The shortest we have is 15 cm., the longest 41 cm., but the usual length is about 25—30 cm. The sticks are generally made of the heavy wooden heads of arrows (generally palm-wood) whittled down, but what was most preferred was the hard wood called *dab*, which was obtained from the Queensland natives through the intermediacy of the natives of Waraber and Half-way Island; sometimes a piece of an old dugong harpoon would be employed as it was made of hard wood. The stick tapers delicately to its upper end and is smooth and neatly made.

The upper surface may be plain, but it is usually decorated in various ways as described in the section on Decorative Art (figs. 378—383, pl. XXXVII. figs. 3, 4).

Very great care is taken of these tops and the better ones are kept in round baskets specially made for them, which are often lined with calico as a further protection for the top. A basket made of coiled basketry is described on p. 82; a polygonal basket is seen in pl. XXVIII. fig. I, but I believe this to be of foreign make. It is very amusing to see elderly men carrying with both hands a top ensconced in its basket with the greatest care; the tops are also very carefully handled, and some are so much valued that we could not induce their owners to part with them. On the other hand, tops could be taken by certain relatives (VI. pp. 100, 101). The stick of his top was hung over the corpse of a deceased man (VI. p. 130).

A top is spun by repeated slow, steady, sliding movements of the outstretched palms and fingers. Formerly they were spun on pieces of melon shell (*Album*, I. pl. 344, No. 4), now pieces of broken crockery or the under surfaces of cups and saucers are employed.

Kolap wed, top songs, are sung during top spinning, *kolap omen*[1]: one of these songs is given on pp. 268, 288.

Stone top spinning was very prevalent during part of our stay in Mer, indeed at one time the people played so assiduously every week-day that they had no time to attend to their gardens, and on Saturday they did not bring in enough food to last till Monday. The Puritan Sunday is in full force, and none would dream of breaking it by gathering food, consequently numbers of children came to school on Monday morning without having had any breakfast. This made them peevish and inattentive, so Mr Bruce had to complain to the mamoose, and an edict was issued prohibiting *kolap* matches

---

[1] The spinning movement of a top is *omen*, or *omen-omen* when spinning fast. When a top is spinning steadily, or as we say "going to sleep," it is called *kolap kus*, and the stopping of the revolutions is called *eiri*.

on Saturday, and the men were told to go to their gardens as heretofore. On one occasion there were thirty tops spinning at the same time (pl. XXVIII. fig. 1). The men sang songs and there was great cheering on of slackening tops, and shouting and jeering when one stopped. At the critical time when one was "dying" great care was taken to shelter it from the wind so as to prolong its "life" a few seconds longer. At one match we timed the four best tops, and found that they spun for 27½, 26¾, 25¼ and 24 minutes respectively. We have seen men of all ages (but no women or girls) engaged in these matches, the grizzled taking as much interest in the performance of their tops as the young men. In the larger competitions one section or side of the island is pitted against another.

Dr C. H. Read (*Journ. Anth. Inst.* XVII. 1887, p. 85) was the first to describe these tops. He says (p. 88): "I do not think it very probable, though it is, of course, possible, that the natives of the Torres Straits islands invented spinning tops for themselves. It is far more likely that they received the idea from a more cultured and ingenious race; for, apart from the rarity of the occurrence of this toy among savage tribes[1], it is evident that the notion of a spinning top, a very complex toy [!], would be little likely to spring ready made into the mind of a people of the mental calibre of the Papuan. We must, therefore, look elsewhere than among the races of New Guinea for the origin of the toy." Spinning tops, such as those described above, can scarcely be considered "very complex" toys, but at the time when Dr Read wrote his paper so little was known about the Torres Straits Islanders that he naturally underrated their mental calibre. Two objects may very well have suggested the making of tops, namely the disc-shaped stone-headed club and the pump-drill (p. 128), but we do not know for certain that they possessed this instrument, though a pump-drill with a circular disc as a fly-wheel occurs in the Gulf District. I see no reason however why the seed tops should not have been directly invented and the stone-headed club may have suggested the stone top, though its shape is never like a split pea except in one specimen from Mer noted on p. 192. Tops spun with the hand occur in North Queensland (Roth, p. 18), and in the Papuan Gulf (Holmes, p. 281).

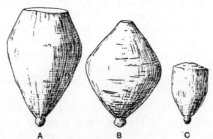

A   B   C

Fig. 262. Peg-tops, Mer. A, 81 mm. long, weight 3½ oz. B, 90 mm. long, weight 4½ oz. C, 50 mm. long, weight ¾ oz.

Two kinds of top spun by means of string were collected by us, the most common being the peg-top (fig. 262), which is also called *kolap*. The form is variable, being

---

[1] The absence of specimens of particular objects, especially a trivial object like a toy, in museums or the omission of their occurrence from the accounts of travellers is negative evidence of extremely little value.

either conical or biconical, the apex in the latter case is frequently truncate; the point is knob-like. It is made of *enoa* (Minnusops) wood. Three other specimens measure 70 × 40 mm., 77 × 39 mm., and 84 × 45 mm. Those which we obtained in Mer were introduced from Mabuiag where they were said to be native, but this is I think improbable. The form of some of them is like that of European peg-tops, others resemble the common form of Malay top (*gasing*) which is found in the Malay Peninsula and throughout the East Indian Archipelago, but as the *kolap* is spun in the European way I think it must have been derived from European and not from Malayan sources.

The second kind of top spun by a string is without doubt of foreign design, though it appears to have been locally made. It consists of a disc of lead 4 cm. in diameter, in a hole in the centre is fastened a cane tube within which is inserted a wooden stick, 148 mm. long, with a swollen conical point (fig. 263). I obtained it at Mabuiag where it was called *wana*; I saw only this one specimen.

I did not come across any whip-tops, but they occur in the Mekeo and Kabadi Districts of British New Guinea, where they certainly seem to be indigenous (cf. *Head-Hunters: Black, White, and Brown*, 1901, pp. 272, 273).

The Islanders had a pastime of throwing sticks along the sand-beach when walking. This is alluded to in a folk-tale (v. p. 45), where Bia threw "a *dukun*, a simple toy spear made of the hard dukun wood, but he only played where there was a sand-beach, and not where there were plenty of stones." The toy consists of a thin rod of hard wood with a swollen fusiform end, something like a miniature dugong harpoon. In Mer

Fig. 263. Lead spinning top, Mabuiag.

we obtained two objects that were used for this mildly competitive game (fig. 264); the rods of our specimens have probably been broken, but if so the fracture was of ancient date. They are called *omaiter* or *aipersi lu*, sliding thing; the word *omaiter* is used also in another sense (figs. 367—370). Similar sticks, commonly known as *wit-wit*, or "kangaroo rat," are used in Australia for the same purpose (cf. N. W. Thomas, *Natives of Australia*, 1906, p. 140, and Roth, p. 18).

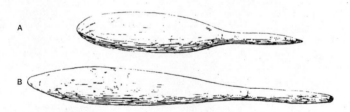

Fig. 264. Toy throw-sticks, *omaiter*, Mer. A, head end 11 cm. long, 31 mm. diam.; total length 16·5 cm. B, head end 14—15 cm. long, 29 mm. diam.; total length 21·8 cm.

The men sometimes had shooting matches with bows and arrows; in the western islands javelin hurling competitions were held. I have also heard of sham fights with blunt arrows.

4. Games of imitation.

Here as elsewhere children delight in imitating the occupations of their elders, and this mimicry forms a not unimportant part of their education. That this was so in the past is evident from the injunction of lads at initiation in Tutu to abstain in future from playing with play canoes and toy spears. Not only are models of canoes still made for boys to play with (*Album*, I. pl. 346, No. 9), but I have seen in Mer fully rigged models of luggers and schooners with which the young men amused themselves, and the spirit of emulation was gratified by racing one against another (cf. Holmes, p. 283).

Toy bows and arrows of *esese* grass stems were made by the boys. Dr Wilson (*Voy.* 1835, p. 311) noticed boys in Mer, "some of them very young, amusing themselves, shooting with bows and arrows, suited to their strength."

On Yam I came across two small heaps of ruddled clam and other shells among some bushes where the boys played at "*augud*" or "*kwod*." The great totem shrines in the *kwod* of that island are described in Vol. v. pp. 373—378. The ceremonies connected with these now obsolete shrines were the most sacred of their religious ceremonies. In this case the boys cannot be said to have exactly mimicked their elders, as they did not know what the real *augud* was like nor how the ceremonies had been conducted, but they "made believe" to their own satisfaction. Heaps of shells are a common feature in the *kwod* of the Western Islanders.

5. Game of divination.

The only divinatory game known to me is that called *koko* in Mer, which is played by girls only. A number of girls bind their heads with bands of leaves or vines and flowers like a garland, or they make a rough sort of leaf basket which they put on their heads, or wear a fillet of a strip of palm leaf to which are fastened vertical or horizontal palm-leaf rings—in fact they adopt as fantastic an erection of leaves and flowers as they can devise. They then walk into the sea until only their heads and shoulders are above the water, form into a line each placing her hand on the shoulder of the one in front of her, and repeatedly sing "*Koko, koko, kaiep maggeb*," keeping time to the music by bobbing their heads up and down. Later they resort to the sand-beach and sitting down in a ring or semi-circle sing "*Kegu-a bamu-a gared-gep*," at the same time they push their hands backwards and forwards palms downwards in the sand (this is called *tag ditiari*, hand shoving), and mutter "*Lar-teregu tarasawem, kwoieru tarasawem, kegu terasawem*" (with fish teeth rub me, with bamboo knife rub me, with charcoal rub me). Finally they examine their hands to see whether they have been cut or whether the bit of charcoal held by each one has made one or two streaks on their palms (pl. XXVIII. figs. 3, 4). Should there be two marks they cry out, "Ah! *keg* has killed a man," and begin again. *Koko* literally means, according to Mr Bruce, to carry on the back as a mother carries her child, it also is the name of a fine weather omen bird

(VI. p. 260), *kokokoko* is a wood used to make fire-sticks, and *kogkog* or *koko* is marital intercourse; *kaiep*, probably the same as *kaip*, a small shell used for scraping food: *wageb*, a Cyrena shell used for the same purpose; *kega* or *keg*, charcoal (cf. VI. p. 146). Mr Bruce states that *bamu*, *gared*, *gep* are in this instance only sounds with no meaning; it may be noted however that *bam* is turmeric and *gared*, south. This game is alluded to in the folk-tale "Markep and Sarkep" (VI. p. 54).

I think I can state definitely that the following games did not occur in Torres Straits: chuck-stones or dice of any kind, gambling games, kite flying.

6. Various Toys.

A "pea-shooter" is made in Mer out of a small bamboo, Abrus seeds ("crabs' eyes") being used as pellets.

Fig. 265. Toy bird made of board, Mer. Tail, wing, ring round neck, and eye red; length 52 cm., breadth 23 cm.

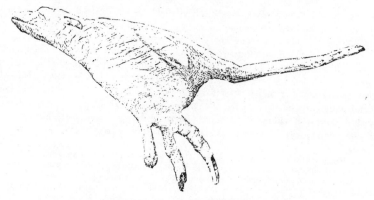

Fig. 266. Toy rat, Mer; 32 cm. long.

Toys for making a noise are described under Sound-producing Instruments. I obtained in Mer a piece of water-worn board carved to represent a bird (fig. 265). A hole was burnt in the board through which, so I was informed, a string was threaded and knotted on the other side. The bird, *ebur*, was put in the sea and the player holding one end of the string ran along the beach. There is a similar specimen with a small central hole, also from Mer, in the Vienna Museum (24,104).

A root which had been slightly touched up so as to make it resemble a rat (fig. 266) was a plaything with some children on Mer. It is quite possible that simple carvings were sometimes made to amuse children. In the British Museum there is a model of a crocodile's head carved in wood, painted red, white and blue, and fastened to a piece of spiral wire, which is evidently a toy. I also obtained in Mer a piece of wood carved to represent a human face with a very protuberant nose (fig. 267), it was merely a toy.

Miriam children play in the sea with the spathes of the leaves of coco-nut palms (fig. 208), pretending they are small canoes. Toy canoes were frequently made for children throughout the islands; I collected one at Mabuiag in 1888 (*Album*, I. pl. 346, No. 9) which is 615 mm. long and is decorated with simple patterns by charring the wood.

Fig. 267.   Grotesque head as a toy, 25·5 cm. long, Mer.

7. String Figures and Tricks.

String figures, *wome* (W.), *kamut* (E.), allied to our cat's-cradle, are universally played by the children and sometimes by adults, but it seems to be dying out[1]. Usually one person plays it alone, in some cases using the toes as well as the fingers, and often bringing the mouth into requisition. The patterns are very varied, and many are extremely complicated in manipulation although the final result may be simple. They are all intended to be realistic; in some cases the object represented is obvious, in others the imagination must be called into play, but other natives invariably recognise them and different islanders make the same figures. There are a large number of undescribed figures in addition to those described below, among which may be mentioned: one child; two children; a woman micturating; coition; a dog; crow *korkor*

---

[1] I first drew attention to this pastime in 1890 (*J.A.I.* XIX. p. 361). In 1898 Dr Rivers and I devised a system of nomenclature for recording. the movements which we published in *Man* (II. 1902, No. 109, p. 147); this paper gave a stimulus to the subject. Several investigators have adopted the useless plan of publishing drawings of the completed figures without any indication of how they are formed. For further information the reader is referred to *String Figures* by Mrs Jayne (1906) and to *Cat's Cradles from many Lands* by Kathleen Haddon (1911), both of which deal with the distribution of the various figures and tricks. I am indebted to the courtesy of Messrs Longmans Green and Co. for the loan of figs. 268—276, 278—284, 294 from the last-mentioned book. The string figures and tricks were collected by Drs Rivers, MacDougall, Mr Ray and myself. I have to thank my daughter for the final form of many of them and Mr W. Innes Pocock for re-writing Nos. 19, 24, and 29 and for other assistance.

(W.); the *pearku* fish; a small fish, *zermoi* (W.), which accompanies sharks; a crayfish, *kaiur* (W.); the larva of the ant-lion, *gobai* (W.); a mouth, *gud* (W.); liana or other climber, *ngal ngal* (W.). The names of the various islands are given where we obtained the figures, but doubtless they occur everywhere in the Straits.

Various movements appropriate to the object represented are also made, thus swinging movements are given to the limbs of the crayfish, other moving figures are mentioned below. In some cases the figures are accompanied with songs, *kamut wed* (E.), which are sung in a low tone. For the translation of these I am indebted, as usual, to Mr Ray, but the words are frequently obscure and cannot be translated with certainty.

The term "string figure" is employed in those cases in which it is intended to represent certain objects or operations. The cat's-cradle of our childhood belongs to this category. "Tricks" are generally knots or complicated arrangements of the string which run out freely when pulled. Sometimes it is difficult to decide which name should be applied.

A piece of smooth, pliable string should be selected which is not liable to kink. A length of about 2 m. (6 ft. 6 in.) is usually the most convenient; the ends should be tied in a reef knot and then trimmed, or sewn together with cotton, or, best of all, spliced.

A string passed over a digit is termed a loop. A loop consists of two strings. Anatomically, anything on the thumb aspect of the hand is termed "radial," and anything on the little-finger side is called "ulnar," thus every loop is composed of a radial string and an ulnar string. By employing the terms thumb, index, middle-finger, ring-finger, little-finger, and right and left, it is possible to designate any one of the twenty strings that may extend between the two hands.

A string lying across the front of the hand is a palmar string, and one lying across the back of the hand is a dorsal string.

Sometimes there are two loops on a digit, one of which is nearer the finger-tip than the other. Anatomically, that which is nearer to the point of attachment is "proximal," that which is nearer the free end is "distal." Thus of two loops on a digit the one which is nearer the hand is the proximal loop, that which is nearer the tip of the digit is the distal loop; similarly we can speak of a proximal string and a distal string.

In all cases various parts of the string figures are transferred from one digit or set of digits to another or others. This is done by inserting a digit (or digits) into certain loops of the figure and then restoring the digit (or digits) to the original position so that they bring with it (or them) one string or both strings of the loop. This operation will be described as follows: "Pass the digit into such and such a loop, take up such and such a string, and return." In rare cases a string is taken up between thumb and index. A digit may be inserted into a loop from the proximal or distal side, and in passing to a given loop the digit may pass to the distal or proximal side of other loops. We use these expressions as a general rule instead of "over" and "under," "above" and "below," because the applicability of the latter terms depends on the way in which the figures are held. If the figures are held horizontally, "over" and "above" will correspond as a general rule to the distal side, while "under" and "below" will correspond to the proximal side. In some cases, when there is no possibility of confusion, we have used the shorter terminology.

A given string may be taken up by a digit so that it lies on the front or palmar aspect of the finger, or so that it lies on the back or dorsal aspect. In nearly all cases it will be found that when a string is taken up by inserting the digit from the distal side into a loop, the string will have been taken up by the palmar aspect, and that the insertion from the proximal side into the loop involves taking up the string by the dorsal aspect of the digit.

Other operations are those of transferring strings from one digit to another and dropping or releasing the strings from a given digit or digits.

The manipulation consists of a series of movements, after each of which the figure should be extended by drawing the hands apart and separating the digits. In some cases, when this would interfere with the formation of the figure, a special instruction will be given that the figure is not to be extended. Usually it is advisable to keep the loops as near the tips of the digits as possible.

There are certain opening positions and movements which are common to many figures. To save trouble these may receive conventional names; the use of these will soon be apparent, but it is better to repeat descriptions than to run any risk of obscurity.

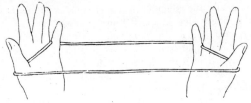

FIG. 268.   Position I.

Position I.—This name may be applied to the position in which the string is placed on the hands when beginning the great majority of the figures.

Place the string over the thumbs and little-fingers of both hands so that on each hand the string passes from the ulnar side of the hand round the back of the little-finger, then between the little- and ring-fingers and across the palm; then between the index and thumb and round the back of the thumb to the radial side of the hand. When the hands are drawn apart the result is a single radial thumb string and a single ulnar little-finger string on each hand with a string lying across the palm.

This position differs from the opening position of the English cat's-cradle in which the string is wound round the hand so that one string lies across the palm and two across the back of the hand with a single radial index string and a single ulnar little-finger string.

Opening A.—This name may be applied to the manipulation which forms the most frequent starting point of the various figures. Place string on hands in Position I. With the back of the index of the right hand take up from proximal side (or from below) the left palmar string and return. There will now be a loop on the right index, formed by strings passing from the radial side of the little-finger and the ulnar side of the thumb of the left hand, i.e. the radial little-finger strings and the ulnar thumb strings respectively.

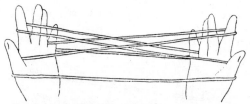

FIG. 269.   Opening A.

With the back of the index of left hand take up from proximal side (or from below) the right palmar string and return, keeping the index with the right index loop all the time so that the strings now joining the loop on the left index lie within the right index loop.

The figure now consists of six loops on the thumb, index, and little-finger of the two hands. The radial little-finger string of each hand crosses in the centre of the figure to form the ulnar index strings of the other hand, and similarly the ulnar thumb string of one hand crosses and becomes the radial index string of the other hand.

The places where the strings cross in the centre of the figure may be termed the crosses of Opening A.

In some finished figures if the strings are pulled apart carelessly a hopeless tangle is the result. To avoid this take the top and bottom straight strings of the figure and pull them apart, and the string will usually resolve itself into a simple loop.

String figures.

1. *Baur*, a fish-spear with several prongs, Mer.
Position I.

Take up with the right index the transverse string on the left palm from its proximal side, give it one twist and return. Pass the left index through the right index loop from the distal side, and take up the transverse string of the right hand from the proximal side and return through the loop.

Drop the thumb and little-finger loops of the right hand and draw the hands apart.

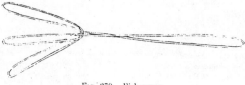

FIG. 270.   Fish-spear.

2. *Dab*, spear[1], Mer.

Opening A. (Left palmar string must be taken up first.)

Transfer right index loop to left index, and the original left index loop to the right index, passing it over the one just transferred.

Release right index and the spear flies to the left; by bringing the right thumb and little-finger close together the handle of the spear appears.

Pick up on right index the string just dropped, and release left index; the spear then flies to the right.

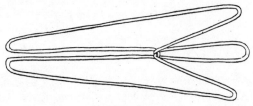

Fig. 271.   Spear.

3. *U*. Mer, *urab*, Mabuiag.   The coco-nut palm.

Pass fingers from the distal side into thumb loops and close hands.

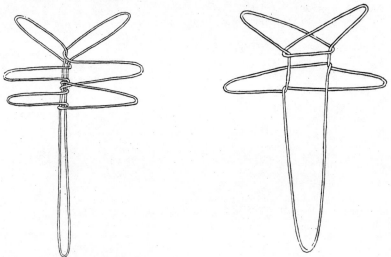

Fig. 272.   Coco-nut palm.

Fig. 273.   Tern.

[1] The name given for this figure was *dab*, which seems to be a misnomer, as the *dab* is a simple spear (p. 156), whereas the figure represents a pronged spear.   "Throwing the fish-spear" would be a more appropriate name.   The same figure occurs at Princess Charlotte Bay and middle Palmer River, N. Queensland, where it is called "Duck in flight."   Walter E. Roth, *N. Queensland Eth. Bull.* No. 4, 1902, pl. V. fig. 6.

Put toe[1] from the distal side into thumb loops, drawing radial thumb string over all other strings, and holding it down.

Exchange loops on little-fingers, the right passing over the left.

Repeat with indices.

Draw tight and work the strings up to form the crown at the head of the tree.

4. *Sirar*, the tern (Sterna Bergii), Mer.

Opening A.

Hold ulnar side of little-finger loop with toe.

With little-fingers take up ulnar strings of index loops from the proximal side, returning proximal to the ulnar strings of the little-finger loop.

Hold radial thumb string with the mouth.

With thumbs take up from the proximal side the radial strings of the index loops and return proximal to the radial strings of the thumb loop.

Release indices and mouth.

Move the hands inward and outward, and the strings will imitate the movements of the tern's wings.

Sing: *O Sirara lubaluba sirara lubaluba neidge kari-gedge doali dogosili.*
      Tern feathers   on rock on my land.

5. *Le sik*, the bed, Mer.

Opening A.

Put thumbs proximal to index loops and into little-finger loops from the proximal side; take up on the backs of thumbs the radial strings and return under index loops.

Pass little-fingers through the index loops from the distal side and into the thumb loops from the proximal side; with backs of little-fingers pick up ulnar thumb string and return through index loops.

Release indices.

Sing: *le sikge,*   *le sikge,*   *ut-eidi,*   *ut-eidi,*   *sik erapei.*
    man on a bed,   man on a bed,   asleep lies,   asleep lies,   bed breaks.

At the word "*erapei*" release little-fingers and the figure disappears.

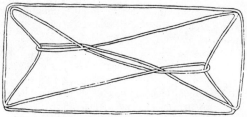

Fig. 274. Bed.

---

[1] The native method of manipulation is given in each case, but although a foot may frequently be used, it is often more satisfactory to get the help of another person, or hook the string on some object.

6. *Tup*, a small fish (p. 155), Mer.

Hold part of the string between the thumbs and indices, the hands being about six inches apart; make a small loop by bringing the right hand towards you and to the left. Hold the loop between the. thumbs and indices so that both the loops hang down, and pass both indices towards you through both loops. Draw the hands apart and turn indices up.

There should now be two loops on each index, with the two radial strings running straight across, while the two ulnar strings cross.

Pass thumbs into the proximal index loop from the distal side, and with backs of thumbs pick up the proximal ulnar index string.

Pass thumbs into the distal index loop from the distal side, and with backs of thumbs pick up the distal ulnar index string.

Pass little-fingers distal to the distal radial index string and proximal to the proximal radial index string; with backs of little-fingers take up this string and return.

Each little-finger is now in a triangle. Pass the indices from the distal side into this triangle, and by turning them up towards you, pick up on their tips the slanting string, i.e. the distal radial index string.

Release thumbs and extend, by turning the palms away from you.

Sing: *Tup   igoli   umi   Waierge,   Waier   kesge,   Waierge   Waier*
      Tup   swim   round   to Waier,   Waier   in the channel,   to Waier   Waier

   kesge.
in the channel.

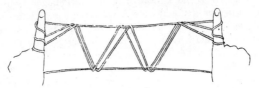

Fig. 275. *Tup.*

7. *Geigi*, king fish, Mer (fig. 314; cf. VI. p. 18); *Dangal*, dugong, Mabuiag.

Opening A.

Release right index and draw out; bend left index into its own loop, thus holding down to palm the string running from left thumb to little-finger.

Release left thumb and little-finger and draw tight.

Put string over left hand as in Position I.

Pass left index over the transverse string of the right hand, and return, twisting the index towards you and up.

Pass right index into right thumb loop from the distal side, and turning the finger up away from you, pick up the ulnar thumb string.

Pass right index into right little-finger loop from above, and by bending it towards you and up, pick up the radial little-finger string, allowing the string just picked up from the thumb to slip off.

Pass right little-finger towards you into the triangle just formed, and hook down against the palm the ulnar thumb string, allowing the original little-finger loop to slip off.

Similarly, with the left little-finger hook down the left ulnar index string. Release thumbs and extend.

Another person puts a hand into the central diamond. If the manipulator leaves go with the left hand and pulls with the right, the fish will be caught; but if he leaves go with the right hand and pulls with the left, the fish will escape.

Sing: *Geigi usar perkori   karem-lar   ko-ditidare.*

deep-sea fish.

Each word is repeated twice, the last word was said to mean, He poke your fin (VI. p. 16).

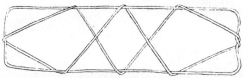

Fig. 276.   King fish.

8. *Laiplaip neur*, girl with large ears, Mer. Make *geigi*.

The figure consists of three lozenges, the outer strings of each lateral lozenge may be described as the upper and lower lozenge strings respectively.

Pass thumbs of each hand above the upper lozenge strings and, drawing these strings backwards, pass thumbs below the lower lozenge strings and take these up and return.

In middle of each half of figure there is now an axial string passing to point of junction of thumb, index, and little-finger loops.

With back of little-fingers from above take up the axial strings and drop indices.

A new figure is produced also consisting of three lozenges.

Pass little-fingers on distal side of lower lozenge strings, take up these strings from above and return.

Sing: *laiplaip neur   tarabuli   urpi   le   a   kolam*

big ear   girl ·both come down fire-ash person and through sexual intercourse

tarabuli.

both come down.

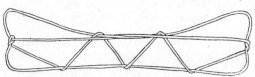

Fig. 277.   Girl with big ears.

9. *Nar*, canoe with two masts, Mer.

Opening A.

Another person must pass his hand distal to the ulnar string, and proximal to the ulnar pair of crossed strings, and take up from above the radial pair of crossed strings at their point of junction, and draw them well out. (The natives perform this action with their right big toe; the loop is therefore called the "toe loop.")

Bend down the right middle-finger through the loop on the right index, and take up the ulnar thumb string on its dorsal surface and return.

Repeat with left middle-finger.

Release thumb, index, and little-finger of each hand.

Draw out large the loop remaining on the middle-fingers and with this go through Opening A.

Pass middle-fingers distal to the little-finger loops and into the toe loops from the proximal side. Then pass them distal to all the transverse strings except the radial thumb string; take up this string on their dorsal aspect, releasing thumbs, and return through toe loops.

Release toe loops and indices and draw tight.

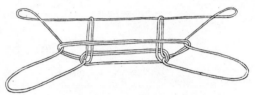

FIG. 278.   Canoe with two masts.

10.   *Pagi*, Mer, *ger*, Mabuiag, a sea-snake.

Opening A.

Pass the right hand round the left hand so that all the strings cross the back of the left hand from the ulnar to the radial side.

Pass the left hand and its strings from the distal side into the right index loop and bring it out proximal to the ulnar index string. Release right index.

Unwind the left hand, bringing the right hand back to its usual position. Release left index.

There is now a single transverse string on the right palm, and a single transverse string on the back of the left hand.

With left index take up from the proximal side the transverse string on the right palm.

Transfer the string from the back of the left hand to its palm and draw tight.

Release left thumb, transfer the left index loop to the left thumb.

Put each index into its little-finger loop from the distal side and take up the ulnar string with the back of the index.

Hold the hands pointing away from the body with the index fingers uppermost. Withdraw left thumb, and with it gently press down the radial little-finger string until the "snake" appears. Gently draw out the right hand and the snake will swim.

It is interesting to note that instead of the pointed tail characteristic of land-snakes, *Pagi* has the broad flat tail peculiar to sea-snakes.

Sing: *Pagia mai nagedim upi etauerida kai amarem[1] pekem.*
  Sea-snake you to where tail strikes I   to side.

Fig. 279. Sea-snake.

11. *Ti meta*, the nest of the *ti* (the sun bird, Nectarinia australis, VI. p. 8), Mer. *Gul*, canoe, Mabuiag.

Opening A.

Insert each index into the little-finger loop from the distal side; bend it towards you and pass it to the proximal side of the radial little-finger string, and bring it back to its original position by passing it between the ulnar thumb string and the radial index string. Release little-fingers.

There are now two loops on each index and a large loop passing round both thumbs. Insert the little-fingers from the distal side into the index loops and pull down the two ulnar index strings. (End of *Ti meta* opening.)

Let go both thumbs gently and insert them into the same loop in the opposite direction to which they had been previously (i.e. change the direction of the thumbs in their loops).

With the dorsal aspect of the thumbs take up from the palmar side the strings passing obliquely from the radial side of the indices to the ulnar little-finger strings, and extend. The inverted pyramid in the centre represents the nest.

Sing: *Ti ti ti mari kesa diteredi kari kesa diteredi.*

This is very obscure, it may mean *Ti* thee property choose, me property choose.

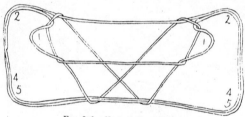

Fig. 280. Nest of the sun bird.

12. *Nageg*, the trigger-fish or leather-jacket (Monacanthus, pl. XXXVIII. fig. 4; see VI. p. 19), Mer.

Ti meta opening.

Drop right thumb loop without pulling tight, and pass right thumb into the upper

___

[1] ? *emarmuli*, rolls about.

central triangle, and press the two strings of the loop just dropped by the thumb towards the right.

Take up with the thumb, from the proximal side, the oblique radial index string and return, letting the two original loops slide off the thumb.

Take right thumb out of its loop and insert again in the opposite direction.

With dorsal aspect of thumb take up the two ulnar index strings and bring them through the thumb loop.

Take out the right little-finger from its loop and place it in the right thumb loop from the proximal side, withdrawing thumb.

Take up with the right thumb from below, and close to the index, the radial index string that passes across to the radial side of the left index. Withdraw index from both loops. (End of *Nageg* opening.)

The loop released by the index will form part of the head of the fish, and the short loop above it is the dorsal spine.

Drop left thumb string without drawing tight.

A big loop is now left which will form the tail of the fish.

Press down with the left thumb, from above, the oblique string from the radial side of the left index till it is below the two straight strings connecting the figure.

Release thumb, and pass it above the straight strings and take up from the far side of the two strings, and from below, the string just pressed down, and extend, keeping the left thumb string in the middle line of the figure.

This string represents the row of spines on the fish's tail.

Sing: *Nageg upi seker   dike,   abele lar   upige   seker   dike.*
        Nageg tail comb[1] it is here that fish on the tail comb it is there.

Another version is *Nagegera* (*Nageg's*) *erakai upige* (on tail) *seker* (comb).

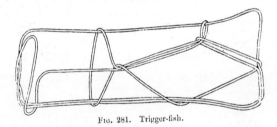

FIG. 281. Trigger-fish.

13. *Saper*, the flying-fox (Pteropus), Mer.

Repeat the previous figure *Nageg* to the end of the *Nageg* opening, only using both hands all through; the figure is then symmetrical.

Extend by passing each index into its thumb loop from the distal side, and picking up on its tip the radial string. Release thumbs.

Say: *a aa*, which is the noise made by the flying-fox.

---

[1] This has reference to the series of small spines at the base of the tail of the *nageg* fish; in the folk-tale *Nageg* is the mother of *Geigi*.

14. *Lem baraigida*, the setting sun, Mer; *Dògai*, a star, Mabuiag.
Opening A.

Pass little-fingers distal to index loop and insert them into the thumb loops from the distal side. With backs of little-fingers take up the radial thumb string and return. Release thumbs.

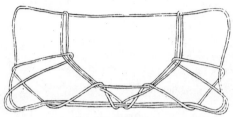

Fig. 282. Flying-fox.

Pass thumbs proximal to the index loops and into the little-finger loops from the proximal side. With backs of thumbs take up the two radial little-finger strings and return. Release little-fingers. By this movement the little-finger loops have been transferred to the thumbs.

Pass little-fingers distal to the index loops and into the thumb loops from the proximal side. With backs of little-fingers take up the two ulnar thumb strings and return. (End of *Lem* opening.)

Transfer loop of left index to right index and loop of right index to left index, passing it over the loop just transferred.

Pass middle-fingers from the distal side through the index loop and take up from the proximal side the two ulnar thumb strings and return through index loops.

Release thumbs and indices.

Pass the thumbs from the proximal side into the middle-finger loops and withdraw middle-fingers, thus transferring the middle-finger loops to the thumbs.

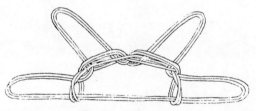

Fig. 283. Setting sun.

Extend the figure with the thumbs towards you; there will then be a St Andrew's cross in the centre of the figure. Insert the indices from the distal side into the lateral spaces of the cross, and into the inverted triangle (the one farthest from you)

42—2

from the proximal side.. With backs of indices take up the respective arms of the cross and return.

Pass middle-fingers through the index loops from the distal side and take up from the proximal side the two ulnar thumb strings and return through the index loops.

Release thumbs and indices, and with the thumbs manipulate the figure so as to make an approximate semicircle with four diverging loops (rays).

Drop middle-fingers and draw out gently and the sun will set.

Sing: *Lem   a   lem   a   gair   lager-lager   tag   a   lager-lager   kokesa kokesa.*
       Sun and   many   ropes   hand and   ropes.

Lager, rope, *lager-lager* may mean stringy (rays of the setting sun); the last three words may be *lagelag,* wishing, *kogiz kogiz,* much sexual intercourse.

15.   *Ares,* fight (two men fighting), Mer.

Lem opening.

There is now a triangle in the centre of the figure; into this insert the indices from the proximal side, and with the back of each index take up its respective side (the radial thumb strings).

Pass the proximal index loop of both hands over the two distal loops on to its palmar aspect (in other words, Navaho the proximal index loop, cf. *Cat's Cradles from many Lands,* p. 5).

Release thumbs, twist the index loops three times to make the "men," and release indices.

Insert the four fingers into the little-finger loops and draw slowly apart.   After the two men meet in the centre only the left string should be pulled, until this becomes free ; the remaining man may then be pulled to the right.

This figure represents a Murray Island man and a Dauar man who meet and begin to fight, and they "fight, fight, fight" (which the performer repeats) until the Murray Island man kills the Dauar man (when the left loop falls), and being a head-hunter, he cuts off his enemy's head and runs home with it (the hindermost loop (fig. 284 B) representing the head).

FIG. 284.   Two men fighting, Mer.

16. *Lar gole*, cuttle-fish, Mer.

Opening A.

Pass fingers from above into the thumb loops and close hands.

Put toe from above into the thumb loops drawing the radial thumb string over the other strings.

Pass thumbs under the index and little-finger strings and draw back the ulnar little-finger strings on the backs of the thumbs, returning through the thumb loops.

Release the little-fingers.

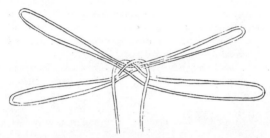

Fig. 285. Cuttle fish.

17. *Epei*, a basket, or *Kanaur*, a Shell (? *kanai*, the mitre shell, Mitra), Mer.

Opening A.

Pass thumbs proximal to the index and little-finger loops and take up the ulnar strings of the little-finger loops and return.

Take up the straight string between the thumbs in the teeth, and lift it over the tips of both thumbs.

Release little-fingers.

Pass little-fingers proximal to the index loops into the thumb loops, bend them towards you over the radial thumb strings and return, thus picking up these strings.

Release string held by the teeth.

Release indices and the figure disappears.

Sing: *Kanaurede kanaurede   epei   tuepeli kerisor topaidili* (? *tupaiteredili*).

basket   shell   spill again.

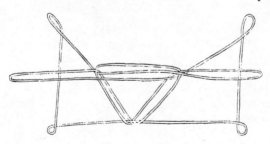

Fig. 286. Basket.

18. *Omasker*, children, and Gazir and Kiam, Mer.

Opening A.

Pass thumbs proximal to the index and little-finger loops, hook back both little-finger strings on their dorsal aspect and return.

Pass each little finger over its index loop, take up the ulnar thumb string from its proximal side and return.

Release all thumb strings.

Pass thumbs over index loops, and insert proximally into proximal little-finger loops, hook up ulnar strings of distal little-finger loops and return through the proximal loop.

Release little-finger loops without extending the figure, and passing little-fingers over the index loops insert them in the thumb loops in the same direction as the thumbs.

Stretch thumbs and little-fingers widely apart and alternately raise and lower each hand. The row of "children" will then dance.

Sing: *Omasker segur   batuglei   segur ki bau waba dada wabawaba waipeda*
        Children play two go round play we   you middle yourselves go round ?
utimdeda[1]   *wa mo wa ma sigezima sigazema*[2] *wa mo ma sigezima.*
throw away ? yes.

This was explained as, Children play and sing and run away and hide.

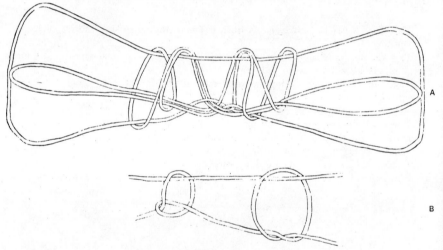

Fig. 287. A, Children. B, Gazir and Kiam.

Drop the index loops, one a little before the other, and draw the hands apart.

Two rings will be left on the strings, one of which is larger than the other. The larger one is Gazir, the smaller, Kiam, these are the sacred grounds in Mer at which the Bomai-Malu masks were exhibited (VI. p. 284); the ceremonies performed at Gazir and Kiam were of a similar nature, but the former were the more important.

[1] Perhaps *itimdeda*, shoot.   [2] Perhaps *sigazi* (W.) from afar, or *sizarima* (W.) come up.

Recite: *Kiam kebi gaire Gazir au gaire.*
Kiam small lot Gazir large lot.

19. *Tamer atkamer le. Tamer* snatching man, Mer.

Extend loop with both hands and place the middle of both strings round the big toe.

Keeping the strings parallel, pass the right loop of the string through the left, and the one now on the right through the other.

Let go strings and pick up through the loops the portion of the loop that was left on the toe and play.

Sing: *Bua! Bua! Bua!* (or *Bub! Bub! Bub!*) *He! He! He!*

The figure was described as "two legs and no body." It is intended to represent the passing of one of the sacred Malu clubs (*Tamera*) (VI. p. 296) from one *Beizam boai* to another during Bomai-Malu ceremony at Las (VI. p. 310).

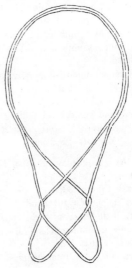

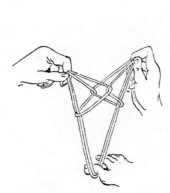

FIG. 288. Man passing the Malu club *tamer*.

FIG. 289. Cough.

20. *Kobek,* cough, Mer.

Stretch the string and place it behind the neck, bringing the ends in front.

Opening A.

Pass middle-fingers through the index loops from above, take up the palmar strings and return through the index loops.

Release all except middle-fingers, and make a coughing noise.

Sing: *Kobek dawĕna*[1] *kapumita*[2] *dawĕna kobek idid lu sabsab lu.*
Cough greasy thing sour thing.

[1] ? *ada-waean* from *adaka wai* (W.), send away.
[2] Said to be a song-word with no meaning, but perhaps (W.) *kapu,* good, *mita,* taste.

21. *Kuper*, maggots, Mer.

Opening A.

Release right index and draw tight.

Pass middle-finger of left hand under the index loop, hook from above the radial thumb string and return.

Release thumb and little-finger of left hand.

Insert left thumb proximally into the index loop of the left hand.

Pass left index distally into the right little-finger loop, hook up from below the radial little-finger string and return.

Pass left thumb distally into the right thumb loop, hook up from below the ulnar thumb string and return.

Pass proximal loop on left index and thumb over the tips of both digits.

Apply the point of the left thumb to that of the index and transfer the index loop to the thumb.

Insert right thumb in its loop in the opposite direction.

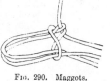

Fig. 290. Maggots.

Take right thumb and little-finger loops on all the fingers of that hand.

Replace left middle-finger by left little-finger in the opposite direction.

Take out left thumb from its loops, pull with right hand, and the maggot goes along to the right.

Slue round right hand pulling smartly and the maggot disappears.

Sing: *Kupera   zariz*[1] *zariz upi eupamada.*

    Maggots go along   jump up.

22. *Kai*, ball (playing ball), Mer.

Opening A.

Release thumb loops.

Twist index of right hand.

Twist little-finger of right hand.

Transfer little-finger loop of right hand to index, and take up both loops in the four fingers of that hand.

Insert left index from distal side into the little-finger loop, and transfer it to index. Take up both loops in the four fingers of that hand.

Holding the strings taut, work the figure up and down by moving the hands.

Sing: *Kai   tupitari   kai tupitari   abu-kak   kai o   atimed-kak   kai o.*

    Ball they hit back ball   not falling ball   not throwing ball.

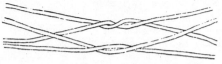

Fig. 291. *Kai.*

[1] Evidently the Western *uzariz*, goes along. The song was explained as "Fruit he stink, maggot jump inside."

23. *Azrik le*, man going backwards, Mer.

Position I.

Pass left index over the ulnar string, take it up from below on tip of finger and return.

Let go right hand.

Pass little-finger of right hand under the oblique string from the little-finger to the index of left hand. Hook down ulnar index string and draw out.

Retaining loop on right little-finger pass right index distally into left index loop, pick up on dorsal surface the palmar string from thumb to little-finger and draw out.

Release indices and little-fingers of both hands gently.

Insert left little-finger into thumb loop.

With right hand draw the figure along by the central strings.

Sing: *Lokoi*   *dirmeda, Lokoi itimeda.*
          (a man's name)   Lokoi shoots.

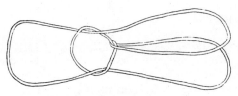
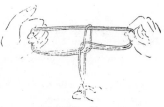

FIG. 292.   Man going backwards.   FIG. 293.   *Sinaur.*

24. *Sinaur*, Mer.

Opening A.

Pass the right foot between the right thumb and index loops and pull down the radial index string with the big toe.

Release right index, stretch the toe string, and drop the other right hand loops, letting them hang loose.

Insert right thumb and index into the left index loop and pick up the ulnar thumb and little-finger radial strings and return.

Drop the index loop and put all the left hand fingers through the thumb and little-finger loops.

Work the loop up and down the strings. This gives a sawing movement, the hands approach as they rise and are drawn apart as they sink.

25. *Kokowa*, a land crab, Saguane, Kiwai Island.

(This figure was collected by Mr S. H. Ray.)

Make *Ti meta* (No. 11).

Put the little-fingers from the proximal side into the thumb loops. Release thumbs.

Pass thumbs away from you through little-finger loops and to the palmar side of the double strings running from index to little-finger. With backs of thumbs take up these strings, returning through little-finger loops. Release little-fingers.

Pass little-fingers from the proximal side into the thumb loops, and release thumbs.

A straight string passes from index to index. Take up this string from the proximal side, close to the indices, with the thumbs. Release indices.

Put indices into thumb loops towards you and withdraw thumbs.

A loop passes from the centre of each palmar string to the outer angle of the central lozenges; take up with the thumbs from the proximal side the string of this loop that lies nearest to you.

Bring thumbs together, tip to tip, and exchange the loops, the left passing under the right.

Pass the middle-fingers distal to the index loops and take up the ulnar thumb string from the proximal side.

Release thumbs and pass them into the middle-finger loop from the distal side, and take up the ulnar middle-finger string from the proximal side. Release middle-fingers.

By these two movements the thumb loops are taken off the thumbs, twisted once, and replaced.

With the thumbs take up from the proximal side the radial index strings, and return through the thumb loops, allowing original thumb loops to slip off. Release indices.

Pass indices from the proximal side into the thumb loops and withdraw thumbs.

One of the two radial little-finger strings of each hand goes across the figure and crosses the corresponding string from the other little-finger in the middle within a central triangle. (If not apparent this triangle will become so by a slight manipulation.)

Take up these strings from the proximal side at the point at which they cross the triangle with both thumbs, so that there is a double string running from thumb to thumb.

With the thumbs, from the proximal side, take up the radial index strings and return through the thumb loops, allowing original thumb loops to slip off.

Release indices and extend.

This figure represents a land crab with its nippers held up.

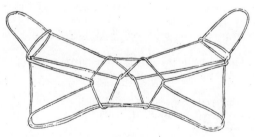

Fig. 294. Land crab.

Tricks.

26. *Mònan*, a lizard, Mer; *Maita*, intestines of a turtle, Mabuiag.

Hold the string in the left hand so that the loop hangs down from it.

Pass the right hand through the loop away from you, then turn the fingers downwards and pass them round the right string towards you; pass the hand between the hanging strings and your body, and bring it forward to the left of the left string; turn the fingers up and bring it back towards you between the two strings.

Pull the hands apart and the right hand is released.

Sing: *Mònan bapitili Peibriem   enau   enau   aroem.*

    Lizard   rolls to Peibri a fruit (p. 133)   for eating.

27. *Kebi mokeis*, the mouse, Mer.

Hold the left hand with the thumb uppermost and the fingers directed to the front. Put the whole left hand through the string letting the loop fall down its dorsal and palmar aspects from the radial side of the thumb. There will then be a pendant palmar and dorsal string on the left hand.

Pass index of right hand beneath the palmar string and between the thumb and index of the left hand, then hook it over the dorsal pendant string, bringing it out between the thumb and index of the left hand. Give the loop thus made a twist clockwise and place it over the left index. Pull tight the pendant strings.

Again pass right index beneath the pendant palmar string and between the index and middle-fingers; hook it over the dorsal string as before; bring this string out, twist the loop clockwise and put it over the middle-finger. Pull tight.

Repeat so as to make similar loops over the ring- and little-fingers. Pull all the strings tight.

Remove the loop from the left thumb and put it between left thumb and index.

This loop represents the ear of the mouse appearing through a crack. Make a squeaking noise, and, when another person (the cat) attempts to catch the mouse, pull the palmar string with the right hand and make the mouse disappear suddenly.

28. *Au mokeis*, the rat (*Uromys cervinipes*, Gould), Mer.

Hold one end of the loop with the right hand and the other end down with the wrist of the left hand, palm downwards.

Pass both strings between index and middle-finger of the left hand.

Release strings of right hand, and, keeping strings parallel, take up the transverse string of the palm through the others and pull tight.

Pass loop with right hand over the whole left hand, and pull tight.

Bring back both strings between index and middle-finger.

Pass both strings between thumb and index and round thumb to palm, and back between index and middle-finger, keeping radial string uppermost all the time.

Bring together index and middle-finger to hold the strings in place, and bring the loop forward over the whole hand, passing the radial string to the radial side of the hand. Draw tight.

Pass loop over from distal to proximal side beneath the transverse palmar string.
Pull tight and pass the loop backwards over the whole hand.
Release loop.

Take off the two distal loops of the thumb, and doubling them back, hold the ends firmly between index and middle-finger.

Take hold of the loose string on the back of the hand, squeak and pull tight, releasing the loops held between the thumb and index. The string will run out.

29. *Zermoi*, the pilot fish (Naucrates) that accompanies a shark, Mabuiag.

Put the loop on the left middle-finger, the strings lying midway on the back of the hand.

Put the free end of the loop over the left little-finger, without twisting the loop, so that the two fingers have the same radial string.

Bring the little-finger loop over across the other loop and round between the thumb and index to the palmar side, drawing it tight. Bring the middle-finger loop over the middle-finger to the palmar side, so that the dorsal cross strings are nipped by a simple loop on either side of the middle-finger.

Turn the palm towards you. Take up a small loop of the middle-finger ulnar string and pass it proximally through the little-finger loop. Through the new loop thus formed take up a small loop of the middle-finger radial string.

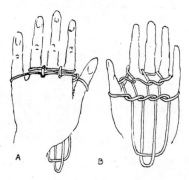

FIG. 295. Pilot fish.

Repeat successively with the distal and proximal strings which pass between thumb and index. Put the last loop on the thumb and pull the free-strings till the figure is tight.

Pat the face with the left hand and sing:

Zermoi zermoi kozia wara daku nguzi wara daka nguzi aigitaian.

Repeat five times on each side of the face and head and also the top of the head.

Release the thumb, keep on pulling and sing while the figure dissolves:

Ziai ninu guba, e Waura ninu guba, e Naigai ninu guba, e Kuki ninu guba.
South thy wind,   East   thy wind,   North thy wind,   West thy wind.

Take the loop off the little-finger and gently pull out the two strings which pass round the index to the back of the hand and sing:

Tabu tabua   wada   gudia   sugu   gudia   iangeta mata miz.
Snake   fish (p. 157) mouth octopus mouth.

Release the string from middle-finger, keeping it in its cup-like loop, put the chin in the small loop and bobbing it up and down sing:

Ibu ibua waruna ibua boina ibua dangalau ibua kaitena ibua.
Chin   turtle   dugong.

30. *Lewer*, food, Mer; *Ai*, food, Mabuiag.

Position I.

Pass indices over the little-finger strings and take them up from below. Return, bringing the part raised in an oblique line across the fingers.

With thumbs take up this oblique string from below and return below thumb string.

Pass little-fingers over the ulnar index string, and take up from below with the backs of the little-fingers the radial string of the oblong.

With thumbs take up from below the remaining string of the oblong (now become the radial string) and return.

Release index loop of left hand, letting it lie loosely on the palm.

Offer it to another person and say " Will you have a yam ? " when he says, " Have you any food for me ? " pull the strings and the yam disappears, and say at the same time, " I hav'nt any."

Repeat with right hand.

31. *Buli*, a fly, Mabuiag.

Hold the string between the index and thumb of each hand about 6 inches apart. Make a small circle by bringing the right hand towards you and to the left, and place the string it has been holding between the left index and thumb to the near side of the string already held.

Put this double string between the teeth with the small loop hanging down and hold the long loop straight out with the left hand.

Put the right index from below into the long loop, then bending it towards you, hook it over the small ring, the tip pointing downwards.

Turn the finger up towards you and to the right until it points upwards, then bring it between the two strings of the long loop from below and put the tip on your nose.

Release the strings held in the mouth, at the same time pulling the long loop and protruding the tongue. The string should come off the right index.

BALL BOUNCING CUSTOMS AND RHYME IN AUSTRALIA

Dorothy Howard

By Dorothy Howard
Fulbright Scholar, 1954-55
University of Melbourne

BALL BOUNCING CUSTOMS AND RHYMES IN AUSTRALIA[1]

BELOW THE EYE-LEVEL of most Australian adults, their children play hundreds of traditional games (unseen and unrecorded by their academic elders[2]) controlled by their own peer laws. Many games have developed uniquely Australian adaptations worth recording and studying. Others, it appears, have adhered closely to traditional games brought from the British Isles and show close kinship with cousin-games in the United States. Ancient ancestors fathered them all.

Australian children observed in 1954-55 played many games in which balls were used[3] and the games were of several varieties. One variety deserving special attention involved ball-juggling with a hollow rubber ball the size of a tennis ball (or a tennis ball) accompanied by the voice chanting numbers or jingles and by dramatic body movements. Boys and girls (though more often girls *than* boys) played in pairs, taking turns going through a set ritual which had a definite name such as "Sevens", "Drunken Sailor" or "Oliver Twist."

Children played with one ball, with two balls or with three balls; and Mr. Jim West of York, Western Australia, reported that a few York children could manage four balls at a time. Most of the children I observed were girls; but in Western Australia where government schools have less segregation of the sexes and less differentiation between boys' and girls' games, I saw more ball-bouncing boys than in any other state.

Not only did Western Australian children appear to have more ball-juggling activities but theirs were the most intricate seen in all Australia. In fact, the most dexterous juvenile ball-bouncers I have ever seen anywhere were in Perth, one of whom was an eleven year old girl who juggled three balls while she chanted verses that told of a princess like "Briar Rosebud" and at the same time made dramatic gestures of a prince climbing a castle high, kissing a princess, and ringing the wedding bells. She promised to write the verses and directions for me but her bouncing skill evidently exceeded her writing interest for the written report never came.

The children played ball-bouncing games on the school yard more than at home, they told me. At home, mother might not be pleased with the sound of a ball clump-clumping against a clean brick or clapboard wall; in fact, at one school I visited, children were forbidden to play ball-bouncing games because the building was new.

To play any of the bouncing games, the children said they needed: a good bouncy ball, a brick or masonry wall and firm ground or hard surface (bitumen covered play yard) beneath.

The children stood facing the brick wall of the school building, about three feet from it and bounced the ball against the wall, on the ground and threw it into the air (underhand or overhand, according to rule). The bouncer and the waiting partner, with sometimes others joining in, chanted directions like the calls in a country dance, while the bouncer added the acrobatic stunts to follow the calls, such as throwing a leg over the bouncing ball, clapping the hands between catches, whirling the body, curtseying, kneeling, and kissing.

Time did not permit a study and analysis of the rhythm patterns of Australian children's ball-bouncing games and rhymes.[4] It is to be hoped that scholars "Down Under" will someday undertake that pleasant task, a task which necessitates spending many, many hours observing one game as well as trying to learn to play it. The results of such an analysis can be of value to both scientists and educators.

Oneses (the simplest of the bouncing games)

Reported by Errol, (age unknown) a child in the Concordia College, Adelaide, S.A. (1955) who wrote: "You bounce the ball with one hand and the one bounces it the most is the winner."

Two ball (the simplest of the ball-juggling games)

Reported by a school-master from the Guildford Government School in Perth; and by Wendy, eleven year old pupil in the Carlisle Government Primary School, Perth, who wrote: "Get two tennis balls and throw them on the wall til you get out. If you don't know how, straight away, just go slow. But when you are sure you are good, you can go very fast. Some girls can play one-handed. When we have 'standstills,' if the ball goes higher than your head, you are not allowed to move."

Sevens (One-ball game)—Version One

Reported in written essay by Edward, eleven years old, Scotch College, Launceston, Tasmania, 1955.

"This is played with a tennis ball. You bounce the ball against the wall, let it bounce on the gound, then catch it. Do this seven times.
"Next—bounce the ball against the wall six times. This time you do not let it bounce. You catch it.
"Next—bounce the ball against the wall five times.
"Next—toss the ball under your leg against the wall and catch it. Do this four times.
"Next—bounce the ball against the wall, turn around twice and catch it.
"Next—bounce the ball against the wall, turn around twice, clap hands twice and catch it.
"Next—standing still—you mustn't move your feet—go through all the steps again.
"Then—kneel down and do the whole thing over again. On the other hand, if you have missed, the next person tries.
"The next time it comes your turn, you begin where you missed before."

Sevens (One ball)—Version Two

Reported in written essay by Kay, a child—age unknown—Whyalla, South Australia, 1955:

"First—you throw the ball against the wall and catch it before it bounces on the ground. Do this seven times.

"Second—you throw the ball against the wall, let it bounce, then catch it. Do this six times.

"Third—bounce the ball on the ground and catch it. Do this five times.

"Fourth—throw the ball under your leg against the wall and catch it. Do this four times.

"Fifth—you bounce the ball on the ground, hit it with your hand to make it bounce against the wall, then catch it. Do this three times.

"Sixth—the same as five except you bounce the ball twice against the wall before you catch it. Do this twice.

"Seventh—you throw the ball at the wall, let it bounce once while your hands are behind your back, then catch it.

"If you miss, you give the ball to your pardner. The first to finish all sevens, wins."

Sevens (One ball)

Undescribed, reported by Glenys, twelve years old and by Carel, eleven years old, East Camberwell Girls' Secondary School (government school), Melbourne, Victoria, 1954.

Sevenses (One ball game)

Reported by Ann and John Howe and Dorothy and Scott Campbell, teachers in government schools, Canberra, A.C.T., 1954.

This game is played like *Sevens,* Version Two, above, to the fifth play.

"Fifth play—three bounces on the wall, one bounce on the ground, one bounce on the wall and catch.

"Sixth play—bounce ball on the wall, bob down *("bob" means squat)* once before catching; then repeat.

"Seventh play—bounce ball on the wall, turn around before catching.

"When a player makes a mistake, he stands aside until another player takes a turn and makes a mistake. Then he carries on from where he missed.

"(Ten and eleven year old boys and girls play this game)."

Sevens (Two ball game)

Observed on the playground of Collier Government Primary School, Perth, Western Australia, where twelve couples of girls, ten, eleven and twelve years old, were lined up before the brick wall of the school building, playing the game. Reported in written essay by Lenore, eleven years old of Colliers School, 1955.

"First—using both hands, bounce the two balls against the wall—one at a time—until each ball has bounced seven times.

"Sixes—with one hand, you bounce one ball against the wall and as it comes back, drop it to the ground for a bounce before you catch it. While you do this, with the other hand you are doing the same thing with the other ball. You do all this six times.

"Fives—you bounce both balls on the ground—one at a time but both going at the same time—five times using both hands.

"Fours—you throw both balls into the air four times, using both hands.

"Threes—you throw one ball underhand at the wall and the other overhand at the wall. Do this three times.

"Twos—you bounce one ball on the wall while you throw one into the air. You do this twice.

"Ones—you bounce one ball on the ground with one hand while you bounce the other on the wall with the other. You do this once."

Tens (One ball game)

Reported in written essay by Lenore, eleven years old, Colliers Government Primary School, Perth, Western Australia, 1955.

"For *tens* you bounce the ball ten times on the ground.

"For *nines* you clap and bounce the ball nine times on the ground.

"For *eights* you bounce the ball and clap your hands behind your back eight times.

"For *sevens* you bounce the ball and throw your leg over the bouncing ball. Seven times.

"For *sixes*, you bounce the ball, then clap your hands first under your leg, then over your leg, then catch the ball. Six times.

"For *fives* you bounce the ball, whirl your hands around each other and catch the ball. Five times.

"For *fours* you hold your dress hem with one hand, then put your other hand through the hole and bounce the ball and catch it. Then change hands and repeat. Two times with each hand.

"For *threes* bounce the ball on the wall, clap the hands under the leg three times, then catch the ball. Three times.

"For *twos* bounce the ball on the wall; then hold the hem of your dress with one hand making a hole; let the ball fall through the hole to the ground and bounce; then catch it. Two times.

"For *ones* bounce the ball *hard* on the ground and while it is in the air, clap hands in front, in back and in front again before catching the ball."

Thirteen (One ball game)

Reported with brief, vague description by a college student in Adelaide, South Australia, who had observed the game between 1948 and 1954; probably similar to Tens *and* Sevens.

In some play groups and in some communities ball bouncing was accompanied merely by counting in a chanting voice in rhythm with the clinking ball as it hit the wall and the ground. In others, verses were chanted demanding dramatic acts as a part of the game.

A, B, C's (Two ball game)

Observed on the Double View Government School playground, Perth, March, 1955. Twelve girls of seven and eight years old were playing in pairs, standing in line before the brick wall of the school building, about two feet from it. The balls were thrown underhand against the wall alternately until the word "learn." On "learn" the right hand threw the ball overhand, then caught the second ball, raised the right knee, threw the ball under the knee and against the wall underhanded; meanwhile, catching the first ball as it came back from the wall (with the left hand). Consequently the "under the knee" act took place on "A,B,C's." The rules were identical in each of the six games going. Not the slightest variation was observed.

> I go to school
> To sit on a stool
> And learn my A,B,C's.

Ball, Ball Bouncing

Reported in writing with no description, by a child, Brian (no age given) Concordia College, Adelaide, South Australia, 1955.

> Ball, ball, bouncing
> Bingo in the bath
> Bunny's eating lettuce
> Up the garden path
> Mouses's in the ladder
> Geese rather lame
> So ball, ball bouncing
> Let us have a game.

Drunken Sailor (One ball game)

Reported in writing by Lenore (and demonstrated by her), eleven years old, Collier Government School, Perth, Western Australia, 1955. Lenore half-chanted, half-sang the words:

> What shall we do with the drunken sailor
> What shall we do with the drunken sailor
> What shall we do with the drunken sailor
> Early in the morning.
>
> Put him in the tub and turn him over   (3 times)
> Early in the morning.
>
> Who you and up she risers   (3 times)
> Early in the morning.
>
> Put him in the tub and turn him under   (3 times)
> Early in the morning.

On the first verse, Lenore kept time with the words by tossing the ball into the air, catching it first with one hand, then with the other. In the second verse, on the word "over", she began tossing the ball into the air, overhand. In the third verse, the ball was held in the hand until the word "risers", then tossed high into the air. In the last verse, the ball was tossed into the air until the word "under", then bounced on the ground.

Hello, Hello, Hello, Sir (One ball game)

Reported with no description by Mrs. N. W. Stanford, who played the game as a child in Indooroopilly, Brisbane, Queensland, (probably, 1925).

> Hello, hello, hello, sir
> How do you do, sir
> I've gone and caught a cold, sir
> Up at the North Pole, sir
> What were you doing there, sir
> Catching a polar bear, sir
> How many did you catch, sir
> One, sir, two, sir, three, sir
>   (and on until bouncer misses).

My Mother Said (One ball game)

Reported in written essay by a child, Wendy, (no age given) Concordia College, Adelaide, South Australia, 1955. Wendy wrote: "You bounce the ball on the ground until you get to the word "woods." Then you throw the ball into the air, turn around three times and

catch the ball. If you drop it, you are *out* and your partner takes
your place."

> My mother said I never should
> Play with the gypsies in the woods.

Number One (One ball game)

*Reported, without description, by a school mistress at Mt. Lawley
Government School, Perth, Western Australia, 1955.*

> Number one, touch your thumb
> Number two, touch your shoe
> Number three, touch your knee
> Number four, touch the floor
> Number five, touch your side
> Number six, pick up sticks
> Number seven, jump to heaven
> Number eight, lay them straight.

Old Mother Mop (Three ball game)

*Observed on the Double View Government School playground, Perth,
Western Australia, March 1955.* Two ten year old girls took turns
juggling three tennis balls against the brick school building. Each
time on the word "pop," the third ball was thrown into the air while
the other two continued to bounce against the wall. One hand was
used to handle both balls bounced against the wall while the other
took care of the ball thrown into the air.

> Old mother mop
> She had a big shop
> And all she could say
> Is candy pop pop
> Candy pop pop
> A penny a sop
> Catch the ball
> And don't let it drop.

Oliver Twist—Version One

*Reported in written essay by a child (no name given) Guildford
Government School, Perth, Western Australia, 1955, who wrote:*
"Two people play. You bounce the ball against the wall and catch it.
You do the actions too."

> Oliver Twist, you can't do this
> So what's the use of trying
> Touch your nose and under it goes
> Touch your knee and around the tree.

Oliver Twist—Version Two

Reported by Joyce, eleven years old, Errol Street School, Melbourne, Victoria. Joyce wrote: "First you get any kind of ball and get a good wall. Then you stand in a good position. You throw the ball against the wall and catch it. And you say:

> Oliver Twist, can you do this
> If so, do so,
> Touch your knee and then your toe
> (and you do this before you catch the ball)

"Next you say:

> Oliver Twist, can you do this
> If so, do so,
> Then your heel and down you go
> (and you bob down)

"After that, you do 'Claps,' 'Whirly Whirls,' 'One Hand,' 'Dumbs,' and last, 'Stand Stills.' If you fail to catch the ball, another player must have a go."

Oliver Twist—Version Three

Reported with brief, vague description in a written essay by a child (no name given) in Whyalla, South Australia, 1955. The rhyme apparently went like this:

> Oliver Twist can't do this
> What's the use of trying
> Touch your knee or touch your toe
> Touch your heel and down you go.

P.K. Chewing Gum (Two ball game)

Observed on the Double View Government School playground, March, 1955. Eleven year old girls were playing in pairs. Two balls were bounced against the brick school building. On the words "gum," "chew it," "stick it," and "gum," the left hand threw a ball under-hand against the wall. On the words "packet," "crack it," "jacket," and "packet" the right hand threw the other ball overhand against the wall.

> P.K. chewing gum, penny a packet
> First you chew it, then you crack it.
> Then you stick it to your jacket
> P.K. chewing gum, penny a packet.

Plainsies, Clapsies

Reported in writing by a child (no name given), Guildford Government School, Perth, Western Australia, 1955, who wrote: "Two peo-

ple or more can play. You bounce the ball against the wall and catch
it and say the words while you do the actions."

> Plainsies, clapsies
> Round the world to Baxies
> First your heel, then your toes
> Bounce the ball and under it goes.

Ball games are ancient, we know. One of the oldest descriptions
of a girls' game of ball is in the Odyssey where, in the palace of
Alcinous, Nausicaa presided over washing-day activities which con-
cluded with bathing in the river, lunch, and a game of ball while
the clothes dried on the rocks by the river.

Current ball-bouncing games, no doubt, owe their widespread
popularity to the world-wide availability of india rubber and the
tennis ball; to school buildings with smooth, brick walls and hard-
surfaced play yards; and to the decreasing amount of play space (a
ball-bouncing game can be played in a small spot) in cities the
world over.

During my brief stay in Australia, I saw and heard far more
than I could record of ball-bouncing play among children. This is
a meager collection. The subject deserves further time and attention.

Notes

[1] This article is based on two sections of a collection and study of Australian children's traditional play customs. The information came from:
observation (I also played with children) of ball-bouncers in Brisbane, Sydney,
Melbourne, Adelaide, Perth, Hobart, and Launceston (Tasmania); and written
reports from children and schoolmasters and mistresses in York (Western
Australia), Swansea (Tasmania), and Whyalla (South Australia).

[2] Among elementary classroom teachers and their children I found much
lively interest in recording play lore. Among Australian academicians (with
important exceptions) I found that folklore has little or no prestige yet.

[3] Some ball games such as "French Cricket" and "Hand Cricket" were
juvenile adaptations of professional Cricket (just as "One-Eyed-Cat" in
America is one of many "Cowlot" adaptations of professional baseball). Many
unsupervised ball games in Australia showed kinship with the academic "sports
programs" in school syllabi but variations from community to community
in rules for playing indicated clearly that oral tradition had played a role in
transmission of ball games from one generation of children to another. What
Australian syllabi indicated (but physical educationists in Australia—as well
as in America—were loathe to admit) was the real relationship of formalized
school-sports-program to folklore. The games in school syllabi were (many
or most of them) adaptions of traditional games. Whether the physical educationists' adaptations were improvements or not is a matter of pedagogy, not
anthropology. Games played with balls were: Ali Baba, Ass, Ball and Cup,
Beam, Blow Football, Bob Ball, Brandies All Over, Branding, Broken Bottle,
Captain Ball, Corner Spry, Cross Ball, Daisy, Danish Rounders, Donkey,
Duck in the Pond, File Gap, First to a Hundred, Five Stone, Fourpence, Free
for All, Keep the Ball, King Ball, Leader Ball, Ledger Ball, Midnight, Pig
in the Middle, Poison Ball, Pounds-Shilling-Pence, Queenie, Rotten Egg,

Rough and Tough, Rough and Tumble, Sick-Dying-Dead, Slag Ball, Street Football, Tip and Run, Tippy-Go-Go, Travellers and Wolves, Tunnel Ball, Two Fields, Uppany Over, Who Is It and Zig Zag.

[4] Dorothy Howard, "The Rhythms of Ball-Bouncing and Ball-Bouncing Rhymes," *JAF* (April-June, 1949), 166-172.

[5] Credit and appreciation for the information in this report go to: informants named in the article; also, Miss M. Jageurs, Miss Margaret Lyttle, Father Francis I. Kelly, Mr. C. G. Humphries, Mr. Andrew McLay, Mr. C. B. Newling, Mr. Elliott Phillips, Mr. John Woods; and to hundreds of Australian lasses and lads who bounced hundreds of balls while I watched with great interest.

MARBLE GAMES OF AUSTRALIAN CHILDREN

Dorothy Howard

Marble Games of Australian Children[1]

by DOROTHY HOWARD

ALTHOUGH American imports into Australia during and since World War II, including ideas as well as manufactured goods of both excellent and shoddy quality, may have influenced the so-called Australian-way-of-life, as some Australians believe, no evidence was found in 1954–5 of the importation of marble tournaments now rampant in the United States. In the U.S.A. national marble tournaments sponsored by schools, city recreation departments and other adult-supervised organizations have established a standardized marble game with printed rule-book in use from the Atlantic to the Pacific (I do not yet know about Alaska and Hawaii); with standardized marble gauge, national marble championship

[1] In 1954–5, the author spent ten months in Australia as an American Fulbright Research Scholar sponsored by the University of Melbourne, collecting and studying Australian white children's traditional play customs. Information was obtained: by visiting playgrounds and classrooms of both government and non-government schools; visiting public playgrounds; visiting in homes; loitering on streets and public beaches where children were playing; from written compositions of school children and letters from older people; by talking with school masters and mistresses, fathers, mothers, educationists, physical educationalists, ministers, priests, anthropologists, psychologists, people on buses, trams, trains, and planes; by studying school syllabi; searching libraries; visiting toy shops; and through publicity in newspapers and magazines throughout Australia and radio addresses in Canberra and in Perth.

Search of Australian libraries revealed: no collections of Australian children's traditional games; no copy of the Brian-Smith manuscript collection of New Zealand children's games — see *Folklore* Vol. 64, September 1953. Ethnograph monographs on aborigine games around 1900 were found in the library of the University of Queensland and in the South Australian Library, Adelaide. Also the South Australian Library, *Early Memories* (a manuscript) written by Sir Joseph Verco, described his childhood games from 1860–70. In the Mitchel Library in Sydney, a file of old newspapers purportedly carried some information on children's games before the turn of the century but library rules, red tape and protocol forbade use of the material during the author's brief stay there.

Australian adults said repeatedly and regularly that their children had no traditional games, yet a ten-month search produced enough factual material to demonstrate that traditional games and customs were alive in the process of adaptation and evidence of more material ready to be collected.

No attempt was made to study aboriginal Australian children's play nor to assess the interaction, if any, that may have taken place between the English-speaking children and the aborigines. A visit was made to one government school in New South Wales (The LaPerouse School) where the children were aborigine or part aborigine. Mr C. P. Mountford, South Australian anthropologist, who

cups; and a standardized motto: 'All championship marble shooters play for fair' enforced by an official referee.[2]

Although Australian educationalists (like Americans) have been tampering with children's traditional play customs for some time thinking to improve folkways, they had, apparently in 1954–5, overlooked marble games. To my delight, I found considerable variety in game names, terms and game ways (characteristics of folk customs everywhere).

This happy omission on the part of scheming adults did not mean that a changing adult-imposed environment had had no effect on Australian children's marble games. According to the memoirs of Sir Joseph Verco: 'In those days (1860–70) . . . the footpaths belonged to the small boys as much as to the city council, and they had no compunction in digging their 'nuck' holes wherever they wanted to play and neither the citizens nor the police ever interfered with their mining operations nor with their play.' Even as late as twenty-five years ago, I was told, children played on open paddocks, earthy playgrounds and sandy footpaths; and could dig their marble holes anywhere they chose. In the nineteen-fifties, with the population concentrated more and more in city areas with more hard-surfaced playgrounds and footpaths, the old hole marble games seemed to be diminishing in favor of surface games played on diagrams of various shapes. With urban areas becoming more congested, leaving less play-space for children, adult supervision of school playgrounds had increased. The amount of adult supervision varied from state to state and community to community. On some, though not all, city school playgrounds, all play was supervised in groups segregated by age, sex and social class (a social class system existed as the result of 'state' and 'non-state' school systems); and the play programmes were set down in state syllabi. I saw no marble games in progress and found no evidence of them

had spent many years living with tribes in the Northern Territory held the opinion that there had been little, if any, play exchange between the two groups of children; that any possible exchange would have been the imposition of white children's play upon the aborigines, most of whom live in the 'outback' away from city influences, charges of the Commonwealth Government. No evidence of marble games or similar games was found among aborigine children.

[2] Peter and Iona Opie (*The Lore and Language of Schoolchildren*, Ox. Un. Press, 1959, p. 249) reporting on Good Friday celebrations say: 'At Tinsley Green, just north of Three Bridges, a marble championship (now, with American participation, assuming an international character) continues year after year. . . .'

on the supervised city playgrounds. I also found no marble games, as such, included in sports syllabi; in some cases, however, syllabi were not made available to me. During World War II, I was told, marbles (which have always been imported) were unavailable in Australian shops; therefore one whole generation of children went without marbles except for those inherited from parents and uncles and aunties. In consequence, the game languished for a time. Surviving a fast-changing environment by the process of adaptation, Australian marble games in 1954–5 had thus far eluded scheming adults. What the situation now is in 1961 I do not know.

This report on Australian marble games is selected data from a larger collection of sometimes fragmentary facts which may one day be useful to scholars with more time, opportunity and skill to collect information and delve into the whys and wherefores thereof. The selected facts include: names of games, kinds of games, ways of playing, kinds of marbles used, game terms, and beliefs of Australian adults about marble games. Very little analysis has been attempted and no moral judgments pronounced. A tourist-collector, such as I, may profitably report a few careful observations. That is all. Wise conclusions demand many years of field work and study.

Chasing games were the simplest of Australian children's marble games. The first one I saw in progress was played by two boys about nine and eleven years old on the carpeted floor of three adjoining lounges in a Canberra hotel. One boy tossed his marble on to the floor at some distance. The second boy tossed his after, trying to hit the first. If he hit, he picked up the first player's marble, put it in his pocket and the first player then tossed out a second marble; if not, the first player took a turn tossing his marble at the second one. The game continued in silence, the rules apparently understood and accepted by the two. I tried unsuccessfully to engage the players in conversation but they picked up their marbles and disappeared from sight, perhaps seeking another playing field secure from a meddling foreign-sounding adult.

Subsequently, I found that the most common name throughout Australia for this marble-chasing game was 'Follow-Me-Taw' (pronounced 'Tor').[3]

[3] Other marble-chasing games were called: 'Follow' — Brisbane; 'Black Track' — Melbourne; 'Track Taws' — Perth (Mt Lawley Government School);

Eventually I decided that the marble games could be categorized as *hole games* and *surface games* (chasing games being the simplest of the latter type); with a third category lazily designated as *miscellaneous* to label games employing special devices such as: a board with carved arches (similar to 'Nine Holes' as described by Gomme, Strutt and Sutton-Smith[4]); a cardboard pyramid ('Prince Henry'); 'Wall'; and non-marble games in which marbles functioned only as gambling currency ('Toodlembuck' or 'Stick on Scone').

Other *surface games*, more complicated than the simple chase games, were played on diagrams on the ground or hard-surfaced play yard, marked with chalk, stick, slate, stone, or by hand, foot or penknife. The diagrams were: circles (of various sizes), half circles, ovals, squares, triangles and lines. Nine circle games were observed or reported.[5] Sir Joseph Verco described 'In the Ring' as he played the game in 1860–70:

On the hard smooth surface of the original red loamy soil of our un-tilled and undisturbed land, as in the school playground a circle was marked out with a pen knife or a piece of wood or a stone. The size of the circle would vary with the skill and the age of the players. The smaller and less skilful would have a ring of two or three feet in diameter, the older and more capable would draw one of a couple of yards across. In the centre a short straight line would be drawn and on this the two opposing players would arrange an equal number of marbles of equal value, whether commonies, stoneys or glassies. They would then toss up for 'first fire' or more commonly (as money, even pence, was then rather scarce), one boy would put his hands behind his back, and then bring his closed fists to the front, in one of which was a marble. His opponent would guess which fist enclosed the marble. If on opening both hands it was found that he had fortunately guessed correctly he had the advan-

'Tractor Kelly' — Perth (Carlisle Government School); 'Tractor Taw' — Perth (Collier Government School); 'Kiss and Span' — Perth (Geraldton Government School). In Scottsdale, Tasmania, a small country community, a Mrs Chugg told of her 'Follow-Me-Taw' game as she played it in 1900 and of the day she won one hundred marbles on her way to school and on her way home in the afternoon.

[4] A. B. Gomme, *The Traditional Games of England, Scotland and Ireland*, Vol. I, London, 1894, pp. 413–14. J. Strutt, *The Sports and Pastimes of the People of England*, 1801 (new edition, J. C. Cox, London, 1903), p. 222 and p. 304. B. Sutton-Smith, '*The Games of New Zealand Children*', *Folklore Studies*, 12, Berkeley and Los Angeles, Un. of Cal. Press, 1959, p. 89.

[5] Circle games: 'The Ring', 'Circle', 'Big Ring', 'Little Ring', 'Big Circle', and 'Little Circle' were current names throughout Australia; 'Poison Ring', 'Jumbo', and 'Eye Drop' were reported from Brisbane; and 'Pyramids' (with marbles dubbed up in a circle) from St Helens, Tasmania.

tage of first 'shot', if wrongly, the other lad led the attack. Down on his knees, he would take his 'taw' between the knuckle of his thumb and his forefinger, and from the line of circumference of the ring fire his taw at the marbles in its centre, with the object of knocking some of them out of the ring. All he knocked out belonged to him. If one of them stopped absolutely on the line of the ring it was put back to the centre. If his taw came out of the ring whether he had knocked out any of the marbles or not he ceased firing and his playfellow had his opportunity. If he had knocked one or more marbles out of the ring, and his taw remained in the ring, he had the privilege of firing his taw at any marble still anywhere in the ring and if he knocked it out of the ring it became his; and if his taw was still in the ring he could repeat the process time after time. A skilful player might thus knock out one marble after another until every one originally on the central line had been accounted for and he had 'skun the ring'. If however the first player had hit the marbles on the line in the centre of the ring and scattered them about but had knocked none of them out of the ring, or had in any other way 'finished his shot' the marbles were not put back on the central line for the next player, but were left where they had been scattered, wherever they might be. Some would be close to it and fired at with a side stroke at close quarters might easily be knocked out of the ring and be secured as his. He would also try, while he knocked out this marble to so strike it as to keep his taw in the ring, and if skilful enough would at the same time strike the marble in such a way as to rebound so as to 'fetch up' near another marble in the ring and so secure as many of them as possible. In this way a great amount of skill could be acquired and displayed in the game, which in some respects resembled the more patrician game of billiards.

Some boys instead of keeping their knuckles on the line when firing their taw would jerk their hand forward into the ring so as to get nearer their mark before releasing their taw for the impact. This was denominated 'funnicking' and directly it was noticed it raised the cry of 'fen funnicks' or 'none of your funnicking', and the practice had to cease as unfair.

Three current circle games — 'Poison Ring', 'Jumbo' and 'Eye Drop' were described in writing by a school mistress in Queensland. Of 'Poison Ring' she wrote:

To make a ring, place the heel firmly on the ground and twist the foot around in a circle. The marbles dubbed up are placed in the imprint of the heel. The ring is called 'Poison'. Then players pink to see who has first go. Any player who pinks into the ring is out. If a player's taw stays in the ring when he hits a marble out, he must put his winnings back in the ring and he is out of the game. If a player hits a marble out of the ring and his marble (taw) does not stay in the ring, his taw then becomes 'Poison'. When a poison taw hits another taw, that man is out. To 'dub up' means to place marbles in the ring before pinking. This is a boys' seasonal game.

Another circle game — 'Pyramids' — was described by a twelve-year-old boy, St Helens, Tasmania:

One player builds a pyramid with his own marbles and draws a little circle around the pyramid. Then another player, by paying the pyramid-owner a marble, is allowed to shoot at the pyramid one shot. If his aim is successful, any marble that rolls out of the circle belongs to him. Then the pyramid is built up again for the next player. The owner makes his profit out of those who aim without hitting. A marble must be paid for every shot. The game continues until all marbles are knocked out of the ring. No taw can be taken but the owner of the taw must hand over another marble.

Most surface game names were delightful metaphors.[6] 'Football' played on an oval diagram, was described by an eleven-year-old girl in Scottsdale, Tasmania:

A football is drawn and a line is drawn down the middle long ways. Each player places one marble on the line crossing the football. Then each player stands back at the shooting line and throws a marble trying to come as near the football as possible to see who will have first go. If a player goes into the ring, then all must throw again. The one who has first go shoots to knock the marbles out of the ring. If all agree he may keep the marbles he shoots from the ring. He shoots until he misses. The game is over when there are no more marbles in the ring. Boys and girls play this.

A twelve-year-old boy in Perth wrote a description of his game of 'Fats':

This game is played by two people. You can play it on sand or clay; or you can play it on asphalt. But if you play it on sand or grass, your marble will not bounce or roll or go into the 'Kill' or 'Fats'.

[6] Half-circle games: 'Half Moon' and 'Townsey' — Brisbane; and 'Mooney Ted First' — Perth. Oval diagrams: 'Football' — Scottsdale, Tasmania; 'Fats' — Perth (Doubleview Government School); 'Eye Drop' (similar to the circle, 'Eye Drop' in Birsbane) — Perth (Collier Government School). Triangle diagrams: 'Killy' — Adelaide, South Australia, and 'Three Corner Killy' — Perth (Geraldton Government School). Square diagrams: 'Square Ring' — Perth (Collier Government School). Line diagram: 'Liney' — Perth (Geraldton Government School).

And he ended his composition by commenting:

This game is exciting when you win all the other boy's marbles but it isn't when you lose all yours.

Of the *hole games*, five one-hole games (current or obsolete) were observed or recorded.[7] No evidence was found of two-hole games either current or obsolete; and no current three-hole games were found though Sir Joseph described a three-hole game of his childhood called 'Nucks' or 'Nux'. Five four-hole games were observed or reported.[8] One eleven-hole game called 'Poison Hole', played in Canberra by eleven-year-old boys, was reported by two schoolmasters and two schoolmistresses in the A.C.T. government schools.

Sir Joseph described 'In the Hole' (one-hole game):

A hole about as big as a breakfast cup was dug in the ground. Each player put down an equal number of marbles, and lots were drawn as to who should have first throw. The fortunate lad stood toeing a line drawn at a measured distance from the hole; it might be ten or twenty feet according to mutual agreement. With all the marbles in his hand he bowled them toward the hole, and as many as rolled into it and remained there were his. The remainder were now thrown in the same manner by the other player, and the game proceeded until the last marble had been holed, when the players could count up their losses or gains and start again.

'Goot' a current one-hole game was described by a twelve-year-old girl, Melbourne (East Camberwell Girls' Secondary School) who gave a demonstration, then wrote the following description accompanied by a diagram:

The first thing to do in this game is to dig a small, shallow hole in the ground. This is called the 'Goot'. Next a line at an agreed distance from the hole — one yard is about right. Now with everything ready for the game to start the two or more players each get their marble and fire it to stop as close as possible to the goot. The person whose marble is nearest

[7] One-hole games: 'Basins' — Mallee Country, Victoria ('played in years gone by'); 'In the Hole' played by Sir Joseph Verco in 1860–70; 'Bunny Hole' — Melbourne (Errol Street Government School); 'Holey' — Fremantle Government School; 'Goot' — Melbourne (East Camberwell Girls' Secondary School).

[8] Four-hole games: 'Castles' played about 1890 in Sea View, South Australia and about 1945 in Horsham, Victoria; 'Pot Holes' — Perth (Mt Lawley Government School); 'Holes' — Brisbane; 'Poison' — Brisbane; and 'Basins' — Swansea, Tasmania.

it is the first to start playing. The others follow in order of their marbles. The leader fires again from the line towards the hole and tries to place his marble in it. If he fails the marble is left where it is and the others have their turn. But if he succeeds in getting into the goot he may fire out of it a little way and wait for another person to fire from behind the line.

When they have done this, the next turn he has, he can chase them and try to 'kill' them. To kill, you have to hit another person's marble three times in succession and then he is out of the game.

Once he kills one person he has to get back into the goot once more, before chasing another. All the other marbles do the same of course, and when everyone except one person is killed, he is the winner.

In Goot it is a rule that you can only have one shot when it is your turn except when you have hit another person, or when you have got into the goot. In each of these cases, another shot may be had at a marble, but if it misses you may not have another shot until your next turn. By then probably the other marble will have moved away or shot at you and the chase begins again.

'Nucks' or 'Nux' (three-hole game described by Sir Joseph):

One of their games they called 'Nucks' or 'Nux'. How it was to be spelt is unknown, never having been seen in print. Three holes about the size of small saucers had to be dug in the ground with a pen knife they were about a yard apart, and in a line with one another from a 'starting' line about half a yard from the first hole the player had to make his first shot. He had a marble which he called his 'taw', and of which he was very careful; because as he became used to it in his many games he was more able to do what he wished with it. This 'taw' he fired with his right thumb and two fingers, so as to locate it in the nearest of the three holes. If it was lodged in this, he went up to this hole, and took from it his 'taw' and with his thumb as a centre at the further margin of his first hole he spread out his fingers and described a semi-circle, and from this in advance of the first hole he 'fired' his 'taw' to try and lodge it in the second hole. If he succeeded he continued the same progress into the third hole, and if successful he proceeded to carry out the same man-oeuvres on the reverse journey, and this play was continued up and down until such time as he failed to lodge his taw in a hole. Then he had to leave his 'taw' wherever it might have stopped. Now it was his op-ponent's turn to try his hand in the same way. If at any point he found his taw anywhere near the first player's marble, he had the privilege of firing carefully at this, and if he struck it very gently, or 'kissed' it as the touching was called, he had the privilege of firing as hard as he pleased at the enemy marble and knocking it as far away as he could, and then continuing at his own progress from hole to hole. As soon as he missed fire in any way or play No. 1 player took his turn again and tried to get into the hole which he had previously failed to enter; and he may have been knocked so far away that it would need two or more attempts before he managed to gain it. The boy who first went up and down the series of three holes three times had won the game. It had to be played necessarily kneeling down, and no otherwise and, so tended to produce a definite bagging of the trousers at the knees, and the wearing of holes there, as well as an accumulation of dirt and even of abrasion at the knuckles of the hands.

'Poison', a four-hole game was reported by a teachers' college student in Brisbane and described as her nine-year-old brother and his friends played it:

Four holes are made — three in a line and one about five feet to one side of the last three. This last is called 'Poison'. The player pinches into the first hole, then into the second, the third; and then back to first, second and third again. Then he goes on to 'Poison'. After 'Poison', he can go into any hole; if in doing so, he hits a marble, he can claim the marble.

'Basins' as described by a twelve-year-old boy, Swansea, Tasmania, illustrates varying terminology from state to state:

Boys and girls, mainly boys ten years old, play this game at home. Four or five holes are dug in the ground. Two people stand back about two yards from the first hole. The players in turn flick marbles at the holes in order. The first player who gets in all the holes is 'Poison'. If 'Poison' can hit the other player's marble, he wins the game. When you get in a basin (hole), you take a span before flicking for the next hole.

In the miscellaneous category of marble games are four: 'Prince Henry', current in 1955; 'Toodlembuck', or 'Stick on Scone', current about 1910; Sir Joseph's un-named game (similar to 'Nine Holes') 1860–70; and 'Wall'.

'Prince Henry' as demonstrated by an eleven-year-old girl, Coromandel Valley Government School, South Australia, employed a cardboard pyramid with a hole at the apex of the cone into which each player, in turn, tried to shoot his taw from a position on the ground some three feet away from the foot of the pyramid, meanwhile chanting:

> Prince Henry had a thousand men
> And a thousand men had he

173

He marched them to the top of the hill
And he marched them down to the sea
And when they were up they were up
And when they were down they were down
And when they were half way up
They were neither up nor down.

The first player to place his marble in the hole collected a marble from each of the losers (if playing for keeps; and this rule was decided before the game started).

'Toodlembuck' as played in Ballarat, Victoria about 1910 was described by Dr T. H. Coates, University of Melbourne. The same game, called 'Stick on Scone' was current in Melbourne around 1900, according to Professor G. S. Browne, University of Melbourne.[9] For apparatus the game required two four-inch lengths of one-inch-diameter broomstick and one trousers button, in addition to a pocket full of marbles for currency. According to Dr Coates:

A circle was drawn on the ground, usually by putting the thumb down as a centre and using the little finger to describe the circumference. In the centre of this circle one stick was placed upright with the button sitting on top. Three yards from the circle a line was drawn and from this line the player had to bowl the second stick, trying to knock the first stick over in such a way as to make the button fall into the ring (or outside the ring — I forget which). Marbles, which we always called 'alleys' were staked on the result. The entrepreneur would sing or rather chant:

'Try your luck on the toodlembuck
An alley a shot and two if you win.'

Dr Coates also related stories of the difficulties boys had at home over missing trousers' buttons donated to toodlembuck games.

Sir Joseph's old game employed a board with seven arches of different sizes into which marbles were bowled (Joseph Strutt's similar game employed a board with nine holes); no similar current game was found in 1955, unless by a stretch of analysis, the game can be linked to the Australian adult-gambling-game, 'Two-up', which employs a board, minus arches, with money for currency where the skill is on one side 'the plausibility on the other'.

[9] 'Notes and Queries', *Journal of American Folklore*, Vol. 73, No. 287, pp. 53–4, gives a description of an entirely different Australian game called 'Toodlembuck'.

Some boys played a game, if game it could be called [wrote Sir Joseph] When the skill was all on the one side, and the plausibility on the other. The latter provided himself with a board of some length in which holes were cut of different heights and widths gradually increasing from one end of the board to the other, and over each hole was a number, the lowest No. 1 over the widest hole and the highest No. 7 over the smallest hole. [The holes in Sir Joseph's diagram were semi-circular arches.] This board was held upright on the flat ground by its owner and at a certain distance off a firing line was marked. From this a boy fired his taw, and sought to send it through one of the holes. If he shot it through No. 1, he was given one marble as his prize, if he failed to get his taw through any hole, he had to forfeit a marble. If he were an expert shot he might win quite a number of marbles, but unless he were an expert marksman, he forfeited more than he won and the owner of the board profited to the extent of the difference.

Another game defying classification was 'Wall', reported current in Deloraine, Tasmania, about 1938. The object in the game was to toss a marble against a wall and hit an opponent's marble on the bounce or ricochet, then take it.

With the trend toward surface games, Australian marble games of the mid-twentieth century were less leisurely than those of the mid-nineteenth and early twentieth centuries. Old games surviving were simplified, required less skill, and had lost much accompanying verbal ritual. It appeared that there were fewer kinds of marbles, and fewer marble names and terms.

Two kinds of marbles seen were: agate and glass; of two sizes — one, about three-fourths inches in diameter and the other, about five-eighths.

The only marble names I heard from children were 'Taw' and 'Agate Taw' (pronounced 'Tor'). The first was in general use throughout Australia; the second, I heard from one twelve-year-old boy in Adelaide, South Australia. When I asked what they called other marbles — not taws — , the answer was 'marbles'. Photographs of Melbourne and Perth games show that all the marbles in each game are the same size. The 'Taw' means the favourite marble for 'firing' or 'drizzying' — the playing marble.[10]

---

[10] J. Strutt reported (page 304) 'Taw' as the name of a game where players each placed a marble or marbles in a ring and then shot at them to knock them out. A. B. Gomme, Vol. 1, page 350, lists 'Long Tawl' as the name of a marble game.

Adults told me that the words 'Commonies' and 'Steelies' were current among children in 1954–5 as in past years but I did not hear them. 'Alley' as a general word for marble was reported in use in Ballarat, Victoria, about 1910. 'Stanker' for 'taw' was a favourite term in Balwyn, Victoria, in 'years gone by'.

Sir Joseph Verco, reporting on marble names of 1860–7 wrote:

There were no fewer than five different genera, — 'agates', 'glass allies', 'stoneys' and 'commonies'. 'Agates' were the most costly and of course the most prized, and one agate was equal to several glass allies, more stonies and still more commonies. They were ground out of special kind of stone whence their name or manufacture and burned and coloured with some opaque polish. It was an achievement to win an agate in a game.

The name 'glass alley' indicates its structure. It varied in size from a small cherry to a walnut and was made of clear glass, and had a very wide range of ornament inside it, both as regards the colouring and pattern and figuring.

The 'stoneys' were mostly about the size of small cherries, were white and opaque and without any colour pattern.

The 'commonies' were of the same size, but of a mud colour, opaque.

Marble language of 1954–5 included various words to indicate rules for use of the taw. Rules were rigid in each play-group and included stance in kneeling, squatting or standing; and manner of holding the taw for 'firing', 'flicking', 'pinching', 'shooting', 'dribbling', 'dribbying', 'drizzying', 'pinking', 'throwing', or 'bowling'.

Photographs taken in Melbourne and in Perth demonstrate two peer-group rules for holding the taw: Perth boys held the taw between thumb and tip of forefinger of the unsupported right hand while squatting to fire; Melbourne boys held the taw between thumb and crook of forefinger of the right hand supported by the left fist — forefinger pointed — resting on the ground, with right knee kneeling. Sir Joseph described two methods of holding the taw for firing: 'The "taw" he "fired" with his right thumb and two fingers....' Later he said, 'with thumb and finger'.

Terms used when a player shot at a hole or at another marble were: 'Fire' (in general use throughout Australia); 'flick' (in Tasmania and in Perth); 'pinch' (in Brisbane); and 'shoot' (in St Helens, Tasmania).

When players stood and bowled or tossed their taws either

toward a line, leaf or some designated object to determine who would fire first in the game, or on to the field simply to start a game such as 'Follow-Me-Taw', the following terms were in use: 'dribbling' (in Canberra); 'dibbying' and 'drizzying' (in Perth); and 'pinking' (in Brisbane).

Other marbles-game-language included: 'kill', widely used when a player hit another player's taw and thus put him out of the game. 'Kiss', heard in Perth, meant the same thing. 'Span' (Perth) meant coming within a hand-span of another player's taw or of a hole or of a line; or taking a hand-span after hitting a marble or going into a hole before firing again. 'Dub' or 'dubbed up' (Brisbane) meant stacking the marbles in a pile in the middle of a ring, square or other geometric figure. 'Poison' which named a game in Brisbane, also meant a place (Brisbane) 'where you go when you fire and get caught in the ring' as well as a marble in Swansea, Tasmania, where 'first the player who gets his taw in all the holes is "poison" and if "poison" hits another player he wins the game.' 'Draw' (Perth) 'is when two boys drizzy and their marbles are even they call it a draw and the drizzy again.'

Two charms called 'moz' were reportedly used in marble games in Victoria from 1910–20. To bring good luck, a player chanted:

'Under the Kaiser's hoof.'

To bring bad luck to an opponent he chanted:

'The poor old Kaiser's dead
He died for want of bread
They put him in a coffin
He fell through the bottom
The poor old Kaiser's dead.'

A widely held belief among Australian adults was that marbles is a seasonal game. Adults who were questioned always answered emphatically either 'spring' or 'autumn'. I actually saw marble games in progress in different parts of Australia in early spring, late spring, early summer and in autumn but I could find no seasonal pattern in what I saw.

Dr Brian Sutton-Smith, in his 'Observations on the "Seasonal" Nature of Children's Games in New Zealand'[11] wrote:

[11] *Western Folklore*, Vol. XII, No. 3, p. 186.

The supposedly mysterious way in which children's games come and go, wax and wane . . . has been remarked upon at great length by the romanticists of children's games. It is a favourite theme, and the complexity of the factors involved lends itself easily to mysticism . . . . It can be shown that children's play seasons result from the interaction of children's groups with a variety of influences in their environment.

And he continued to say later that 'climatic seasons represent one factor among many' Among mid-twentieth-century Australian children, hard-surfaced playing fields make an environmental factor affecting marble games — as well as other games — the year round.

Australian adults considered marbles a boys' game. The degree of accuracy in that belief is problematic. Many Australian girls were playing marbles. That boys and girls played their games in separate groups at school was the result of separate playgrounds. Outside of school I saw boys and girls playing together and reports indicated that home and neighbourhood marble games were often mixed groups. Perhaps the male proprietary attitude was more fancy (aided by controlled environment) than fact.

Australian children's play environment is changing as the nation changes from a '98 per cent British people' to include other ethnic groups; from a pastoral to an industrial arrangement of the population. In addition, modern modes of mass entertainment and recreation are not condusive to self-motivating activities like marble games which require skill developed through patient practice. With increasing adult-supervised, adult-motivated and adult-rewarded play (badges and championship cups), incentive for peer-approval decreases. Hence, marble games — old gambling games of individual skill — change or disappear; a pocket full of marbles is not sufficient reward; the gambler prefers the adult's golden cup.

Scholars differ in their points of view about adult supervision and standardization of children's play life. They differ about how much adult-imposed change has taken place in traditional play and they differ about the moral and psychological aspects of those changes. Paul Brewster and Norman Douglas lament the modern adult-supervised playground.[12] Brian Sutton-Smith, psychologist and former physical educationalist, defends it. He says: '. . . society of today does not require that children be craftsmen of play; it

[12] P. Brewster, *American Nonsinging Games*, Norman, Oklahoma, 1953, p. xx. N. Douglas, *London Street Games*, London, 1931, p. xi.

requires, rather that they be competent social mixers in play, or to use a term of some current vogue, it requires that they be "gamesmen" '.[13] The Opie's newest book (*The Lore and Language of Schoolchildren*), encyclopedic in size and nature, indicates that children — English, Scottish and Welsh children, at any rate — are making tradition as fast as designing adults can annihilate it.

Whatever the moral and psychological implications of adult-imposed changes in children's play may be, the study of no other traditional play custom illustrates the extreme adult intervention found in marble tournaments.

It is yet to be seen whether or not Australians will import marble tournaments along with American comic books. If they do, the old games of 'Goot', 'Three Corner Killy' and 'Rabbit Hole' will disappear. The time may come when children, the world over, will play one standardized marble game. Perhaps the time may come when an Australian child, an American child and an English child will compete in a world marble championship tournament on a space platform anchored somewhere in the wild blue yonder. In this event, this world will surely be left a dull, brave new world.

NOTE:

Credit and appreciation for the information in this report go to: informants named in the article; to adults — Miss Margaret Outridge, Miss Christine Brown, Miss Betty Watts, Miss Marjorie Warham, Professor F. J. Schonell, Dr McKenzie and Mr R. A.K. Brooks (Queensland); Dr Harold Windham (New South Wales); Mr J. F. Bingham, Mr and Mrs Howe and Mr and Mrs Campbell. (A.C.T.); Miss M. Jageurs, Miss Margaret Little, Miss Gladys Beckham and Mrs Joan Mowson (Victoria); Mr Harry Dodson, Mr R. H. Dean, Miss Ann Harris, Mrs Chugg, Miss Jill Suter and Dr Michael Grounds (Tasmania); Miss Mavis Wauchope, Dr H. H. Penny, Mr C. P. Mountford, Mr C. S. Chaney and Mr E. L. Shaw (South Australia); Dr T. L. Robertson, Mr Wallace Neal, Dr D. K. Wheeler, Miss Milligen, Mr Norman Elliott and Mr Garrett (Western Australia). Credit also goes to hundreds of Australian boys and girls who played marble games while I watched and to those who wrote compositions describing their games: D. Kennetts (Queensland); Leona Howlett and Suzanne Cory (Victoria); Billy Gray and Rosalind Beattie (Tasmania); Robin Eden (South Australia); Ken Kenkin, Colin Chipper, Ian Ballantine, Chris Warwick, Max Eartledge, Ian Richter, Richard Dempter, John Setlak and John Bingham (Western Australia).

[13] B. Sutton-Smith, *The Games of New Zealand Children*, pp. 160–4.

INDIAN CHILDREN'S GAMES

[Edited by E. F. Im Thurn]

Indian Children's Games.—The games of Indian children, when untouched by European civilization, appear, as I have elsewhere said, tentative imitations of such things as will be their serious occupations in after life— hunting and fishing in the case of the boys, cooking in the case of the girls. But there must be in these, as in children elsewhere, a natural element of mere sportiveness, however indiscernible this may be to the eye of the stranger. For as soon as these children are brought nto contact with civilization, either at the mission stations or elsewhere, as soon, that is, as the stern necessity of learning to hunt and learning housewifely cares is no longer allowed to occupy their whole time, then the natural sportiveness develops. I have lately been watching certain Indian children in this half-civilized condition. One Ackawoi boy who lives with me, seems as playful as any happy English child. One of his amusements is to catch a sandwasp, and, having tied to it one end of a long fine hair, to the other end of which a bright coloured flower or a scrap of paper is fastened, to let the insect go again, and then to chase it, just sufficiently flower-burdened as it is to prevent its either flying too fast or falling too easy a prey. Or this same boy amuses himself by stripping the green part from a cocoanut leaf leaving only the branched woody midrib, and on this he threads innumerable corollas of bright flowers, making the whole into a brilliant fan. Or, at other times he plaits palm leaves into fantastic crowns, or makes of them eccentric boxes and baskets. Once, too, at a mission I watched a boy—there appeared to be only one who could do it—who running on all fours as fast as the others could on their two legs, chased his companions and almost invariably caught them, the whole party being clamorous, throughout the game, with shouts of joy. And at this same mission I once saw the children play for a whole evening at a most organized game, which they must have been taught ; it was a version of our own childish game of ' oranges and lemons'; each player as he was caught being asked whether he would join, not the oranges or the lemons, but the sun or the moon.

A NOTE ON CHILDREN'S PASTIMES

H. E. Lambert

A NOTE ON CHILDREN'S PASTIMES

H.E. LAMBERT

The terms and expressions used in children's games, riddles and the like can afford linguistic diversion, if nothing of greater value. A few of them, all from the North, are given in this note.

GAMES

Two games rather like Hide—and—seek are commonly played. One is called Kivumbubumbuka. In this one child hides and the rest call *"Kivumbuvumbuka! Tule nyama!"* The hidden child dashes out suddenly and tries to catch one of the others. Any child caught is *"beaten up"* gently and it is then his turn to hide. The phonetics of the name suggest that this game was introduced from the South.

The other form of Hide—and—seek is called Koriṭilo. In this all the children except one hide themselves and the other calls *"Koriṭilo!"* The hiding party answer *"Ado"*, meaning *"Bado"*, until they are well hidden, indicated by *"Ndiyo!"* from each one. Then the search begins and the first child found becomes the seeker in the next round.

A sort of Blind—man's—buff is called Kibe. In this one child is blindfolded and called the *kizuizui* or *mkongwe*. This child calls out *"Kibe kibe!"* and the others answer *"niyao!"* (I am coming). They then sing *"Mkongwe msichana, haya mṭaue mumeo ṭ'awa"* (Aged damsel, come on now, choose the louse your husband, come on, choose your husband the louse) if the blindfolded child is a girl, and *"Mkongwe mvulana, haya mṭaue mkeo ṭ'awa etc."* if a boy.

In a game called *T'aso*, played by boys and youths, two teams of about six each line up in the middle of an open space. The object of each team is to get one of its members through to the *"goal"* (a convenient tree stump or other spot previously selected) of the opposing team without his being touched by one of them. The *"goal"* is called *mko*, pl. *miko*. In Lamu this game is called *Karo*.

There is a guessing game called *Kiba Fute*. One child invites another to guess how many objects he has in his closed hand. Such objects are usually immediately edible, such as cashew nuts *(korosha)*, ground—nuts *(njugu)* or pop—corn *(bisi)*. The challenge is *"Kiba fute!"* and the answer *"Moya fute, mbili fute etc."* according to the number guessed. If the guesser thinks there are none he says *"Hamna fute"*. If his guess is correct he demands *"Nipa moya yangu, mbili zangu etc."* or *"Nipa hamna yangu"* (Give me my none—inside). In some places *papu* is used instead of *hamna*. The poser pays the appropriate number; *hamna* is paid for by one only. (Cf. Velten *"Desturi za Wasuaheli"*, Gottingen, 1903, p.29).

TONGUE—TWISTERS

A favourite amusement is the posing of sentences suposed to be difficult to pronounce rapidly, A child who accepts the challenge must say the sentence clearly, accurately and very quickly. A few such sentences are given here. They are called *"Maneno ya kupisanya"*.

(a) *"Ng'ombe uko nyuma ya ngome"* (The cow is behind the fort). This sentence would appear to be a test of a small child's ability to pronounce the various nasals without hesitation.

75

(b) *"Tunda pumba tumwandike p̓unda"* (Collect a clod, let's load up the donkey).

(c) *"Mwalimu uṭindie k̓uku kwa kisu kinisikiṭishacho kamacho"* (Teacher has slaughtered a fowl with a knife the like of which makes me sorry — *uṭindie, U. amechinja; kamacho = kama hicho)*

(d) *"nyiza na wana wa nyiza na hizo nyiza awanyizanani"* Strips of palm leaf and the children of the strips — i.e. split strips — and those strips share among yourselves) (Cf. Velten, *op. cit.* p.37).

RIDDLES

The northern word for riddle is *"chondowi,* pl. *zondowi (Siu etc. dhondowi)"* and the formula corresponding to the southern *"Kitenda-wili! Tega!"* is *"Chondowi! Kwete! (Siu etc. Kweche)".* If the riddle is not correctly answered the poser may say *"Nipa ng'ombe"* or *"nṭ'i"* (land) or *"liwa"* (plantation) or *"mui"* (village), or something of the sort, but there is no actual payment. Here are a few riddles.

(a) *Ki papo hukioni.* Answer: *Kishogo*
It is there, but you don't see it. Answer: The back of your head)

(b) *Papo upekeche.* Answer: *Chumbo*
(You carry it just there in your lap. Answer: Your stomach)
This is in the Siu form. *"Upekeche"* = southern *"umepakata".*

(c) *Mwanang'ang'a hulia mwituni.* Answer: *Kitoka*
(*Mwanang'ang'a* cries in the forest. Answer: An axe)

Mwanang'ang'a, used as a name, represents the ideophone *ng'a!*
ng'a! or *ng'o!*, the sound of an axe striking a tree)

   (d) *Wanangu wawili mtana huchecha, usiku hupachana.*
     Answer: *Mlango*

     (My two children quarrel by day but agree at night.
       Answer: A double door, which is open during the day and
         shut at night)

This is in the *Siu* form. *"Huchecha = Amu etc. "huteta"*

DANCES

   There are many children's dances. In the one called *Ukuti*
(Siu etc. Ukuchi), danced on moonlight evenings, the children form
themselves into a ring round the song—leader *(mwimbizi Siu etc.*
mwimbidhi):, join hands and move slowly round, raising and lower-
ing their hands rhythmically. The song is as follows:

Leader: *Ukuti ukuti*   Others: *Wa mnazi wa mnazi*
Leader: *Ukingia pepo*   Others: *Watetema*
Leader: *Ukingia pepo*   Others: *Watetema*

The children then jump up and down and shake their shoulders in
imitation of the rustling tremble of the palm fronds in the evening
breeze.

LULLABIES

   Lullabies *(tumbuizo)* are numerous. They can hardly be said
to be children's pastimes, but children like them and may join in
the singing, and young girls sometimes sing them to their dolls
(watoto wa bandia: Gunya, vachocho va bandia). Here is one from
Siu.

77

Howa muchocho, nyamaa silie;
Ukilia wanilidha na mie.
Howa muchocho, nyamaa silie,
Matodhi yaweke hata nifie
Ipije makonde unililie
Na wachu waye wakushikilie.
Howa muchocho, nyamaa silie.

("Now, child, stop your crying; if you cry you make me cry too.
Now, child, stop your crying, put by your tears until I am dead,
then beat yourself with your fists and weep for me and then let
people come and pick you up. Now child, stop your crying".
The implication is "You've got me, so you've nothing to cry about.
Keep your tears for my death, then weep for me. If you can't weep,
hit yourself till you do. Then no doubt people will pick you up,
which is what you want me to do now").

NURSERY RHYMES

Nursery rhymes, as understood in Europe, do not appear to be
much in vogue among Swahili children. Some of the songs sung by
their grown—ups would seem to be very suitable, but though children
know them and like them they do not often sing them. Here is one
from Lamu.

Kandu yashitaki   "*Qadhi niamuwa,*
Mimi sivaliki,   *mbona navaliwa?*
Nimeoza ziki   *na pa kukaliwa*".

(The *kanzu* complains 'Kadhi, judge my case, I am unwearable,
why am I worn? I am threadbare at the collar and the place which
is sat on')

BABIES' RATTLES FROM 2600 B.C.
AND
OTHER ANCIENT TOYS

Richard A. Martin

BABIES' RATTLES FROM 2600 B.C. AND OTHER ANCIENT TOYS

By Richard A. Martin
Curator of Near Eastern Archaeology

Rattles, such as are used to pacify babies, have a long history. Field Museum is in possession of several children's rattles, made of pottery, dating back to 2600 B.C. Some of these are in the shape of animals, such as hedgehogs or goats, while others are very similar in form to those used to-day. They are hollow and contain one or more pebbles which make the noise. These rattles are from the ancient city of Kish, and were excavated by the Field Museum–Oxford University Joint Expedition to Mesopotania. One of these rattles might have belonged to Sargon of Akkad, whose youthful days were spent in Kish, or perhaps to a playmate of this founder of a great dynasty.

Also in the collection is a whistle, the sound of which was heard on the radio-drama about life in Kish given June 23 over WGN, in the series "From the Ends of the Earth" currently being presented by Field Museum and the University Broadcasting Council. Among other toys are models of chariots such as those mentioned in the broadcast.

In general, outside of modern Europe and America, rattles have been used more by adults than by children. In India, however, native children are given rattles to play with. Among the Chinese, various sorts of bronze rattles were formerly used as musical instruments, and the Museum has on exhibition a set of this type of rattles which was used by an ancient Chinese military orchestra.

A large and varied collection of rattles used in the magical rituals of African tribes is on display in the halls of African ethnology. Various tribes of American Indians used rattles similarly in religious ceremonies, and various types made by them are included in the Museum exhibits. In ancient Egypt a sort of rattle, called a "sistrum," which consisted of a staff with metal rings dangling on its end, was used by priests in very solemn religious ceremonies. A bronze sistrum is exhibited in Hall J.

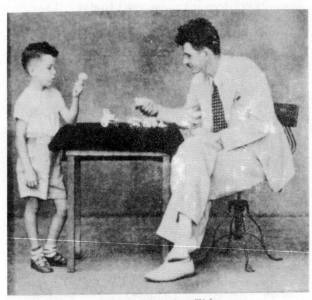

Toys from Ancient Kish

Donald Miller, 7 years old, of Springfield, Illinois, on a visit to Field Museum, learns from Curator Richard A. Martin about toy chariots, animals and rattles made for Sumerian children about 4,500 years ago.

THE JUGOSLAV CHILDREN'S GAME *MOST*
AND
SOME SCANDINAVIAN PARALLELS

Jelena Milojkovic-Djuric

THE JUGOSLAV CHILDREN'S GAME *MOST* AND SOME SCANDINAVIAN PARALLELS

by Jelena Milojković-Djurić

ANY GERMAN VARIANTS of the widely known arch game under discussion have been described by Mannhardt.[1] In these the children pass under a "bridge" formed by the upraised arms of two of the players. One after another the captured players have to choose between "Sonne und Mond" (variant from Westphalia), "Himmel und Hölle" (variant from Bremen), and "Teufel und Engel (variant from Tübingen). Sometimes the arch game ends here. More often a tug of war takes place between the two groups of children lined up behind their respective leaders. These two groups represent opposing forces struggling against each other. The tug of war is not present in the German variants quoted but frequently appears in Jugoslav analogues. It occurs also in certain Swedish variants (*Dragkamp* and *Bro, bro, breda*)[2] and in some Czechoslovakian forms of the arch game such as *Zlatna brana*.[3]

Let us examine the Jugoslav variant of the arch game called *Most* (Bridge). This particular variant is played by the children of Soko Banja, Serbia, and is unaccompanied by singing.[4] Two players stand facing each other, their hands clasped and raised above their heads to form an arch. The others form a long line, each holding around the waist the player in front, and begin passing under the arch, which is referred to as the "bridge." The two forming the arch have previously decided between themselves which is to be "Heaven" and which is to be "Hell." To the other players, however, they are, e.g., "apple" and "pear" (cf. the English "Oranges and Lemons"). The first player in the line calls out, "Is the bridge firm?" The two players clasping hands reply, "As firm as a rock." The first then asks permission to pass over. This is granted, but he is warned that the last in line will be captured. The captured player is asked whether he prefers "apple" or "pear." When he has made his choice, he takes his position behind the one he

---

[1]Wilhelm Mannhardt, "Das Brückenspiel," *Zeitschrift für Deutsche Mythologie und Sittenkunde,* IV (1859).

[2]Carl-Herman Tillhagen, *Svenska folklekar och danser.* 2 v. Stockholm, 1950.

[3]J. Feifalik, "Nachtrage zum Brückenspiel," *Zeitschrift für Deutsche Mythologie und Sittenkunde,* IV (1859).

[4]See Paul G. Brewster and Jelena Milojković-Djurić, "A Group of Jugoslav Games," *Southern Folklore Quarterly,* XX (1956).

has chosen and puts his arms around the other's waist. This continues until all have been captured. When they form two lines, one headed by the "apple" and the other by the "pear," the two players who composed the bridge inform the rest whether they are in "Heaven" or in "Hell." Sometimes the game ends here. More often, however, the leaders of the two lines grasp hands firmly and the game ends with a tug-of-war.

Another variant of this game is the singing game "Prolazite, prolazite, poslednja je naša"—"Pass, pass, the last is ours." This game is well known among the children of Belgrade, whert this variant was recorded. Here also two players form an arch, but they sing while the others are passing under their arms, holding one another around the waist. As the last girl is passing, the players forming the bridge let down their arms and imprison her. She must then bend backward over their clasped hands, when she is asked in a very low voice whom she chooses. The choice is usually between "devil" and "angel" or "Heaven" and "Hell." The lining up of the players behind their respective leaders and the tug-of-war are present in both variants of this game. The song which accompanies it runs:

In the following variants of the game "Most"—"Bridge" from Danilovgrad (Montenegro), "Prolazite, prolazite, no Moravu dolazite" —"Pass, pass, come to Morava" from Belgrade, and "Elem, belem, cedilo" (meaningless) from Soko Banja (East Serbia), the names of the two leaders have changed in the course of time to more common ones belonging to the child's own world, e.g. a doll and a plane. Sometimes the choice is between two kinds of fruit.

The variant from Danilovgrad runs as follows: Two players facing each other as previously described form an arch. They start to sing, while the other players one after another pass under their unpraised

arms. Prolazite, prolazite	Pass, pass,
Najzadnjega ostajiste.	Leave the last.

Pro la-zi-te, pro la-zi-te po slednja je na ša

As pointed out in the song, the last player in the row has to stay. Then he is asked, "What do you wish, a plane or a doll?" When he has made his choice, he takes his position behind the leader who represents the one he has chosen and puts his arms around the waist of the player in front of him. When all the players are divided into two groups, a tug-of-war follows. The group whose members succeed in pulling the others across a line between the two parties is the winner.

In the Soko Banja variant, players hold hands, forming a chain (*lanac*), as they pass under the upraised arms of the two forming the arch. At the last syllable of the song which the latter sing, they suddenly squat and encircle the player's waist with their arms. He must then choose either "the golden queen" or "the golden princess." After all are lined up behind the leaders, a tug-of-war takes place.

Elem, belem, cedilo,

Mama mesi ledilo,	Elem, belem, bag,
Čuj Kato, Katice.	Mummy bakes ledilo,
Orom, šorom šorice,	Listen, Kato, Katice.
Cica maca zazubac.[5]	(These last two lines are meaningless)
El-em, bel-em ce-di-lo	ci-ca ma-ca za zu-ba-ca

The same game was observed in the vicinity of Soko Banja in the village of Jošanica. The children in that village use the word "gate" to denote the arch formed by the upraised arms of the two leaders. Otherwise there is no difference either in the method of play or in the words of the song. Only the final tug-of-war is missing.

There is also an interesting variant of the arch game known under the name "Laste, prolaste" or "Prolazite, prolazite," familiar to many children. As in the variants previously described, here again two players form an arch. The other participants one after another pass under holding one another round the waist. All the players sing as the line passes under. The choice is usually between two fruits or two toys, and a tug-of-war ends the game.

Observing children and their games during the summer and fall of 1959, I noticed the following variants of the song accompanying the game. The game itself was always played unchanged.

La-ste pro-la-ste na Mo-ra-vu do-la - ste

A group of girls and boys aged 12-14 from Belgrade accompanied their game with the following verses:

Laste, prolaste,	Pass, pass,
Na Moravu dolaste.	Arrive at Morava.

[5]Some of the words in this song are used solely because of their rhythmical value, the number of syllables, and their agreement in the terminal sounds of their rhymes. Others, however, have some meaning. *Cedilo* is a word used in East Serbia to denote a bag made of hand-woven woolen cloth; *cica maca* is a pet term applied to a cat. The use of nonsense words is much more common in counting-out rhymes, where it often forms the essential part of a verse.

Moja gora uvela	My wood is Welken (?)
a vaša je zelena.	But yours is green.
Kalopero, Vero, Vero,	Kalopero, Vero, Vero,
Otvori mi vrata Jelo,	Open the door to me, Jelo,
Da prodje vojska Vero, haj!	That the army may pass, haj!

Another group ranging in age from 7 to 9 and also from Belgrade sang:

Prolazite, prolazite,
Na Moravu dolazite.
Vaša gora zelena
a naša je uvela.
Halo Pero, Vero, Jelo,
Otvori mi vrata Jelo,
Da prodje vojska mlada, haj!

The only remarkable difference between these last two songs is in the fifth line. The word "kalopero" is in the second version replaced by "halo Pero." *Kaloper* is a kind of grass (*Balsamita maior*). This plant is not often seen in gardens nowadays, and the children do not know what the word means. Accordingly, they have replaced it with a phrase having the same number of syllables and somewhat the same sound. More important, it has a meaning for them, being actually a call to a comrade. According to some of the players of the second group, the game sometimes includes a little *postludium*. At the moment when the stronger players have pulled the weaker group across the line, all participants must squat as quickly as they can. The one who is last is called "the devil," and the others mock him:

U djavola crne noge a u mene bele!
Devil has black feet, but I have white ones!

As they sing this, they alternately rise partway and then squat again. The "devil" tries to touch one of them while he is still partly upright. If he succeeds, the other must then take his place.

This game was noted also in Soko Banja, where the players, a group of children 3-6 years of age, sang these verses:

Laste, prolaste,	Pass, pass,
Iz dolinu dolaste.	Come from the valley.
Alo Pero, alo,	Hallo, Pero, hallo,
Donesi mi plavo.	Bring me the blue.

The children could not explain what is meant by the last line. They answered simply, "Just what we sing: pass, pass, bring me something blue." The explanation of these shortened verses may lie in the assumption that the rhymed poetry from the towns has exerted an influence upon them. Even the contemporary Serbian folk lyrics sometimes contain very rough verses of the same kind. The melody of the song accompanying the just-mentioned variant belongs to the widespread recitative type; it is almost a declamation formed of four bars. The whole range of the melody is within a fifth, with a medial cadence and a final one on the tonic.

All the textual variants of the song "Laste, prolaste" include in their second part verses beginning with "Kalopero . . .," which formerly belonged to another folksong. In 1862 the Serbian composer Kornelije Stanković published an album of folksongs among which the following lines can be found:

Kalopero, Pero	Kalopero, Pero,
Što me zoveš Jelo?	Why do you call me Jelo?
Otvor' gradu vrata	Open the door of the town
Da provedem vojsku, &c.	That I may lead the army through, &c.

In the preface to that album the composer wrote that he had collected these songs while traveling among the Serbian folk. There is no comment as to the occasions on which they were sung or whether the singers were playing during the singing.[5a]

Ka - lo pe - ro, pe - ro ka lo pe ro-pe - ro, ka - lo pe - ro, pe - ro

In 1907 the well known ethnologist Tihomir Djordjević noted in his book *Srpske narodne igre* a game with the title "Kalopere, Rajo." According to him, the game was played chiefly by girls and young married women. Two groups are formed, one representing an emperor with his army, the other a host and his home or a knight and young girls. The whole game bears a strong resemblance to wedding ceremonies. The song which accompanies the song is in dialogue between the two groups, explaining the successive actions of the game, e.g., the wooing of a girl and the describing of her qualities, which are humorously denied by the others:

Kalopero, Rajo,	Kalopero, Rajo,
Što me zoveš, Jelo?	Why do you call me, Jelo?
Otvor' gradu vrata.	Open the door of the town.

A sto ce ti vrata?	Why do you need the door?
Da provedem vojsku, &c.	That I may lead the army, &c.

The group which follows the emperor sings and passes between the (double?) row of other girls lined up in front of them. As they pass, the latter take one of them.[6]

In 1931 Vladimir R. Djordjević noted a similiar variant and stated that the song was sung during the càrnival season.[7]

Kaloper, Pero, Rajo,	Kaloper, Pero, Rajo,
Što zoveš lepu Maru?	Why do you call the pretty Mara?
D' otvori gradu vrata	To open the door of the town
Da provedem vojsku.	That I may lead the army through.

Ka - lo - per - o Pe - ro, ra - jo, Pe — ro

After having noted all these examples, we may conclude that the children's song "Laste, prolaste" consists of two different parts which form a whole. The first part is the children's song "Laste, prolaste. The second is a variant of the first four verses of the quoted song "Kalopero, pero."

One of the corresponding Swedish variants is the singing game "Bro, bro, breda."[8] This variant has been strongly influenced by the game "Syster, syster, ädla min." The romantic little drama of the latter has passed over to the game "Bro, bro, breda," and both are played like a circle dance (ringdans). In this variant the "bridge" is not formed by the upraised hands of two players as in the quoted Jugoslav form, nor are the imprisoning, the choice, or the tug-of-war present.

Another variant, from Östergothland, is played like an arch game.[9] The children pass singing under the arch until the last verse, when the two leaders try to capture the last player. The one caught must leave the game. There is no choice between two sides and no tug-of-war. The last verse of the song

[5a]Srbske narodne pesme. Bec. 1862.
[6]However, the one taken is not necessarily the last in line.
[7]Srpske narodne melodije (predratna Srbija). Beograd, 1931.
[8]A. I. Arwidsson, Svenska fornsånger, I-III. Stockholm, 1842.
[9]Ibid., pp. 253-254.

Sa när som den, som efter är,   The one coming after
Han skall i brona ligga.   Shall lie in the bridge.

supports the opinion of Gomme[10] and Newell[11] that this game is connected with the widespread superstition that a bridge or other building will not be firm unless a human being or an animal is built into it. The same motif is present in the old Serbian epic "The Building of Skadar on Bojana." Haddon has cited some Greek folksongs with the analogous motif of building a human being into a bridge.[12]

The "Bro, bro, breda" of Tillhagen[13] is very similar to the first variant of this game described by Arwidsson, each having a lyric *postludium*. It resembles the arch game in that the captured player must utter "the dearest name" in order to win his freedom. Sometimes, too, this games ends with a tug-of-war (*dragkamp*). The choosing between the players forming the arch (Sun and Moon) and the lining up are the same as in the nonsinging game *Dragkamp*.[14]

The non-singing game *Dragkamp* has more similarities with the Jugoslav variant "Most." There is a choice between the two leaders (Sun and Moon), which form an arch with their upraised arms. There is also the lining up behind them. Only the players are captured one after the other, not always the last one. In this Swedish game the tug-of-war is not a collective action, but the leaders try to pull each other over a line.

It may be of interest to compare the two Serbian games given by the Danish ethnologist Feilberg[15] as analogues of the variants described above. The first Serbian variant, quoted under the name "Erberečke," is a well known and still-played game, known also as "Jelečkinje, Barjačkinje."[16] It is played by boys and girls. They divide into two groups of equal size and arrange themselves in parallel lines facing each other. The distance between the lines depends upon the size of the playground, but is ordinarily about 10 meters. All the children in one of the two rows call out to those of the other, "Erbetutor" or "Jelečkinje." The other group answers, "Erberečke" or "Barjačkinje." The first then calls, "Whom do you wish?" Those in the other row give the name of a player of the first group. This player then runs as fast as he can toward the other line and tries to break through at what he thinks

[10]A. B. Gomme, *The Traditional Games of England, Scotland, and Ireland.* 2 v. London, 1898.
[11]W. W. Newell, *Games and Songs of American Children.* New York, 1911.
[12]A. C. Haddon, *The Study of Man.* London, 1898.
[13]*Op. cit.,* II, 320.

is a weak point in it. If he succeeds, he is allowed to return to his own group taking with him one of the two players between whom he broke the line. If he fails, he must remain on the side of the opposing group. The two sides alternate in challenging each other, and the game goes on until one of the groups has practically all the players and the other can no longer continue playing.

This game bears no similarity to the different variants of the arch game either in dialogue or in action. Maybe it was used as the closest parallel available at the moment.

The second game in Feilberg, quoted as corresponding to the arch game, is "Lese." As it is described in the text of the song, all the players, holding one another by the hand, sings:

> Twist, twist,
> We are twisting ourselves to a network
> And we untwist us again,
> Like the chains
> We are twisting, us bachelors.

While singing the first three lines of the song, the whole row passes under the upraised arms of the last two players.

There is an analogous Jugoslav singing game "Kolariću, Paniću, we are twisting ourselves," in which the players pass under the upraised arms, twisting themselves as in the former game. The way of performance is quite different from that in the aforementioned "Bro, bro, brille." The players do not pass over a "bridge"; the upraised arms do not represent symbolically the bridge. They are passing under the upraised arms, holding one another by the hand and making a complicated figure, the "knot." Here is the song:

Kolariću, Paniću,	Kolaricu, Panicu,
Pletemo se samiću,	We are knitting ourselves.
Sami sebe zaplićemo,	Ourselves we are twisting.
Sami sebe otplićemo.	Ourselves we are untwisting.

The game "Lese" described by Feilberg, together with "Kolariću, Paniću," belongs to another type altogether. As a further analogue to

[14]*Ibid.*, I, 123ff.

[15]H. F. Feilberg, "Bro brille legen," *Svenska landsmålen och Svenska folkliv,* XII, 4 (1905).

[16]See Brewster and Milojković-Djurić, *loc. cit.*

[17]Paul G. Brewster, "Notes on Some Games Mentioned in Basile's *Il Pentamerone,*" *Folklore,* V (1950).

[18]Ljubica and Danica Janković, *Narodne igre,* I. Beograd, 1934.

these "twisting" games may be mentioned the American "Twist Tobacco."[17] The Serbian "Oj, Jovo, Jovo" from Montenegro[18] belongs to the same group. There exist a number of similar variants in the whole territory of Bosnia and Hercegovina.[19]

Trying to explain the origin of the arch game, Mannhardt has pointed out that the motif of crossing a bridge is present in the epic *Edda,* in which the dead man rises to Hel over a bridge called Gjallarbru. Feilberg mentions the same motif, with an additional reference to an inscription on a gravestone at Winnipeg (England).

Another important motif is very often present in these games: the struggle between two groups under the leadership of two opposing forces. In the Middle Ages the motif of an allegorical fight for a human soul is very often present in folk tradition and in tales. Even some other games of children include such a conflict. Such, for example, are the Serbian children's game "Cincili, bomboli"[20] and the Czechoslovak "Angel and Devil."[21] Among English-speaking children the latter is usually known as "Colors."

However, some variants of the children's arch game known nowadays under different names have lost from their verses any connection which permits an explanation of their origin as due to some mystical heritage. There is seldom a choice between "Himmel und Hölle," "Teufel und Engel," as quoted by Mannhardt, but between a doll and a plane, two kinds of fruit, or a princess and a queen. The conclusion may be that the arch game influenced other children's songs (cf. the verses which accompany the game from Soko Banja, "Elem, belem, cedilo," or "Laste, prolaste" in all mentioned variants), which assimilated the way of performance unchanged, but in turn the arch game accepted some elements from other children's games.

Paul G. Brewster
Tennessee Polytechnic Institute

[19]J. Dopudja, "Narodne igre Kupreskog polja," *Bilten Instituta za proučavanje folklora* (Sarajevo, 1953).
[20]See Brewster and Milojković-Djurić, *loc. cit.*
[21]Feifalik, *loc. cit.*

RECREATION OF BAIGA CHILDREN

Dinesh Mishra

Recreation of Baiga Children

by

Dinesh Mishra

Tribal Research Institute, Chhindwara.

"Recreation is activity engaged in during leisure and primarily motivated by the satisfaction derived from it".[1] Activity takes place for its own sake.

Recreation of the children of Baiga Chak[2] consists in playful activities which are mostly physical in nature. Simple movement of legs and hands in a haphazard manner forms a play to an infant. There is no question of leisure in it. Lying in the sling which is hung on the shoulders of a Baiga mother, the infant cooes and makes various babblings. It plays with the necklaces and 'chhuta'[3] of the mother while she is engaged in discharging some domestic duties or working in the farms. Various activities of an infant, besides making it happy, bring rejoice to the adults as well. Mainly the parents and some of the older siblings constitute the social life of an infant. But as it begins to crawl and then to walk, its social life extends. Various accessible materials of the home form the objects of its play and many persons are befriended. It plays with them.

Most of the time of a child, between three and five years of age, is spent in playing. All children of the neighbourhood—boys and girls together gather in the open spaces or in the alleys and play. They go to their houses only when either they are hungry or thirsty and sometimes when called by their parents. Otherwise they are all seen playing together.

Both boys and girls take sticks and play what they call 'ghorha' (a horse). A longer stick is taken behind between the legs and it is 'beaten' with a smaller one as if they are riding a horse and driving it with a whip. At times sticks are fixed in a piece of soft ground or in the sand. This fixing of sticks and then taking them out repeatedly is also a play to them.

The children whose parents are particular about the play of the children get wooden wheeled toy-carts prepared for them. They are seen dragging them along the lanes in the neighbourhood. Very few children have toy-carts because many of them do not get opportunity to see the actual bullock-carts. The hilly and mountainous tracts do not permit the Baigas to use carts and hence all the children are not tempted to ask their parents for toy-carts.

Children between five and nine years of age are engaged in play for hours

---

1. H.D. Meyer and C.K. Brightbill : *Recreation Administration*, Prentice Hall, 1956, Pp. 1.

2A reservation area in Mandla District, Madhya Pradesh.

3. 'Chhuta' is a sort of necklace made out of multi-coloured beads, beautifully threaded in five to seven threads.

together, This is the age when the period of their playing is the longest though with many intervals in between. In the earlier part of this stage of life, the children are very irregular and unsystematic in plays. They try to imitate various adult activities through play.

An older boy drives a group of younger children as if he is driving his cattle. Semetimes the children throw dust in the air showing that they are winnowing the corn. At other times, pleasure is derived by throwing stones and lumps of clay from one place to another. Every piece of wood and stone forms an object of their play. They play but do not compete with one another; they fight but they try not to hurt anybody. They make much noise while playing.

Towards the end of this period, the children are more definite in their games. They follow some of the rules of the game and insist on others also to follow them. The team games enter into their plays and the spirit of competition with the opposite team through cooperation of the players of one's own them is developed. Breaking and regaining of friendship with a playmate which is an amusing characteristic of younger children is not made by an eight or nine year old child. One thing which is viewed towards the close of this period is the grouping of children according to sex. Boys begin to play more strenuous and vigorous games like climbing up high on a tree and swimming in a flooded river, while girls mainly imitate the female occupations of the community and assume them to be their play. If a boy of eight or nine years of age joins a group of girls,

they frankly say, 'a boy need not play with girls.' Other boys also condemn a boy who keeps away from playing with boys and likes to play with girls.

Two important favourite games played by the children of this age, are known as 'ghar-gundalia' and 'goru-goru'. Both of these are played in a make-believe way and the charm of these is retained even in the later life. In 'ghar-gundalia' an older girl conducts the game. The activities of a well established family like getting married, cooking and serving of meals, entertaining the guests, attending on a sick person, drinking liquor, bringing firewood and allied economic and domestic duties, are imitated by children. A five or six years old boy acts as the head of the family. The game should not be seen by the male adults of the community. The other game is known as 'goru-goru' ('goru' means a cow). Two concentric circular boundaries, one smaller than the other, are made by fixing thin pieces of wood in the ground; wild brinjals represent cows in the bigger circle and calves in the smaller one. Various pastoral and cattle rearing activities are then mock-played by the children.

Organized plays or games are played when children exceed roughly the age of eight or nine years. At first, they gather where older children are playing and observe them. Sometimes they request the older ones to allow them to join in the game and the request is granted if the former want some players. By thus observing and occasionally participating in such games, the smaller children learn the rules of the various games and after understanding them fully, they play with their age-groupers. They may be guided by older boys in their play if so desired.

Among the organized games, the first to mention is 'Killo' which is played with a stick and a number of semi-spherical flat wooden blocks. The blocks are put vertically on the ground in a line and from a distance of eight or ten feet a block is pushed with one end of the stick. The number of blocks brought down by the push are the marks scored by the player. Another game is known as 'Kukra-pat'. Here a single player called 'Kukre-choon' brings other players to his team by dragging them out of the circle in which they gather themselves. The next game is just like 'Atya-patya' played in urban areas. It is locally known as 'Hudua'. In this game, all the members of one team must enter all the 'rooms' of the patch and then once again gather in one 'room'. Then they are said to have purchased 'namak' (i.e. salt). Every 'room' is guarded by the players of the other team. If any player of the party purchasing salt is touched by someone of the other team, the whole team is out.

Besides these, a number of other games are played with 'gend' (a ball prepared out of rags tied with fine twine) and 'gilli-danda' ('gilli is a four or five inches long wooden piece pointed at both ends and 'danda' is a stick of one and half feet in length). Children are very fond of making 'gilli' with a small axe which they always carry on their shoulders, At this age, they also learn to make ropes with their own hand and they can therefore prepare 'gend'. Hence, these games are popular in this area.

The age of maturity comes early in the Baiga Chak than in urban areas. The Baiga children, especially the girls are supposed to assume the responsibility as adult members of the family earlier. They have to compulsorily discharge the domestic and agricultural duties which are assigned to them. For the whole day they are busy in one way or the other and in the evenings, they gather at one place, sing in a chorus and play on musical instruments. When the girls and young women of the community join them, all dance together. The songs and dances form the acceptable means of recreation for the grown ups and they replace the games and plays. In the 'Karma' dance, the girls dance round the boys who sing and play on musical instruments. In 'jharpat the groups of girls and boys dance facing each other and singing while receding and going forward, turn by turn. 'Rina-Rana' is an exclusively female dance.

The age of childhood is the age of play and it is emphasized that a Baiga child gets sufficient time to play. Through active play their arms, legs, brain and muscles of the body, are developed. Play becomes to them, "the working partner of growth, for activity is as vital to growth as food and sleep."[1] Besides the bodily growth, various instincts in the child are also modified, emotions get expression and faculties of its mind are developed.

The activities of an infant are activities for the whole body. It is simply

---

1. Folsom M.B. : Children's Bureau Publication No. 324, Washington 1949, Pp. 31.

because it has not yet acquired the control of muscles. As soon as it begins to crawl, it derives enough pleasure in reaching various objects and persons. Different activities of the organs, make it possible for the child to use its body with increasing effectiveness as its life unfolds,

Up to seven or eight years of age it is found that the children engage themselves in many 'make-believe' types of plays. Most ordinary things represented in their plays are actually very important in adult life. They manipulate ways of extracting pleasure and through imitation of the adult activities informally and unconsciously, they prepare themselves for their later life. These activities encourage their scope of imigination as well.

Change in the size of the play-group is observed with the growth in age. At first, the group consists of very few children—those outside the immediate famiiy. The group is indiscriminate in sex. There is nothing like organisation and hence leadership is assumed by anybody depending upon the proficiency to play. Age is a major consideration for the role of leadership. The group feeling, sacrificing one's self-interest and the spirit of give and take are developed through the plays at this age. Further the plays and games demanding leadership regulate the instinct of self-assertion

As a child reaches the age of early teens, many organized and team games are played by him. The success of a team depends upon the mutual co-operation of its members. Each is given a definite role as in the game of 'Hudua' and a single player is made responsible for the defeat of the whole team. Thus, the sense of responsibility is inculcated in the team games involving competition and skill. The team games also develop and modify the herd instinct in them to social advantage

By this age, a child has several experiences of life in his home, neighbourhood and community. Sometimes he is annoyed, frustrated, disappointed, his longings are repressed, and sometimes he is filled with excessive joy. These feelings find expression in their play. The play may be said to be utilized to supply vent to or yield a substitute for crude emotional reaction. Little harm is done to one's emotional mental life if he plays out his pent-up feelings.

The sex instinct finds expression and is satisfied when children are initiated in dances. The dances are mixed and the songs are in the form of questions and answers between the boys and girls. The analysis of the songs shows that they are conversations full of romance. The Baigas believe that a person should never dance along with his children. If one's son is dancing he will not participate. Hence it is observed that the group of dancers consists of youngsters only. In this way, the youngsters are quite free to dance and enjoy.

They play organised games, participate in the community dances and recreate themselves after the hard labour of the day, Thus, energy for the next day is regained and the chain of hard work and recreation goes on smoothly.

THE INDIAN CHILD AND HIS PLAY

[Parts I and II]

Dhan K. Mistry

The Indian Child And His Play*

Dhan K. Mistry

Games of Early Childhood

The games mentioned earlier consist mainly of simple activity and imaginative play. In early childhood neuro-muscular control and skill increase and group activity is found to be more interesting. But complete loyalty towards the group develops much later. Games which give a chance to exhibit individual glory and valour find favour with children, who as yet cannot play for the group, Competitive and other games in which the individual has to withstand the attack of the whole group attract children between the ages of five and ten.

Play at this stage extends over a longer duration and is more systematic. Generally all the games begin with counting in order to determine the chaser, but at times skill too has its part to play. Chance or skill determines the victor or the victim from among the players.

In competitive play all the players have equal opportunity. Running, high jumping, jumping from heights, climbing and descending stair-cases and trees, and successfully turning some of the difficult types of somersaults are forms of competitive play prominent among our children. Although one or two of them may give proof of their ability and superiority several times, others are rather slow in acknowledging defeat and insist on trying over and over again. Girls too participate in several such competitions but they prefer competitions of singing, acting and dancing.

We have a rich variety of games of skill and chance and also those of slight endurance. We shall here describe some of the popular games of children under the age of ten.

The Indian Child and His Play

This is a complex form of chase and tag. It is played like the ordinary game of chase and tag but for one important difference—as the chaser tags one player after another, they all join him and continue the chase. The chasers, however, do not act individually but join hands so as to form a chain and run together to chase others. Once

Continued from page 147 of Vol. VII, No. 2.

all the other players are tagged by the chain of chasers, the game begins all over again.

There is another interesting variety of chase and tag, very popular with this age group. The chaser is asked to choose one name from the following—stone, cement, iron and wood. Articles made of the material he chooses have a special charm. Any player as long as he touches one of those articles cannot be tagged by the chaser. The players run about from one such article to another. The one tagged by the chaser in turn begins the chase.

*(M) Una Una Sawali (G) Tadako Chhayado (E) Dhup Chham (P) Dhup Chham (Ta) Weyyulam Nilalum (Te) Yanda Nida (K) Neralu Bisilu (B) Chhaya Dhora

An open sunlit place with a little of shade scattered all over is essential to this game. The chaser stands in the sun light and he can only tag the other players when they are not under some shade. Each player tempts the chaser by exposing himself to sunlight but quickly rushes to the protection of the shade when approached, thus giving the chaser a hard time. This continues till one of the players is tagged by the chaser when not under the refuge of shade. This player becomes the chaser and the game starts all over again.

(M) Sat Talya   (G) Sat Tali   (H) Sat Tali   (P) Sat Tali (Ta)   (?)   (Te) Educhapatta Ata (K) Ailu Chappale (B) Sat Tali

The chaser faces one of the players from the group while others stand near the latter, ready to run away. The player facing the chaser gives him seven claps. The last clap is the signal to run. All the players run, followed by the chaser who tries to tag one of them. The player who is tagged becomes the chaser. This is again a more complex form of the game of chase and tag. It involves dodging as well as the dictates of a given signal. This game demands right action at the right time, a quick move and complete alertness before action.

(M)Lapandaw (G) Santakukadi (H) Chhipa Chhipi (P) Lukkan Mitti (Ta) Kanna Muchchi (Te) Dagadu Mutta (K) Kannu Muchchata (B) Luko Churi

This game of hide and seek is accompanied by a good deal of shouting in a loud singing voice. The seeker stands facing a wall

M—Marathi; G—Gujerati; H—Hindi; P—Punjabi; Ta—Tamil; Te—Telugu; K—Kanarese; B—Bengali.

with his eyes closed while the others hide. After some time the
seekers calls out, "Are you ready. I am coming". Generally the reply is,
"No, not ready, don't come". After all the players have found a hiding place they call out, "Coo-ook". The voices give the seeker an
indication as to the places where they may be hiding. As he spies one
player after another, they come out of their hiding place. If however one of the player enters the den of the seeker without being
observed by him, the seeker is said to have failed in his task and he
must begin over again, giving all the players a chance to hide once
again. When all the players are spied, the game begins anew with
a new seeker. The player who had been spied first in the last game
becomes the seeker this time.

The game demands a proper use of the ears and complete
alertness.

(M) Dole Jhak (G) Andhali Khiskoli (H) Ankh Michauli (P) Anna
Jhota (Ta) Kana Katti Wilayatta (Te) Grudivani Ata (K) Kannu
Katti Muttu (B) Kana Machhi

A small area is fixed for playing this game. One of the players
is blind-folded and made to stand in the midst of this fixed area. He
is the blind man. The other children run about in the fixed area
trying to escape the blind man. Anybody caught has to be correctly
named by the blindman who is allowed use of his sense of touch in
determining the identity. If identified, he is blind-folded, the old
one is released and the game begins again. This play is rendered
more difficult by locking out completely the sense of sight.

(M) Khambe Khambolya (G) Char Khuna (H) Char kone (P) Char
Kone (Ta) Mulaittachchi (Te) Nalugu Stambala Ata (K) Kambadat
(B) Pakhir Basa

This is a dodging game. It can only be played in a place which
has four or more corners or poles at equal distances to form a square,
pentagon, hexagon etc. To every corner or pole there is one player,
besides these there is an extra player who stands at the centre.
Players at the poles or corners exchange places while the one at the
centre tries to get into one of these interim vacant places. So quick
is the act of exchanging places and so much of movement is there all
around that the player at the centre has to rush from pole to pole.
The exchange of places, in all possible directions, goes on till the
player at the centre succeeds in occupying one of the vacant places.

The player now deprived of the place comes to the centre and play begins all over again.

(M) Gupchup Toba (G) Dam Gotilo (H) Rumal Chhipana (P) Kotla Chapaki (Ta) Kaikutta Wilayattu (Te) Chetigudu Ata (K) Toppige Ata (B) Rumal Churi

All the children sit in a circle facing inside. One of them runs around outside the circle with a well-knotted piece of cloth or a big handkerchief. Quietly and swiftly he puts it behind one of the players. Each player is attentive and as soon as he senses the presence of the cloth behind him, quickly picks it up and runs around the circle, chasing the player who threw it behind him. The latter, however, runs up to reach the vacant place, or else he could receive a few smart hits from the chaser. In case of failure to detect the piece of cloth behind oneself, the seated player is rudely shaken by several good hits with that same piece of cloth. So, a good beating is always in store for the inattentive whereas quick and gentle action gives another the pleasure and the right to spank. Attention plays as important a role in play as in any other pursuit.

(M) Wagh Bakari (G) Akra Bakarani Jhanjhar (H) Ser Bakari (P) Ser Medha (Ta) Adum Puliyum (Te) Meka Puli (K) Meke Huli (B) Bag Chhagol

One of the children is made the tiger and another the shepherd. All others are the lambs. They line up behind the shepherd, each holding firmly the waist of the child in front of them. The tiger with all his ferocity comes up to the shepherd and asks for one of the lambs. As the shepherd refuses this demand, the angry tiger tries to pull away as many of the lambs as he can. The shepherd with both his arms tries to keep back the tiger. At times, the shepherd is allowed a knotted piece of cloth or twisted rope for the protection of his lambs. The tiger makes repeated efforts, inspite of all the beating he gets, till he captures all the lambs. Sometimes this game becomes very rough, especially when it is played by the bigger boys and the shepherd is allowed a twisted rope for defence. The game calls for a good deal of endurance and rough handling and therefore attracts boys of nine or ten but is much more popular with the bigger boys.

(M) Langada Tonaga (G) Khodiyo Pado (H) (?) (P) Langa Dhodha (Ta) (?) (Te) (?) (K) Kuntata (B) Ek Paye Dhora

One of the players is made the buffalo. He is tied to his knee so that he becomes the lame buffalo. In this position he has to limp and chase the rest of the players. They, however, can run only within a restricted area. Anyone tagged by the lame buffalo has to become one in his turn. Often this game is played as a chase on one leg only.

(M) Gonde (G) Tappi Daw (H) Thapaki Lagana (P) Khidu
(Ta) Pantu Wilayattu   (Te) Banti Ata   (K) Puta Kakuw Ata
(B) Bol Chaprano

Lobbing the ball and lightly hitting or tapping it with the palm is a competitive game frequently played by our children. Each player has the chance to lob the ball till he misses a hit and the number of lobs indicates the score of each player. The player with the highest score is the winner.

This game is popular both among boys and girls. The girls prefer to sing as they lob the ball rather than count the number of lobs. The game calls for simultaneous action of the eyes, the ears and the hand, accompanied by speech and rhythm.

(M) Bada Badi (G) Dhabba Dhubi (H) Dhaba Dhubi (P)   (?)
(Ta) Pey Pantu (Te) Chandat (K) Damba Dabi (B) Daba Dubi

One of the boys tosses up a ball in the air and all the others try to hop it. The one who gets hold of it is free to strike anyone nearby except those who tag him immediately after getting hold of the ball. And so anyone who gets hold of the ball has a chance to hit any other player, except those who have already tagged him. This random striking, modified only by the tag, goes on as long as the players wish to continue it.

(M) Bhatta (G) Patthar Takawa (H) Patthar se Khelna (P) Thanu Khelna (Ta) Kal Atam (Te) Gurichchuchi Kottu (K) Guri Todi Hodiyuwudu (B) Pathor Nirikh

Aiming at a particular mark or object has its own peculiar appeal to our little children. Usually two little boys play this game. One of them throws his pebble some distance away from a line. The other aims at it, toeing the same line. From the spot which his pebble reaches who has the presence of mind to call out, "I play first", has his turn first, and the one who says, "I second", plays second, and so on.

The player stands outside the ladder and begins play by throwing his stone into the first rung or square. If by chance, the stone cuts any of the sides of the square or falls outside it, the player loses his turn. If all is well, the player jumps on one leg over the first rung into the second square and then into the third till he reaches the sea with both his legs on the ground. Whilst returning the player stops before the square that contains his stone, bends down, picks it up, jumps over that square and out of the ladder. In this way, he climbs up the ladder conquering each rung till he reaches the top. On reaching the top, he acquires the right to mark out his "house" in any of the squares except the big one called the "sea". Any such marked square has to be jumped across by the rest of the players whereas its "owner" may place both his legs in it and rest.

In this way each of the players has his turn. The one who makes the largest number of houses on the ladder is the winner.

A quick call for a turn, proper aiming so that the stone falls into each square without cutting any lines, jumping on one foot, balancing while bending to pick up the stone, taking long jumps on one foot over the houses of the other players are the major demands that this game makes upon the players. A good deal of exertion and endurance are essential and the reward is the comfort of a "house".

This game seems to teach the child the one important lesson that success can be achieved gradually, stage by stage and that too, after hard work and by fresh effort at each stage. At the same time, the child learns to exercise his right over that which he acquires as well as recognises the right of others over their possessions.

(M) Gotya (G) Lakhoti (H) Goli (P) Goti (Ta) Goli
(Te) Golilata (K) Goli Ata (B) Guli Khela

Games of marbles demand a greater amount of skill. Each boy tries to hit the pebble of the other and so the game continues. Each instance of correct aiming gives a fresh feeling of delight to the one who aims and an impetus to the other who longs to pay back. In some parts of the country, especially in the South, this game is plated with nuts and the one who aims correctly gets a nut from the other.

(M) Sagar Gote   (G) Sagar Gota   (H) Sagar Gota   (P) Cita
(Ta) Kayattam   (Te)   (?)   (K) Ani Kallu   (B) Sagor Guti

Our girls too have their own pebble games. Big round seeds, shells, pebbles, shreds of pottery and at times even little pieces of coal serve as ready material. The pebbles are thrown up into the air and an effort is made by the player to catch as many as possible with the palms turned backwards. These are again hurled up into the air and caught with both the hands, the palms facing upwards this time. Thus each player goes on playing till she drops down all the pebbles.

This game of pebbles has a more complex form also. A number of pebbles are thrown on the ground. The player picks up one of these, tosses it up in the air and before hopping it again, picks up one or two, and sometimes a large number of pebbles all at once.

The skill of the player lies not only in the quick and subtle collecting of the pebbles from the ground but also in throwing them on the ground in such a way as to enable her to pick up the required number in groups, without disturbing the rest of the pebbles.

(M) Sidi   (G) Nisarni   (H) Sat Kundi   (P) Kidi Kahra
(Ta) Pandi   (Te)   (?)   (K) Palle Ata   (B) Ekka Dokka

A peculiar variety of hop-scotch is found to be a very common form of play among our children. A ladder with seven rungs is drawn on the ground. The first six rungs are equal in size while the last one is bigger than the rest and is called the sea. Each of the players has a flat little stone or a piece of broken pottery and each of them plays by turn. Marbles are played in several different ways by boys in all parts of the country. Of these, the one most widely played are described below. A small round pit, big enough to contain a marble, is dug in the ground. From a line about ten feet away from the pit, each of the boy tries to throw a marble into the pit. The one whose marble falls nearest the pit plays first, the others have their turns according to the places they hold near the pit. The boy who has acquired the right to play first, picks up his marble and from the spot where it was lying, tries to throw it into the pit. He holds the marble between his index finger and thumb and pushes it with the middle finger of the other hand, towards the pit. If the marble enters the pit, the player has a chance to hit the marbles of the other boys. With every successful hit, a point is scored. The player has to score twenty-two such points to win the game. Failure to cover the pit (that is, to throw the marble into the pit), or failure to aim correctly at the marble of another player means loss of turn. Then the second player begins play from the place in which he finds his marble, and so on till all the players have had their turns. The one who scores twenty-two points first is the winner, the others generally give up their marbles to him in appreciation of his success.

Besides the variety mentioned above, we have another very popular marble game. In this one of the boys takes a distinguishable marble from each of the players and tosses them towards the pit. He goes on repeating the process till all except one marble have gone into the pit. That marble which has not acquired the merit of finding its way into the pit is the victim of the attack that follows. The other players take their turns according to the order in which the pit was covered. The victim of the attack is kept near the pit and one after another, each player tries to hit it with his marbles as far away as possible. This hitting however is modified by a peculiar rule. As soon as the marble aimed at is found to be nearer the pit than the one hitting, the player loses his turn. In this way every player tries to remove the marble as far away from the pit as he can. Now comes the turn of the owner of the marble. He is given a chance to rescue it thus—he has to pick his marble up with his toes while he balances himself on one foot, jump on one leg to the pit and place the marble in the pit. If he drops the marble while carrying it to the pit or rests both his feet on the ground, his marble remains unrescued. Once again it has to face the attack of all the other players. A rescue on the other hand ends the game.

(M) Patang   (G) Kanakawo   (H) Patang   (P) Guddi
(Ta) Pattam (Te) Gali Pattamu (K) Gali Pat (B) Ghudi Okano

From the beginning of October to the end of January, one is bound to notice little coloured specks high up in the air. These are the kites of our boys who are enjoying the kite-flying season that precedes and follows the well-known festival of "Shankranti". Hoisting up a kite is as good as a challenge to anybody to have a "kite-fight," as it is called. For these fights a special kind of thread treated with powdered glass and gum is used. Usually two boys backed by a host of companions fly their kites closer and closer till they meet in a fight. Each boy so handles his kite as to cut off the thread of his opponent.

94

(M) Langar Ladhdwine (G) Langar (H) Langar (P) Kamtien
(Ta) (?) (Te) (?) (K) (?) (B) Kata Kuti

Sling fights are usually held during the kite-flying season. As broken pieces of thread used for kite-flying are easily available, our boys make a little weapon out of it. A small stone, a piece of broken tile, or any little thing slightly heavy in weight is tied to one of the ends of a thread. This thread is approximately as long as the outstretched arms of the player. As many slings as there are players meet together in a contest and each player so handles his sling as to snap the threads of his opponents' slings.

These snapped or broken pieces of string are not wasted, they provide another enjoyable game. This game is played by two boys. Each boy is armed with a small piece of string, the ends of which he holds in both hands. The boys so rub their threads as to snap one another's threads. The one whose thread does not snap is the winner.

(M) Bhomwara (G) Bhamardo (H) Lattu (P) Lattu
(Ta) Pambaram (Te) Bongattamu (K) Bugari Ata (B) Lattu Khela

With care and accuracy, either from their bigger brothers or their friends, our boys learn to spin the top. The top is twirled with a long string, one end of which is held between the middle and the ring finger. The top is held between the thumb and the index finger and whipped on the ground so as to land spinning on its spike. Once the boy learns to spin the top, he can participate in several interesting games. Here we shall deal with three of the most favourite top games.

(i) Two boys spin their top at the same time. The player whose top spins longer is the winner. Such a competition is held several times till finally, the winner is given the chance to notch the top of the loser as many times as the latter proved second best. This game is meant specially for the beginner. It seems to prepare the player for the more difficult varieties of top games.

(ii) A small circle is drawn on the ground and a stone kept at its centre. All the players spin their tops aiming at the stone. The top that does not spin or fails to hit the stone has to replace it. This time the players spin their tops aiming at the top in the centre so as to hit it as forcefully as they can. Only if the spinning top gives a proper hit can the player have another turn. If not, his top too goes to the circle to receive the notches that it well deserves. Often the top spins correctly in the circle but fails to strike any of the tops in it. Then the players who have their tops in the centre of the circle get a chance to rescue them. Such a player entangles the spinning top with his string, throws it up in the air and makes a hop with it. One of the other players may come to the aid of the spinning top. He may compel the losers to give up their chances by spinning in his top before the necessary conditions for rescue may be fulfilled. If timely aid does not arrive, the player who fulfils the conditions of rescue gets his top back, while the top of the player who gives him this opportunity goes to the centre of the circle for notching.

(iii) Two circles are drawn on the ground at a distance of about ten to eleven feet. A stone is placed at the centre of each circle. Every player spins his top, at first in one circle and then in the other so as to strike the stone in each of them. The players whose tops do not strike one or the other of these stones, place their tops at the centre of one of the circles. The other players hit the tops in the circle by turns. With each effort, the tops of the losers are gradually pushed further and further towards the other circle. Tops are even spun on the palm and thrust upon the victimized tops to be further pushed into the second circle. Then the players who have been successful throughout, that is, those who have their tops neither in the first nor in the second circle, thrust the spokes of their tops into the tops of the losers. The number of thrusts that each winner gives are fixed at the very beginning of the game.

Then begins the second stage of the game. This time the tops from the second circle are to be pushed back into the first circle. If successful, the winners give half the number of thrusts as they did in the second circle.

In this as in the second one, the losers always have a chance to rescue their tops. The conditions of rescue are similar to those described in that game.

(M) Chak Phirawine (G) Paidum Chalawu (H) Pahiya Chalana
(P) Chakkar (Ta) Wattam (Te) Chakramu Triputa (K) Bandi Ata
(B) Chaka Chalana

It is not an uncommon sight to see boys with little sticks or very thin iron bar about a foot and a quarter in length, running behind an iron ring. The ring rolls on and on urged by the little stick in the boy's hand. One hasty or miscalculated push and the ring, losing its balance, falls to the ground, to the great disappointment of the player.

To keep the ring rolling is indeed a difficult task. It demands complete correlation of the muscles of the eyes, the hands and the legs. Proper judgment, alertness and quick movements are absolutely essential to this form of play. Our boys love to have ring-rolling races, especially after they have acquired mastery over the ring.

(M) Chor Sipayi (G) Akkal Bhuli (H) Chor Sipahi (P) Chor Sipahi (Ta) (?) (Te) Donga Sipayi (K) Kalla Polis (B) Indur Bidal

All the boys except two stand in a circle and raise up their arms. They then hold hands so as to form an arch or a window as they call it. The two boys outside the circle then come in, one chasing the other. The chaser has to pass and repass as many windows as the other player who is generally called the thief. If the chaser or the policeman as he is called, gets into the wrong window while chasing the thief, he is said to have lost the thief. He joins the circle and another policeman is appointed to carry on the chase. As the old thief is caught, another takes his place and so the game continues till all the players have had their turns.

This game is often called the cat and the mouse game so as to distinguish it from the complex team game of robber and police played by the bigger children.

The Indian Child And His Play[*]

Dhun K. Mistry

(M) Itee Dandu (H) Gulee Danda (Ta) Kittee Pill (K) Chini Phani (G) Moi Danda (P) Gulee Danda (Te) (?) (B) Dang Gulee[*]

As interesting as the game of cricket, this game greatly resembles it. The equipment for play are a thick stick about an inch in diameter, and about a foot and quarter in length. It is flattened at one of its ends, and is generally called 'danda'. A small piece of wood about three inches long, thick at the centre and tapering at the ends, completes the equipment necessary for this game. This little piece of wood is called 'etee', 'gulli' or 'chini'.

A small pit about an inch and a half deep is dug in the ground. A player from the team which wins the toss comes out to bat, and the players from the other spread out for fielding. The 'etee' is placed horizontally or vertically in the pit supported by the flattened end of the 'danda'. The other end of the 'danda' is firmly held by the player, who pushes the 'etee' forward as far away from the pit as possible. He has to be careful enough to see that the fielders do not make a catch with his 'etee'. If caught that player goes out and another player from the batting team comes in.

If the 'etee' falls on the ground, the player either holds the 'danda' vertically in the pit or places it horizontally on the ground, at a distance of one 'dan' from the pit, in the opposite direction from the fielders. One of the players aims at this 'danda' with the 'etee'. A right hit dismisses the player and another from the same team comes in.

If the 'etee' fails to hit the 'danda' aimed at, then, the player picks it up and holding 'danda' in his right hand places the 'etee' on it, so as to touch his fist. He tosses it up, and hits it towards the fielders. He goes out on missing the hit or on being caught. If no such misfortune overcomes the player, he again faces the fielder who tried to block him by throwing the 'etee' into the pit, or within the radius of a 'danda' from it. The success of the fielder means the dismissal of the player. If the 'etee' falls away from the pit, with or

* Continued from page 96 of Vol. VIII, No. 1.

* M—Marathi;   H—Hindi;   Ta—Tamil;   K—Kanarese;
  G—Gujarati;   P—Punjabi;   Te—Telugu;   B—Bengali.

without a hit by the player, the distance between the 'etee' and the pit are measured by means of the 'danda'. Every seven dandas' equal one point. So the player begins to score.

The further stage of the play depends upon the number of 'dandas' scored, in addition to the complete point of seven 'dandas'. The number of additional 'dandas' over the complete point determines the beginning of the next stage. Each of the 'dandas' measured has a separate name, the sort of play to be continued in the next stage of this game is called by that name.

The first 'danda' above the complete point is called the 'vakat'. The player begins by resting the 'etee' on his foot near his toes, throws it up in the air and hits it with the 'danda' towards the fielders.

If the score is two 'dandas' above the complete point it is called 'rend' and the game continues in a different way. The player holds one end of the 'etee' the other facing groundwards. Then with a gentle hit with the 'danda' he makes the 'etee' fluster and strikes it before it falls down.

Three 'dandas' above the complete point that is 'moond', involves a different form of play. The 'etee' is placed on the fist of the left hand, jerked up in the air and hit by the 'danda' before it falls on the ground.

Additional four 'dandas' above the complete point that is 'nal' fixes another form of play. The player places the 'etee' horizontally between the index and the little finger, throws it up in the air and hits it with the 'danda' towards the fields.

'Aar' or five 'dandas' above the complete point demands a truly difficult task or rather a stunt to be performed. The player closes one of his eyes and places the 'etee' upon it by inclining the head a little backwards. Then he jerks the neck tossing the 'etee' up in the air and hits it with the 'danda' before it reaches the ground.

As compared to the one who continues with the 'aar', the one who scores six 'dandas' above the complete points is more fortunate. Raising the left hand in level with the shoulder, he places the 'etee' on the bent elbow. As usual he jerks the 'etee' up in the air and hits it towards the fielders.

The player who scores all his points complete is the most fortunate. He continues the game in the same manner as he first began the play. Resting the 'etee' horizontally or vertically in the pit supported bv the flattened end of his 'danda', firmly holding the other end of his 'danda', the player pushes the 'etee' forward.

Failure on the part of the batsman to make a correct beginning of this stage of play as imposed upon him by his score or the taking of a catch by one of the fielders gets him out.

One after another each of the players in the team has his turn and the sum of their individual scores becomes the score of the team. Then, of course, the fielders have their batting.

This game with the team-spirit that it inspires, its skill and rich variety of action, its systematic and interesting stages of play may be ranked among the most appreciated and the most popular team games of the world today.

(M) Hutu-tu	(G) Hu-tu-tu	(H) Kabaddi
(Te) Chadugudu	(Ta) Chadugudu	(K) Chedu Gudu
	(P) Kabaddi	
	(B) Hadudu	

This game is played in each and every part of India. It is one of the most well-known Indian team games. It requires no equipment and no special playground or court. A rectangular or square place is divided into two by means of a middle line. Each half is the territory of the two teams. The players of each team spread out in their own territory and then the game begins. A player from one team crosses the boundary line and enters the territory of the other team, saying Hu-tu-tu-tu or any sound resembling, in a single breath. As many players on the other side as are touched or tagged by the 'attacking' player, get out, on his return to his own territory without losing breath. Those who are thus touched are all said to be killed. They temporarily drop out of the game. On the other hand, the intruder may be caught by several of the players when in their territory and be compelled to lose breath. He is then said to be killed and drops out of the game.

For every man killed on one side, one player from the other side comes to life. One of the players lost to the team as dead rejoins the game and play continues. By turns a representative is sent out by each team to launch an attack into the territory of the other. He acquires several heads or is killed himself. The team which loses all its players loses the game.

Our girls too play this game but in a less strenuous manner. Instead of severely pushing the intruder and knocking her down, they merely hold her and stop her from returning to the territory of her team. She is soon out of breath and numbers among those killed. Many of our girls do not like this game, they prefer singing, acting and dancing.

(M) Kho Kho	(G) Kho Kho	(H) Kho Kho	(P) Kho Kho
(Ta) (?)	(Te) (?)	(K) Ko Ko	(B) Kho Kho

In this game as in all other games, the team which wins the toss has its turn first. All the players of the other team except one sit down (double knee bent) in a row, at a distance of about three feet from each player. Each player sits facing the direction opposite to that of the player in front of him. The player who is not seated, stands at the head of the row and is the first chaser. Players from the other side stand in between the seated players or at the end of the row. The chaser runs thrice around the row of players and then the dodging begins. The players of the other team cannot run across the space between the seated players nor can the chaser. If the players wish to cross over to the other side of the row they must run round the whole row. The chaser, too, has to work within limitations. He cannot change the direction in which he runs till he reaches the end of the row. He however has the advantage of utilising the services of any of the other players from his team. The player, who the chaser thinks has the maximum advantage in the chase, is touched on the back with the word "kho" or "ko". This player then begins the chase while the old chaser takes his place. Soon a tag "kho" is said to another and so on, till the chasers have tagged all the players of the other team. Then the chasers have their turns.

This game is played by girls as well as by boys. It is interesting and exciting both to the players and the onlookers. Responsibility is transferred in quick succession from one member of the team to another, to the best advantage of the team. Each player is expected to judge as to which member of his team is, under the circumstances, most suited to do work for the team. This game demands a quick decision, followed by immediate action.

(M) Langadi   (G) Langadi   (H) Langadi   (P)   (?)

(Ta) Nondi   (Te) Kundi Taku   (K) Ontikal Ata   (B) Langadi

This game appears to be a complex form of the game of chase with a foot tied up, or the chase on one leg which we have described among the games of Early Childhood.

A huge square is marked on the ground. The players of the team which loses the toss sit outside the square and those of the other team spread themselves within the square. Then the team outside the square sends in a player. This player has to chase the players of the other team within the boundaries of the square on one leg only. The chaser tags as many players as he can. Several others, too anxious perhaps to escape the chaser, run out of the square to be enumerated among those who are out. When the chaser is tired or when he puts both his feet on the ground, his turn of the chase is over. Another player from his team replaces him. So, one chaser after another enters the square and carries away his victims till the players within the square are out. Then with the other team within the square, the chase begins once again. The team which gets all the players of the rival group out by sending in a smaller number of chasers is the winner.

(M) Kur Ghodi   (G) Dabal Ghodi   (H) Ghodi Ghodi   (B) Gidi Gidi

(Ta)   (?)   (Te)   (?)   (K)   (?)   (P) Ghodi

We may call this a horse-riding game. All the players of one team become horses. A sturdy player from that team bends down and supports himself on all fours. Often he is allowed to rest his hands around the hips of the first player, tucks his head sideways, and firmly holds on to him. This player is well gripped at the hips by the third player and so the whole team files up. These players are like a number of horses harnessed together to bear the weight of the riders.

A player from the other team, that is, one of the riders, comes running up to the tail of the file, swings himself up by supporting both his hands on the back of the last player and tries to sit on the back of the first boy in the file. Only then can all the riders find a seat for themselves. If any one of them is left out then the riders are said to be unsuccessful in their mount and lose their turn.

After each of the riders has mounted the horse, the leader of the team holds out any number of fingers and asks the leader of the opposite team to guess the right number. With every wrong guess, the number of fingers held up is varied, till a correct guess is made. Then the horses get a chance to be riders.

A proper mounting of the horse is absolutely essential to the game. If any of the riders while trying to acquire a seat, slips down then the whole team loses its turn. On the other hand, if the rider is so forceful in the act of mounting that he bears down the horse, all the riders have their turns again.

The horse and rider team game is a tremendously rough type of game, which demands great endurance and a good bit of jumping. It is played exclusively by the bigger boys and is not meant for girls at all.

(M) Lagori	(G) Nagorcho	(H) Satal	(P) Pithu
(Ta) (?)	(Te) (?)	(K) Lagge	(B) Sat Pathor

Seven flat stones or seven little pieces of tile are piled on top of one another. The biggest tile lies at the bottom of the pile and the others are placed in the order of their size with the smallest at the top. This pile is placed in the centre of the playing field and a line is marked at a distance of about twelve to fifteen feet away from it. The winners of the toss stand behind this line while the fielders spread out a short distanct away from the pile, in the opposite direction of the winners. Thus the two teams face one another with the seven tiles between them.

Then one of the players in the' team throws a tennis ball at the tiles, aiming to break up the pile. The ball either hits the tiles and disturbs the pile, or lobs near the pile to be caught by one of the fielders. In case of a catch after the first lob, the player finishes his turn and the next player comes in. If no catch is made or a catch is made only after the second lob, then the player has a second chance. So the play continues till one of the players breaks down the pile.

The breaking up of the seven tiles makes the game immensely interesting. Then sets in the second phase of the game. Only one of the fielders stands near the tiles which are scattered within a small circle (about a foot in radius). All the other players from both the teams spread out on the field. The fielder on the circle tries to hit out any of the players from the other team and he is assisted in this task by the whole lot of fielders who rescue the ball and throw it back to him. The tile-breakers, on the other hand, try to escape a direct hit from the ball but once it lobs on the ground, they try to kick it as far away from the tiles as possible. While a tussle goes on betwen the fielders and some of the tile-breakers, others from the team of tile-breakers rush up to rebuild the pile of seven tiles. Great indeed is the risk to which the rebuilders expose themselves. At any time the ball may be rescued by one of the fielders and thrown directly into the hands of the fielder at the circle. With a single direct hit at one of the rebuilders their whole team can be dismissed. The ball may, however, arrive too late, then the risk is worthwhile. The pile is built up and the builders win a game.

The victors begin play again. They can only be dismissed under three conditions: (i) if they fail to disturb the tiles after each of them has had his turn; (ii) if one of them gets hit in the tussle that follows the breaking up of the tiles; and, (iii) if any of them gives a straight catch or a full lob into the hands of any of the fielders.

(M) Hatwan Pani (G) Mar Dadi (H) Bolka Khel (B) Bom Juddha
(Ta)   (?)   (Te)   (?)   (K) Chendata   (P)   (?)

A line is marked in the centre of the field. The players of both teams on either side of the line face each other. Every player in the game has a ball. At a given signal, the players of each team strike the players of the opposite team with their balls so as to push them behind. Then they advance into their boundary. The team which succeeds in this endeavour wins the game.

(M) Gedi Dada   (G) Gedi Dada   (H) Dadi Mar   (P)   (?)
(Ta)   (?)   (Te)   (?)   (K)   (?)   (B) Polo Bol

This game requires more equipment than any that we have described so far. It is a kind of hockey game popular among the children from the rural areas. Each player must have a long stick slightly hooked or curved at one end. A rag or coir ball specially made by the boys themselves, completes the material requirements.

Two goals are fixed in the opposite direction at two ends of a huge field. After the assignment of a goal to each team, the coir or rag ball is buried in a heap of dust in the midst of the field.

The players of each team stand a little away from the heap of dust facing their goal. A player from each team stands very close to the heap of dust and at a given signal pushes the ball out of the dust towards his own goal. Each team tries to push the ball further and further towards its goal and at the same time stops it from reaching the other goal. The team which scores more goals than the other is the winner.

Beside the game enumerated above, Indian children play a number of Western games. Western team games, especially cricket, hockey, football and net-ball are played all over India. Indoor games like carrom, table-tennis and badminton are also great favourites.

At this stage we cannot maintain that a regular movement for organised play has begun in India. The efforts made by some of the so-called "All-India" societies are petty and poor. India today needs a well-planned movemet for the creative and constructive use of leisure, so as to exploit the educative value of play. In any such programme, Indian toys and games must have a place of their own.

COUNTING-OUT RHYMES OF CHILDREN

Will Seymour Monroe

COUNTING–OUT RHYMES OF CHILDREN

By WILL SEYMOUR MONROE

In the belief that the reactions of children on their play interests would be of service to the student of the psychology of childhood, I instituted five years ago the following investigation among the pupils in the elementary schools of western Massachusetts.

Two sets of compositions were written by two thousand and fifty (2,050) children, the direct aim of the investigation being six-fold:

1. To make as complete as possible a list of the traditional games of Massachusetts school children.

2. To determine the play interest of children as indicated by their preference for certain games.

3. To obtain descriptions of traditional games.

4. To ascertain personal variations in such typical games as tag and hide-and-seek.

5. To ascertain the qualities involved in determining leadership in plays and games.

6. To determine the extent and importance attached to counting-out rhymes in the plays and games of school children.

I now desire to present a brief review of the results obtained on the sixth and last rubric of the investigation. The compositions were written in the schools as a part of the required school work and the papers sent to me. The results were collated, tabulated, and curved by sexes and ages. The ages of the children were from 7 to 16 years, 978 of the whole number being boys and 1,072 girls. Of the more than two thousand children tested but five boys reported that they never used counting-out rhymes in their games. One of these was further questioned by his teacher as to the method employed in determining who shall be "it," and he replied: " I say to the boys, let's play. I'll be 'it' to begin the game."

The incident is introduced not because of surprise that these lads knew no counting-out rhymes, or at any rate made no use of such rhymes, but because the investigation suggests that such rhymes are apparently universal features of the plays and games of children.   Indeed, individual children reported as many as seventeen (17) such formulas.

In all, one hundred and eighty-three (183) different counting-out rhymes were reported, but all but fifty-four (54) proved to be variations of a few pleasing or much used jingles.   The girls throughout mentioned more such rhymes than the boys.   The one oftenest named, being given by 91 percent of the children, is the unmeaning and inelegant :

> *Ena, mena, mina, mo,*
> *Catch a nigger by the toe ;*
> *If he hollers, let him go,*
> *Ena, mena, mina, mo.*

The second in point of popularity, being given by 86 percent of the children, is :

> *One, two, three, four, five, six, seven,*
> *All good children go to heaven.*

And the third oftenest named (given by 79 percent of the children) is :

> *Richman, poorman, beggarman, thief,*
> *Lawyer, doctor, merchant, chief.*

Sex differences were pronounced in the study.   Rhymes involving color and dress were mentioned much oftener by the girls than by the boys, such as :

> *Red, white and blue,*
> *All out but you.*

And

> *As I went up the steeple,*
> *I met a crowd of people ;*
> *Some were white and some were black,*
> *And some were the color of a ginger-snap.*

The same is true of counting-out rhymes which involve love, courtship, and marriage, such as :

He loves me, he loves me not,

being mentioned almost exclusively by girls.

Boys, on the other hand, are far ahead of the girls in counting-out rhymes which involve number combinations, such as :

Little boy driving cattle,
Don't you hear his money rattle,
One, two, three, out goes he.

and

Intry, mintry, coutry corn,
Apple seed and apple thorn ;
Wire, briar, limber, lock,
Three geese in a flock ;
One flew east, one flew west,
One flew o'er the cuckoo's nest,
One, two, three, out goes he.

Boys also lead in rhymes involving animals and natural phenomena, such as :

As I was walking near Silver lake,
I met a little rattlesnake ;
He ate so much of jelly cake,
It made his little belly ache.

Nursery rhymes and jingles are made to do service in the plays and games of children, as is apparent from the frequent mention of such counting-out rhymes as :

Hickory, hickory, dock,
The mouse ran up the clock,
The clock struck one and down he ran
Hickory, hickory, dock.

Also :

Peter, Peter, pumpkin eat her,
Had a wife and couldn't keep her.
Put her in a pumpkin shell,
And there he kept her very well.

Many of the older children were questioned as to whether they ever composed, or had known of their companions composing counting-out rhymes for their plays and games, but none such could be recalled. From the large number of variations, however, it is apparent that children must add to and alter such rhymes. Following are examples of such variations :

> *As I went up the apple tree,*
> *All the apples fell on me ;*
> *Bake a pudding, bake a pie,*
> *Did you ever tell a lie ?*
> *No, but I stole my mother's tea-pot lid.*
> *She kicked me up, she kicked me down,*
> *She kicked me all around the town.*

Compare with the following :

> *As I went up the apple tree,*
> *All the apples fell on me ;*
> *Bake a pudding, bake a pie,*
> *Did you ever tell a lie ?*
> *No, I never told a lie,*
> *But I ate the apple pie.*

These unmeaning and mysterious formulas, according to the testimony of the children themselves, serve a two-fold purpose in the play-activities of childhood :

1. They determine who shall take the undesirable part in a game — a species of casting lots, as has been suggested, but differing in the method of execution. As these Massachusetts children say, the counting-out rhymes enable them to determine who shall be " it " — the use of " it " being purely technical and having distinct meaning in their play-vocabularies, — and

2. They use these rhymes for purposes of divination ; some of them foretell the life-duration of the child ; others the occupation of prospective husbands, probable number of children, etc. Bolton is doubtless right in regarding counting-out rhymes as survivals of the practice of sorcery — spoken charms originally used to enforce

priestly power — and now repeated by children in innocent ignorance of the practices and language of a sorcerer in some dark age of the past.

Although occasionally undergoing changes, being transmitted from one generation of childhood to another through oral repetition, the marvel is that they should survive at all with such apparent purity. This persistence is possible only through a conservatism of children which is as pronounced as it is unexpected, since in most of the matters that concern them, they are reformers of the most aggressive type — wholly oblivious of the traditions and limitations of their environment.

But in all that pertains to their play interests, they are conservative to the core. The formulas of play are clung to with gospel tenacity; and children themselves are most displeased when the canons of games have been violated.

Because of this insistence, this vein of juvenile conservatism, children's play interests and activities, with their counting-out rhymes, are the oldest things in the world, linking the child through his play-life to the mental life of savages and barbarians.

THE GAME RHYMES OF
NEW ZEALAND CHILDREN

Brian Sutton-Smith

The Game Rhymes of New Zealand Children

BRIAN SUTTON-SMITH

DURING THE last two years I have been carrying out research into the historical and psychological significance of the unorganized games of New Zealand children. In this article, I wish to report on the game rhymes which I have collected in respect to their numbers, their nature, and their apparent significance to children. Although I have arranged these rhymes into an interpretative paradigm, I have not gone very deeply into the matter of explanation, as I realize there are innumerable other ways in which these rhymes could be classified. My aims in writing this article are twofold: to give ample evidence that game rhymes are still very much alive in the play of modern children, and to attract the attention of other investigators to the importance of this field of study.

My collection consists of more than three hundred rhymes, two-thirds of which come from children now in school. The remainder of the collection comes from adult informants and refers to games which were played earlier in New Zealand's history. The types of game rhymes are as follows: obscene rhymes, 95; teasing rhymes, 55; skipping rhymes, 54; singing and dialogue rhymes, 50; and counting-out rhymes, 41. In addition, the collection contains also a miscellany of nonsense rhymes, ball-bouncing rhymes, hand-clapping rhymes, and school rhymes.

The majority of the rhymes falls into three categories, namely: rhymes of protest which include obscene, teasing, nonsense, and school rhymes; rhythmic rhymes in which appear skipping, singing, ball-bouncing, and hand-clapping rhymes; and rhymes of chance which consist of counting-out and guessing rhymes.

The rhymes of protest are all rhymes in which, in one way or another, children protest against adult institutions, conventions, or attitudes. Children express the same type of protest also in many other of their play activities, for example, in pranks on adults, raiding orchards, stealing, truancy, smoking, fighting, and in gang activities. Such manifestations seem to be a necessary feature of children's growth in our society. There is a compulsion to rebel against the world which sheltered them in infancy in order to establish independence within that world during adolescence.

The obscene rhymes were not sought after as intensively as the other types of rhymes were for obvious reasons. Nevertheless, more obscene rhymes turned up than those of any other type. In one school, the open-mindedness of the teaching staff, and the intelligence of the pupils brought forth numerous rhyming obscenities. Fifty children, thirty boys and twenty girls, in a Standard Six Class (Grade 8, U.S.A.) whose average age was twelve, were asked to write down all the rhymes they knew of all types. They contributed forty-five different rhymes, thirty of which were printable. Of the fifteen obscene rhymes, nine referred to excretory processes and six were sexual in nature. A later request to the boys for off-color rhymes brought forth twenty-one more items, sixteen of which dealt with sex and five with scatology. We may conclude that the boys felt that the latter rhymes were less serious offenses against the laws of propriety. It must be noted, however, that of the obscene rhymes contributed by younger children, the scatological rather than the sexual element predominated.

Objections may be offered that obscene rhymes should not be termed "game" rhymes at all, and it is true that they are not involved in any recognized formal games of individual or of group competition. Nevertheless, they can, I believe, be regarded legitimately as a species of informal play. Many informants reported the manner in which they competed against each other to see who could tell a new obscene rhyme or the dirtiest joke.

The question must be asked now why children have such an intense interest in rhymes of this nature. In various ways, most children at some time or other have a tilt at the standards of conventional behavior which adults regard as acceptable. There is nothing very unusual about this, as many of these standards directly contradict some of the children's natural interests in sexual, excretory, and other bodily functions. Furthermore, adults are very stubborn about the relaxation of taboos which shroud open discussion of such matters with children. As a result, children's interests of this sort may often become hypostatized, "undergo no development and remain a fixed image in the deeper layer of the mind" (M. Lowenfield, *Play in Childhood*, p. 107). The "bowling-green" mind of many adults, their salacious interest in filthy stories and jests, demonstrates the manner in which these interests, unreleased and untutored in childhood, carry right on through life in their early and most primitive forms. Lowenfield claims that the interest in what we term the "obscene," "if allowed to take place at the proper time 'unobserved' or, more exactly, unreproved, and in circumstances which offer many and varied interests, is played through and disappears of its own accord as the small personality develops and life affords more interesting outlets" (p. 109). It would seem that in obscene rhymes children have institutionalized their lack of recognition. These rhymes represent, in effect, their protest against the fact that adults have not recognized their childish interests and given them adequate "socially acceptable" scope for outlet. They represent the children's own attempts to create a symbolism for these interests when no relevant symbolism is provided for them by adults. My examples from my collection suggest that a large area of human emotion is being untapped and wasted in our culture because it is forced to take surreptitious outlets.

Teasing rhymes have been known in all historical periods and represent one of the most important ways by which children express their individual and group antagonisms toward each other. As A. K. Stimson notes, "The battle cries of children often become formalized, and they belong to folklore as do songs, games, proverbs and riddles" (*Journal of American Folklore*, LVIII, 124). Presumably, children symbolize various of their feelings in these battle cries or teasing rhymes. Our culture demands independence and assertiveness from children yet does not show them how to channelize their aggressiveness on all occasions. Teasing rhymes are one of their ways of expression. The most popular teasing rhyme is:

> Giddy Giddy Gout!
> Your shirt's hanging out,
> Five miles in
> And five miles out.

The response to this is:

> Sticks and stones may break my bones,
> But names will never hurt me.

Most teasing rhymes center about things which children dislike, such as staring, copying, and telling tales. Some refer to personal characteristics (fatness, thinness, hair color, etc.); others to weakness (crying, sissiness). Examples are:

> Have a good stare.
> By the way,
> You remind me of a bear.

> Heh, you copy-cat,
> You dirty rat.

> Stare, stare, like a bear
> Sitting on a monkey's chair.

> Cry, baby, cry!
> Stick your finger in your eye
> And tell your mother
> It wasn't I.

> Fatty in the teapot,
> Skinny in the spout.
> Fatty blew off
> And blew skinny out.

> Jenny funny, Jenny fat.
> Hit her in the tummy
> With a baseball bat.
>
> How long ago did you cut your wig?
> You big fat pig.

There are many others of a provocative nature which are intended to provoke anger in other children.

> Clear the track
> For the maniac.
>
> You big bumble bee,
> You couldn't catch a flea.
>
> Inky, pinky, ponky,
> You're a dirty donkey.

There are special times for some teasing rhymes:

> A duck in the pond,
> A fish in the pool.
> Whoever reads this
> Is a big April Fool.
>
> A pinch and a punch
> For the end of the month.

Some rhymes play upon boy-girl differences:

> Boy, boy, you big saveloy!

Some center upon group differences. Most of these are about religious differences. Some are more modest, for example, the following is based on house colors.

> Green, green, you're the best ever seen.
> Red, red, you don't go to bed.
> Yellow, yellow, you dirty fellow.
> Black and white, you dirty skite.

Many rhymes are directed at the children's parents and at other adults. Most of these rhymes attack the mother, an indication that children feel it is a greater slight to have their mother insulted than to have their father attacked.

> You're mad, you're barmy,
> Your mother's in the army.
> She's got barbed wire stitches
> In her britches.
>
> Cowardy cowardy custard,
> Your mother's made of mustard.
>
> To make your mother dance,
> Put ants in her pants.

Children may protest in nonsense rhymes and other chants against the orders of adult reality by distorting those orders through rhyme and jingle. In their nonsense, children escape from the oppressive world of common sense. In nonsense they can express their many negative feelings about the adult world without having to suffer the rebuke that they are lacking in common sense. Their humor and many of their parlor games find motivation from this source.

> Pounds, shillings and pence.
> The elephant jumped the fence.
> He jumped so high
> He reached the sky
> And didn't come back
> Till the middle of July.

> Poor old Ernie's dead.
> He died last night in bed.
> They put him in a coffin,
> And he fell through the bottom.
> Poor old Ernie's dead.

More common are chants like:

> Yesterday at three o'clock this morning,
> An empty house full of furniture caught a light.
> The fire-brigade came and put it out before it started,
> Ran over a dead cat and half killed it.
> Two naked men came running down the stairs
> With their hands in their pockets.
> Two dead men went to hospital all right.

School rhymes nearly all have a protesting quality. Presumably, schools are often places of oppression to which the children give expression.

> Two more weeks and we shall be
> Out of the gates of misery.
> No more writing, no more French,
> No more sitting on a hard board bench,
> No more walking two by two
> Like the monkeys in the zoo;
> No more spelling,
> No more sums,
> No more teachers
> To whack our bums.

For the unpopular teacher:

> Ole Pa Watson's a very good man.
> He goes to church on Sunday.
> He prays to God to give him strength
> To whack the kids on Monday.

We may wonder why it is that children give rhymed expression to the various categories of protest. We may ponder why children render obscenities, aggressiveness, resentment, and nonsense in rhymed form. In the early primary school years from the age of seven onward there is an upgrowth among children of an interest in words and in their intellectual relationships. There is an interest in riddling, word puzzles, and in the manipulation of sheer verbal confluence of sounds and word echoes in their many diverse relationships. This verbal interest and a feeling for rhythm is common to all children. The interest in the expression of love and hate in terms of obscenity and teasing is also common; but, in varying degrees, children are aware of guilt feelings in connection with these latter interests. Perhaps by expressing interests unacceptable to adults in terms of the acceptable interests, the obscenity, and the teasing in terms of the rhyme, children are able to make a compromise between the complete rejection of any expression of these interests—a rejection which adults demand—and the interests themselves. That is, children use one part of their nature which is accepted by adults and which is beyond suspicion to sugar-coat another part of their nature which is rejected by adults. It is not likely, of course, that adults will be prone to accept the sugar-coating— the "dirty kangaroo sitting on the lamp-post"—any more than they are likely to accept a direct interest in the scatological on the part of children. That situation, however, is not important. The compromise is not immediately between children and adults. It is a compromise between two parts of the children's nature. Children at this age have only partly accepted, because they only partly understand, the adult's rejection of any direct interest in basic functions. Their rhymes are expressions of this partial acceptance. The borderline jokes of adults serve a similar function.

Skipping rhymes are the most numerous of the rhythmic rhymes. Children's play of today has more skipping rhymes than fifty years ago. It seems safe to state that so far as New Zealand is concerned, the interest which girls have in rhyme has transferred from singing games, which are nearly moribund, to skipping games. I have collected about fifty skipping rhymes which are current today, only a few of which are older than 1900. Adult informants could remember the rhymes of their singing games, but their inability to recall skipping rhymes could not be attributed to obliviscence. Furthermore, students of games before 1900 did not record many skipping rhymes. For example, Lady A. B. Gomme in her *Traditional Games*, Flora Thompson in *Lark Rise*, and Alison Uttley in *Country Things* and *Carts and Candlesticks* have relatively few skipping rhymes. After 1900, skipping rhymes began to come into prominence, both in the reminiscences of those I interviewed and in overseas sources, such as Norman Douglas's *London Street Games*.

Skipping rhymes seem to have a variety of origins. Some derive from singing games; others from old counting-out rhymes and other miscellaneous rhymes of childhood. Some are a mixture of many rhymes. "Singing rhymes frequently become tagged onto each other in order to sustain the continuity in skipping. . . . Such enjambment is a perfectly natural way of filling gaps caused through loss of memory" (L. Daiken, *Children's Games Throughout the Year*, 1949, p. 62). Some skipping rhymes are old rhymes from other sources adjusted to the rhythmic nature of the skipping movements. Daiken (p. 69) points out that the metrical system of most skipping rhymes is extremely ancient, and that even new rhymes are so stressed as to contribute to this old meter. Most New Zealand skipping rhymes have come quite clearly from overseas sources. Adequate overseas documentation might well establish the fact that they were all derived from overseas origins.

There are various types of skipping rhymes. All skipping games are, in the first place, tests of skill and alertness, and many of the rhymes reflect that fact. Twenty-four of those collected were specifically of this nature. For example:

> One to make ready and two to prepare,
> Good luck to the rider and away goes the mare.
> Salt, mustard, vinegar, pepper.

Twenty-one rhymes were of a divinatory nature. They were rhymes of chance. In them the skipper sought to find the initial letter of her lover's name, whether he would marry her, in what month they would be married, how many kisses he would give her, how many days she had to live, how many stitches in her britches, how many dishes she had to wash, etc. In all these rhymes the children skipped until they tripped. Meanwhile, the rope turners or chorers, as they are called in Otago, counted out the numbers, letters, or yes, no, yes, no, until the trip established the answer the skipper was seeking. Example:

> My little sister dressed in pink.
> She washed the dishes in the sink.
> How many dishes did she break?
> 1, 2, 3, 4 . . .

Nine rhymes were imitative rhymes in which the girls imitated the actions of various persons, whether Girl Guides, Teddy Bears, Madame Moraleor, or Charlie Chaplin. Example:

> Madame Morale, she went to the well.
> She never forgets her soap or towel.
> She washes her hands; she dries and dries.
> She combs her hair.
> She jumps up high and touches the sky.
> She twirls around until she drops.

A few rhymes made slighting or satirical reference to adults and incorporated something of the motive of protest mentioned above.

> Ching Chong Chinaman bought a toy doll,
> Washed it, dyed it, then he caught a cold.
> Send for the Doctor. Doctor couldn't come,
> Because he had a pimple on his tum tum tum.

The names of the singing games and dialogues which I have collected are as follows:

Down in the Valley
The Jingo Ring
Merry Ma Tansa
Sally Waters
Pretty Little Girl of Mine
Poor Sally (Alice or Jenny) is A-weeping
The Farmer in the Dell
There Stands a Lady on the Mountain
Oats and Beans and Barley
Green Gravels
Jenny Jones
Wallflowers
Up and Down the Street
The Mulberry Bush
When I was a Lady
Cobbler, Cobbler, Mend my Shoe
Punchinello
Lubyloo
Ring a Ring a Roses
Oka Ball
The Three Dukes
Nuts in May
Surrender the Tower
Milking Cans
In and Out the Windows
Rushes and Reeds

Oranges and Lemons
London Bridge
How Many Miles to Babylon
The Eely Iley Oh
Draw a Bucket of Water
Wash the Dishes
Skip a Basket
Ghost in the Garden
Mother, Mother, the Pot Boils Over
Who Goes Round my Stonewall
Hen and Chickens
The Old Lady from Botany Bay
Old Mother Gray
Booby Bingo
Drop the Handkerchief
Kiss in the Ring
Jolly Miller
Will You Lend My Mother a Saucepan
Fire on the Mountains
The Last Couple Out
Duck Under Water
The Grand old Duke of York
Thread the Needle
Roger de Coverley
Baloo Balight

Before 1900, Nuts in May, Oranges and Lemons, The Jolly Miller, and Green Gravels were the most popular of these games throughout New Zealand. Sally is A-weeping, A Pretty Girl of Mine, The Three Dukes,. Botany Bay, Kiss in the Ring, and Drop the Handkerchief were also well known. Today, however, Farmer in the Dell, Punchinello, Oranges and Lemons, and Nuts in May are the only singing games which are played at all frequently by the girls at their playgrounds.

Singing games have usually been interpreted by the folklorists in terms of their origins in primitive ritual and custom. It is doubtful, however, if that type of interpretation is alone adequate to explain the significance which these games have for children or the reason that some of them have persisted in children's play until the present day. To the historical interpretation must be added an explanation in terms of the games' movements, rhythm, rhyme, repetitiveness, verbal content, music, and the social relationships involved in them.

Ball-bouncing rhymes are not as widespread as ball-bouncing games. In many places, a ball-bouncing game, called Sevens is played without the use of rhymes. Even in this case, however, the counting of the bounces takes on a certain rhythmical quality. Most rhymes reported were variations of the O'Leary ball-bouncing rhyme which has ancient lineage.

> One, two, three, O'Leary,
> One, two, three, O'Leary,
> One, two, three, O'Leary,
> One O'Leary, Postman.
> Open the gate and let me through, sir.
> Open the gate and let me through, sir.
> Open the gate and let me through, sir,
> Early in the morning.

The most frequently reported versions of the rhyme are those which refer to mandarins.

> One, two, three, O'Leary,
> I saw sister Mary
> Down by Canterbury
> Eating mandarines [sic].

Another bouncing rhyme reported is:

> Two, four, six, eight,
> Mary's at the garden gate
> Eating cherries off a plate.
> Two, four, six, eight.

Hand-clapping games have very little place in the schools today, and, in any case, they were never very widespread. My Mother Said and Pease Pudding Hot are two which are heard.

Rhymes of chance form a large category. This division includes some skipping rhymes as well as those other rhymes classified under this heading. In all these rhymes, children appear to be symbolizing their awareness of the importance of the unknown and mysterious factors in their lives. No great knowledge or depth of psychology is necessary to realize why children can come to feel that these mysterious factors in their lives are immensely important to them.

Counting-out rhymes have not faded from children's play to the same extent that singing game rhymes have. Nevertheless, it is clear that these rhymes are not as important to children today as they were to children before 1900. Most rhymes of this kind reported by today's children are comparatively simple, whereas quite complex counting-out rhymes were known by old identities. The most widely known counting-out rhymes in New Zealand today are:

> Ickle, ockle, bottle,
> Ickle, ockle, out.
> If you come in my house,
> I will kick you out.
> O, U, T, spells out and
> Out you must go for saying so.

> One potato, two potato, three potato, four;
> Five potato, six potato, seven potato, more.

The most widely known rhymes before 1900 were those that began: ickle ockle; eenie meenie; and onerie, twoerie. Most rhymes collected were based upon numbers or upon distorted forms of primitive numerals. All such rhymes are in a sense divinatory rhymes. There is an element of chance involved in all of them. According to the way in which the luck falls, so a player is chosen fortuitously to be *he* for a game of chasing. In some games, the players themselves pick a word, usually a color, and the letters of that word are then used for counting out the players.

> My mother and your mother were hanging out clothes.
> My mother gave your mother a punch in the nose.
> What color do you think it ran?
> Blue spells B,L,U,E, and out spells O,U,T.

A number of counting-out rhymes contain elements of protest, including slighting references to adults.

> Go heerty, feerty, hally go lum.
> An old man went out to get some fun.
> He got some fun and hurt his shin.
> Go heerty, feerty, hally go in.

There is another class of very brief counting-out rhymes, each of which contains only one or two lines. Presumably these are used by children to speed up the process of counting out the *he*. Significantly enough, nearly all these rhymes are of recent vintage.

> Inky, pinky, penny, winky,
> Out goes she.

> Look up, sky blue,
> All out but you.

> Pig snout
> Walk out.

It has been customary to interpret these counting-out rhymes in terms of their origins in primitive numerals. It is clear, however, that the significance that they have for children today depends upon their connotations, not upon their origins. The jumble of the cumulative: Inky pinky fidgety fell, Ell dell drom and ell, gives to children both a sense of mystery and a sense of something impending, both of which are the necessary elements in the emotional effects they wish to create through these rhymes.

Only a few guessing rhymes were reported, such as:

> Nivy nivy nick nack,
> Which hand will you take?
> The right hand or the wrong,
> Or the old blind man?

Guessing in children's games is just one of the many innumerable examples of the way in which children often use words and names in their games, as if some magical power inhered in the nature of the words themselves. (See C. K. Ogden and I. A. Richards, *The Meaning of Meaning*, Chap. I.)

In conclusion, although children may express their rhyming interest in practically any subject which effects them importantly, they express that interest mainly in terms of the three areas of experience which I have indicated. Their rhymes express chiefly their interest in protesting against adult attitudes, conventions, and institutions; their interest in rhythmic activities; and their interest in the unknown and mysterious factors in their lives. Here in the children's rhymed responses to their untutored experiences lies the psychological foundation of a great deal of folklore material. Here also in the fact that children give so much of their time and attention to these three areas of experience lies a lesson for those interested in the psychology of childhood and in the education of children.

THE MEETING OF MAORI AND EUROPEAN CULTURES AND ITS EFFECTS UPON THE UNORGANIZED GAMES OF MAORI CHILDREN

Brian Sutton-Smith

THE MEETING
OF MAORI AND EUROPEAN CULTURES AND ITS
EFFECTS UPON THE UNORGANIZED GAMES OF
MAORI CHILDREN

By BRIAN SUTTON-SMITH

IN the past two years I have been investigating the psychological and historical significance of the unorganized (traditional) games of New Zealand Pakeha children. In the course of my investigations I have had cause to study the effects of Maori children's unorganized games upon the unorganized games of Pakeha children and *vice versa*. The information that I have received makes it clear that, despite the immense value of Elsdon Best's *Games and Pastimes of the Maori*, there is still a great deal of research to be carried out in this field. As my own study has not been directly concerned with the games of the Maori, and as I am not myself an expert in Maori lore, it is with some diffidence that I make any report whatsoever. I do so, however, in the hope that it will stimulate others, more expert than myself, to record similar data.

In general it can be said that the history of nineteenth century Maori-European conflict of cultures was, in effect, the history of the gradual submergence of Maori culture. To this submergence the disruptive effects of successive Maori wars, the repressive attitudes of the missionaries, the outlook of Europeans, and the policy of Government officials, all contributed.[1] In this article only those Maori children's games which have survived this process of cultural disintegration, are considered. Further, only those games are considered which have been retained spontaneously by children. This means that the organized games and pastimes

---

[1] See for example: Miller, H., *New Zealand*, p. 13; Beaglehole, J. C., *New Zealand, A Short History*, p. 18; Best, E., *Games and Pastimes of the Maori*, N.Z. Dom. Museum Bull., No. 8, p. 11; Butchers, A. G., *Young New Zealand*, p. 120; Polack, J. S., *The Manners and Customs of the New Zealanders*, Vol. 1, p. 1.

which were encouraged by the Maoris themselves, especially after the rise of the Young Maori Party in the 1890's, and which were encouraged by the Education Department after 1930, are not considered.[2]   Again, those games encouraged by the Physical Education Department after 1939 are only considered if they are still played spontaneously by Maori children.[3]   My information is derived from correspondence and interviews with physical education specialists and others who have been educated, or have taught, in Maori schools; the information is derived also from interviews with members of the Maori Club at Ardmore Teachers' College in 1950.[4]

These sources indicate that the following games are still played by Maori children in some areas: Hand games, knucklebones, stilts, whip tops, string games.   In addition there are many other games of a more informal nature which are still played.   These include: Vine-swinging, hunting and fishing, sliding and sledging, throwing and skipping stones and pipi shells, slings, juggling, spears, skipping, sailing flax canoes, penny doctors, *putuputu, hotaka*, head-standing and acrobatics, swimming, mock-fights and racing. It is of some interest that hand games, string games, whip tops, stilts and knucklebones should be the *formal* games most generally retained by Maori children.   All these games had their counterparts in the unorganized play of Pakeha

[2] Sutherland, *The Maori People Today*, p. 40.

[3] After 1939, physical educationalists, stimulated by their Director, Mr. P. A. Smithells, saw the educational value in certain Maori rhythmic games and sought to revive these for use in both Maori and Pakeha schools.   Most of their work was done with hand games and stick games.   They collected these games from Maoris who still knew how to play them (generally the older Maoris).   The games were then recorded and introduced to teachers at refresher courses and in Training Colleges.   Some attention, but not as much, was paid to string games and knucklebones.   See: *Education Gazette*, April, 1941, p. 58, October, 1941, p. 201.   Records of hand games and knucklebones are in the possession of the physical education authorities at Ardmore and Auckland Teachers' Training Colleges. See also Beard, D., *The History of Physical Education in the Primary Schools of New Zealand*, p. 136.

[4] I am particularly indebted to Colin Spanhake and W. G. Johnston of North Auckland and Koro Dewes, Walker Kamata, and Whitu McGarve of the East Coast.   I record their names out of gratitude only.   I would not like them to be held responsible for any of the above interpretations of their reports.   All the material quoted above refers to conditions within the last twenty years.

children. The Europeans brought to New Zealand their own
versions of all these five games. (The European hand
games are known as stone, paper and scissors.) With a few
possible exceptions all the above-mentioned *informal* games
also had their counterparts in the European tradition.

The persistence of these particular Maori games suggests that the existence of the parallel games in the European
culture acted as a permissive factor on the same games in
the Maori culture; that the Maori children were implicitly
encouraged to continue with these particular games in
preference to others, because these particular games were
intelligible to the European mode of life. Perhaps missionaries and others, who are said to have done such damage to
Maori pastimes, even looked with a more lenient eye upon
pastimes that they recognized as the pastimes of " civilised,"
and not just " heathen " children. There may be other
reasons why these particular games have persisted. The
hand games, for example, require no apparatus and can be
played at any odd moment; they may have been carried on
because of their inconspicuous nature and their convenience.
They are reported as still being played by men and women
at odd shearing sheds in the East Coast area. But, if there
are any other reasons why hand games and the other games
mentioned above have been carried on, and all the other
original spontaneous Maori children's games not carried on,
then these reasons are not known. It is certainly true that
there are not any comparable number of distinctively Maori
pastimes which have survived and which do not have their
counterparts in the European tradition. In fact no evidence
was received of any such Maori games which had survived
and which were still of widespread importance.

It can be assumed, therefore, that with all the above-
mentioned games, the respective traditions, European and
Maori, served to confirm and re-emphasize each other. It is
probable that in many cases the traditions of the two cultures
combined so that features of both were preserved in the
ultimate product. The most interesting example of the way
in which this has happened is provided by the case of
knucklebones. The fusion of Maori and European knucklebones in fact, is of some anthropological significance. It will
therefore be reported in detail.

The claim has been made that knucklebones was introduced to the Maoris by the early whalers.⁵ No evidence,
however, has been provided to support this claim. All the
information to hand suggests, on the contrary, that knucklebones was separately a part of both the European and the
Maori traditions. It is known, for example, that knucklebones was an extremely ancient game; that it was played
throughout the ancient world; and played throughout the
Pacific area in pre-European times.⁶ This information
suggests that the European settlers brought their own
tradition of knucklebones to New Zealand, and that the
Maoris already had one of their own before those settlers
arrived in New Zealand.

It is possible to classify all the types and varieties of
Maori and Pakeha knucklebones into four main categories.
Each of these categories refers to a broad type of movement
which includes many subsidiary movements of that type. No
description is given here of the subsidiary movements as
they are irrelevant to the purpose at hand. Details of some
of these subsidiary types can be acquired from the references
given in the footnotes. All types of knucklebone games
include the fundamental movement of throwing a knucklebone up into the air with the right hand and catching it with
the same hand. While this is being done, that is while this
knucklebone is still in mid-air, the four types of movements
that are possible are: (a) catching the thrown knuckle-
bone(s) on the back of the right hand when it falls; (b)
arranging other knucklebones on the ground in various
formations such as rows, circles, squares and diamonds with
the right hand and then catching the knucklebone which has
been previously thrown up with the same hand; (c) picking
up other knucklebones off the ground with the right hand
and then catching the thrown knucklebone; (d) moving
knucklebones with the right hand on the ground, in, over and
about the *left hand* and then catching the thrown knucklebone with the right hand.

⁵ *Education Gazette*, December, 1942, p. 298.

⁶ See the *Oxford Classical Dictionary, Astralgus*, p. 110; Tylor,
E. B., *Primitive Culture*, Vol. II, p. 81; Lovett, E., "The Ancient and
Modern Games of Astragals," *Folklore*, Vol. 12, Sept., 1901; Budd,
E. G. and Newman, L. F., "Knucklebones—An Old Game of Skill,"
Folklore, Vol. LII, 1941, p. 8.

An examination of the English and Maori games which
have been recorded and which I have collected, suggests that
where knucklebones was played in its most complete traditional form the European game often included all the four
movements outlined above and the Maori game only the
first three types. I have collected many early New Zealand
reports of European knucklebones which contain all the
four types and were played in areas in which there was no
great contact with the Maori. In addition, reports of
knucklebones as played in England contain references to all
the four types.[7] On the other hand there are reports of
early Maori knucklebones which do not contain references to
to the fourth type of movement. It can be reasonably
certain that the Maoris playing the games contained in these
reports were uninfluenced by the European tradition of play.[8]
It is worthy of note also that in all the examples of knucklebones from other Polynesian islands which are mentioned
by Elsdon Best, there is no reference to the fourth movement. It should, however, be mentioned in passing, that in
all the reports of Maori knucklebones the movements of the
first three types are developed to a far more advanced stage
than are the same movements in the reports of European
knucklebones which I have collected in this country. Some
Maori games, for example, include juggling amongst the
movements of (b) above.

More recent reports of Maori games also suggest that
Maori knucklebones originally lacked the fourth type of
movement. For example, two recent articles which record
Maori knucklebones include movements of the fourth type,
but these movements of the fourth type, unlike the movements of the other types in these games, are known by
Pakeha terms, not by Maori terms.[9] Obviously it is peculiar
that these Maori names should not contain Maori terms for
this fourth movement when they do contain Maori terms
for the other movements.

[7] Lovett, E., *op. cit.*; Budd, E. G. and Newman, L. F., *op. cit.*

[8] Chapman, F. R., " Koruru, the Maori Games of Knucklebones,"
Journal of the Polynesian Society, Vol. VII, 1898, p. 114; Best, E.,
op. cit., p. 29.

[9] *Education Gazette*, " Jackstones," Dec. 1st, 1942, p. 298;
(Wanganui area) " Koruru, Knucklebones or Jackstones," *N.Z.
Physical Education Soc. Bull.*, No. 4, 1947, p. 105 (Rotorua area).

In order to discover whether English names are generally given by Maoris to the movements of this fourth type when they are included in their games, I collected descriptions of knucklebones from sixteen Maori students at Ardmore Teachers' Training College. Of these sixteen students only two had not played the game at all. These two students came from districts in North Auckland. Four students had played the game without the fourth type of movement. One of these students came from Parapara (North Auckland); one from Okahukura (King Country); and the other two from isolated villages in the Bay of Plenty area, namely Ruatoki and Omarumutu. The other ten students had all played a game of knucklebonès (generally under the name of *huripapa*) which included the fourth movement. Of these ten students, eight students used only English terms for the fourth movements although using Maori terms for the other types of movements. The English terms they used were: " Hurdles," " Stealing Eggs," " Eggs in the Basket," " Piano." All these terms are familiar in English records of knucklebones.[10] These eight students came from the East Coast area, from Nuhaka, Whangaparoa, Whakatane, Horoera, Tekaraka, Rangitukia, Mokai, Manutahi. Two students had a Maori term for one of the movements in the fourth category of movements, but English terms for all the rest of the movements in that category. Thus " Stealing Eggs " was called alternatively by its Maori name *tahae heki*. These two students came from Tikitiki and Whakaangiangi.

When Elsdon Best made his records of knucklebones in the East Coast he did not record any of these type four movements. Yet they are there today, but under English, not Maori names. This certainly suggests that the Maoris have borrowed the type four movement from the Europeans, that they have assimilated into their own knucklebone tradition a type of Pakeha cultural phenomena of a nature analagous to their own. It is probable that they have been able to do this because the Maori tradition of knucklebones was more vigorous than the European tradition. The vigour of the Maori tradition would be responsible both for the assimilation of the distinctive European type of movement

---

[10] Lovett, Budd and Newman, *ibid.*

and for the fact that knucklebones are still played today much more frequently in Maori schools than in European schools. Fourteen of the above sixteen Maoris had played the game at school, whereas the game was well known in only three European schools (Hokitika, Collingwood, Kaiata) out of the thirty-two I visited in various parts of New Zealand. And even at these three schools it was seldom played by the children at school. It was a home game rather than a school game.

There follows an account of the games which have been enumerated above. This is followed in turn by an account of the games which are played today in Maori schools, but which are adaptations of games from the European tradition.

The names of some of the *hand games* that are reported as being still played by Native school children today are as follow:[11] Hei Tama, Homai (Whakaropi); Matemate ra, Hipi Toi, Ropi, Toro Piko (Mokai, Rotorua); Homai, Ropi, Kumute (Materawa); Hei Tamatutama (Nuhaka); Hei Tama, Whakaropi (Horoera); Hei Tama, Whakaropi, Ropi, Mate ra, Hipitoetoe, Toropiko (Rangitukia); Hipitoitoi with thumbs, Toro Piko, Whakaropiropiro, Hei Tama, E Ropi (Tikitiki); Whakaropiropiro, Hei Tama, Horo Piko (Omarumutu); Homai, Tu Tama (Whangaparoa); Hipi Toi (Te Paroa). Of these games one area-organizer in *Physical Education* writes: "These games are often played in North Auckland Maori schools. I have never taught one in a Maori school nor have I met a teacher who has. Several teachers have confessed that when they have professed any interest in the hand game, the children have turned up with many varieties saying, 'Dad told me,' etc."

String games reported are the following:[12] Diamonds 1, 2, 4 (Okahukura); Mouii, Wharekehua (Whakaangi-angi); Whai, Whare Kehua (Tikitiki); Cup and Saucer, Diamonds 2, 3, 4, Waewae pikaokao, Wharekehua (Horo-era); Cot, Mattress, Single and Double Diamond (Te Karaka); Whai wahine, Whai tane, Mouti Mourea, Waewae pikaokao, Diamonds 1, 2, 3, 7, 11, 13 (Rangitukia); Tane,

[11] The names of the district or village are placed in parenthesis. The hand names are recorded as they were given to me. It will be noted that there are often various forms of the same name. I have not attempted to select the correct one.

[12] For details see Andersen, J. C., *String Games.*

Wahine, Diamonds 1 to 13, Canoe, Moti, One Diamond with loops, Cup and Saucer (Te Paroa); Bird's net, Bird's foot, Diamonds 1 to 7, **Mouti-Mourea (Mokai)**; Mauii, Wahine, Tane, Cup and Saucer, Waewae Pikaokao, Wharekehua (Nuhaka). Other areas which have been reported as strong centres of Maori string games are Matauri Bay, Whaka-rewarewa and Kaitaia.

There are several reports of *stilts*. "We played 'follow the leader' games on stilts made out of wineberry tree or *manuka*." (Huirau). "We had fights and races on stilts made out of manuka or old planks." (Horoera).

"*Whip Tops* made from pine cones or with manu-factured tops are common in North Auckland and they are invariably propelled by cabbage tree whips." "We shaped the hardwood into a top and then put a nail in at the point. A medium sized piece of flax was tied on a stick to make a whip. The top was spun by winding the flax around the tops. There were top fights." (Okahukura). "We made tops from manuka and whips from cabbage trees." (Waitaruke). "Tops from manuka and totara." (Rangi-tukia). "Tops from *hinehine*." (Tikitiki). "We played broad-jumping with tops, bowling another top over and jumping obstacles with them." (Horoera).

Vine-Swinging of an informal nature is still common. "We used to swing on willow trees" (Te Paroa). "We had distance tests of vine-swinging as a method of qualifying for entrance to our gang" (Bay of Plenty). "This was a variation of the Maori game of swinging on a vine and flying into a river. A good vine hanging from a tree was selected. The player took a run back, flew through the air and let go. The place he landed was marked. This practice could almost be termed a long jump and some would be really long too. The aim was to gain speed on the run up, then really fly through the air holding the vine. The main ingredient after that was the courage to let go in order to land many yards further on. I can recall a number of injuries." (Kaikohe).

"*Hunting* filled a large part of our leisure time in summer. Eels and birds were the main victims. There was a variety of methods of catching both. Snares from flax were used to catch hawks or pheasants. We tied down a good springy stake of *manuka,* lancewood or *tanekaha.*

The stake was stuck into the earth then bent over and secured by a piece of flax, to which was attached the bait. The bait for hawks was meat or fish; for pheasants a cob of corn. When the bait was moved a little it would release the flax and the stick would spring upright. At the end of the stick would be another piece of flax attached and laid on the ground about the flax in a loop. When the stick was released this loop was supposed to catch on to the bird's legs. The method was very successful with hawks, and sufficiently successful with pheasants for us to keep on trying. With smaller birds a kit or box was used. This was propped up at one end with a stick and seeds and crumbs were scattered under the box. The hunter lay concealed at a distance holding onto a string that was attached to the prop-stick. A little tug was supposed to drop the cover over the birds." (Kaikohe).

"Wax-eyes were caught on an apparatus which consisted of two poles and a cross-bar of string. A decoy wax-eye was swung on the string cross-bar. The wax-eyes were attracted by the hunter who hid in the bush next to the cross-bar. By sucking inward that part of a corn leaf which is like cigarette paper he made whistling sounds like the squeak of the wax-eye. When the birds alighted on the cross-bar, they were knocked unconscious with a flick from a supple piece of *manuka* hardened in the fire." (Huirau).

"In tidal rivers, when the tide is out the entry and exit holes of *eels* are clearly visible in the mudbanks. The method is simply that of putting a hand in each hole, feeling the eel inside and pulling it out. A grip with the middle finger over the top, and the second and fourth fingers underneath is a firm one. Very large numbers can be caught in a very short time. Where holes are very large, discretion is the better part of valour. The most suitable costume for this game is the nude and several of us would spend an hour or two roaming the tidal banks in the nude pulling out eels. We have met parties much older than ourselves similarly clad. Mud banks can be very messy. In swamps a piece of plain wire attached to a stout stick is all that is required. By frequent poking eels can be felt by the quivering of the stick. The eel is then pulled out as before. In soft muddy places they can be felt with the feet. In rivers, night time is the best. A torch made from sacking or the stalks of flax flowers provides a suitable light. A gaff is needed to pull out those attracted to the light." (Kaikohe). " We used a lighted tyre to attract the eels." (East Coast). " We fished eels with a rod. A bait of worms was strung on cabbage tree leaves and *wiwi* was used as a hook." (Nuhaka).

" *Crab* fishing was done at night. A light was used to attract the crabs and they were hooked out with a piece of wire turned up at one end." (Whangaparoa). " We dived for *paua*, sea-eggs and crayfish. Crayfish pots (called *pouraka*) were set at night. Crowds of families would go down at the early morning tide and fish them out. We would compete to see how many sea-eggs we could bring up at one time. This was done in shallow water. We felt around with our feet first then dived to bring them up. The same was done with crayfish. We felt round for their holes with our feet, then dived to bring them up. The sea-eggs could be eaten raw. Some old folks would eat the whole thing." (Horoera).

" *Putuputu* is played by cutting out from tin a piece the shape of a horseshoe. A hole is made in the tin through which a piece of string is threaded about a yard long. At the other end of the string is a knot. This knot is held between the toes. Each player then has his *putuputu* dragging behind and the idea is to give chase and to tramp on the other fellow's *putuputu*." (Kaikohe). The same game is mentioned as having been played with flax threaded through the holes in shells (Omarumutu, Opotiki). Although it is not mentioned by Elsdon Best it is probably a traditional Maori game. An informant from Waitaruke, North Auckland, speaks of threading string through the holes in *paua* shells and walking on them like imitation horses. The two games may have had the same origin.

" *Hotaka* consists of the main stalk of a *nikau* frond. This is almost severed at about four inches from the thick end and is so cut that the nearly severed piece hangs by the outer bark of the frond. The heel plate of a working shoe, which is shaped like a small horseshoe, is attached to the swinging end of the frond. This toy makes a very good imitation of a horse hoof in the sand or dust and smaller children get a lot of fun playing horses with it." (Kaikohe). In most reports of this game, which appears to be widespread, the children use the frond as a horse hoof without

attaching any shoe-plate; in others the children use flax.
The flax-hoof (Okahukura, Omarumutu) or flax-capper (Te
Paroa, Nuhaka) is made by cutting a piece of flax leaf near
the hoof. The stalk is cut longitudinally and then bent
double. Children then run along making a cracking sound
like the hooves of a horse.

There is report of children making *slippers* out of giant
kelp (Horoera).

Children throw *pipi* shells in the air to make them glide
(Te Paroa, Huirau). They skip flat stones and the flakes
of the paper rock (Horoera).

There is mention of *slings* in which an arrow lying on
the ground is slung a distance by the aid of a string looped
over a notch by the arrow head. The string is attached to a
stick and the stick is flicked (Huirau). There is report of
fern root slings which are used to throw stalks of the pampas
grass (called *kakaho*). There are competitions in distance
throwing (Horoera). " A piece of flax slit down the seam
can be shot into the air when the seam is pulled quickly
through the fingers. We aimed at each other and had
distance competitions." (Ohakune).

Natural foods eaten are *tawa* berries, *miro* berries,
totara berries, *koramu* berries and the fibre of the lace
bark (Huirau). " We chewed supplejack and the flower of
the *kia kia*." (Horera).

A *stick game* which is mentioned as having been played
spontaneously is *tititorea* (Ruatoki).

" *Mud-slides* were very unpopular with parents, but
very popular with the children in the winter. All that is
required is a grassy slope. Buckets of water are poured
down this slide. After a time a very slippery surface can
be obtained. Skill is required to negotiate the slide at speed
while remaining standing on two feet. A spill is rewarded by
a patch of mud on the seat of the pants." (Kaikohe). Most
of the sliding that is reported is done on the leaves of
cabbage tree or on *nikau* fronds (Ruatoki) which are used
as sledges (Omarumutu, Rangitukia).

Flax boats are also well known.[13] These are made out of
the pointed piece at the end of the flax leaf. The flax rib
is the bottom of the boat. The ends of the two sides of the

---

[13] See, for example, Morice, Stella, *The Book of Wiremu*, p. 16.

flax are turned round each other and a stick is pushed through to hold them in place. Cross-bar sticks are placed in the middle of the boat to keep the sides apart. A flax sail—another similar piece of flax—can be slid under these cross-bars, brought over the top and fastened by its point to the stern of the boat (Ruatoki). Boats are also made out of the dry flax sticks. These sticks are hollowed out and shaped like a boat. Smaller sticks can be used for outriggers and masts can be put in for the paper sails. A white *pipi* shell is put in for a keel (Russell).

Penny Doctor beetles, also known as "Butcher Bats" is a game widely reported by Wellington Training College students as being played in many parts of the North Island. In this game straws moistened by spittle are pushed down the hole of the appropriate beetle. The beetle seizes the end of the straw. When the player feels the straw moving he or she flicks out the beetle. The player who can catch the most beetles wins the game.

It is worth noting that I received no reports of kites, hoops or darts. Yet these are all games which had their European and Maori counterparts. It is probable that they have faded in Maori schools for the same reason that they have faded in European schools, although they may have both been confirmed and accentuated in earlier years; that is, before road traffic and organized sports became of any great importance, say, prior to 1910.

The *introduced* games which appear to have become of some importance in Maori schools are: marbles, smoking, ball-bouncing, stagknife, bow and arrows, shanghais, pop-guns, windmills and propellors, ball hop-scotch. Others which are also mentioned, but which do not seem to be so widespread, are: *Poka*, buttons, tractors, rotten egg, Toi and Whatonga, rollers, whistles, sending a message. The popularity of marbles and stagknife may perhaps be explained by the fact that the Maoris have always had more pastimes involving manual dexterity than the Europeans.[14] It is worth noting that the Maoris often fire their marbles in the "Mollybar" fashion, namely, off a straight middle finger which is held in two fingers of the other hand and then catapaulted. It is of interest also that while marbles

[14] The American negroes also excel their white counterparts in games of manual dexterity.

faded in many European schools during the war because there were no supplies, the supply was supplemented in many Maori schools from melted down gramophone records which were rolled into a ball shape.

Poka is a game played with a ball and four holes in the ground (Kaikohe). It is an adaption of the marble game of "Holey" which is still to be found among the mining settlements north of Westport in the South Island. Buttons (Kaikohe) is an adaptation of the old Scottish marble game "leggings-out" or "knock-backs." Rotten-egg (Omarumutu, Opotiki, Huirau, Ruawera) is the game of egg cap or egg cup which is still played at Alexandra in Otago.[15] Toi and Whatonga which is reported from Nuhaka, Tikitiki and Whakaangiangi is said to be a game which is similar to draughts but played on an eight-pointed star scratched in the sand. It is said by these informants to have died out in their time (within the last ten years). The shape of the diagram and the fact that the game is not mentioned by Best, suggests it may be nothing but an adaption of Chinese checkers. Sending a message, which is played in a circle formation, and in which the message is conveyed by a squeeze of the hand, may be an adaption of the well known English parlour game of slip the button (Mataraua).

It was noticeable in all reports that there were a large number of typically rural pursuits mentioned. This was not unusual as a large number of Maori settlements are still of a predominantly rural nature. There seemed also to be more attention to games starring war parties. For example: "There were many varieties of war parties. Our weapon consisted of a *tanekaha* stick about two feet long—any supple and springy wood would do—and a ball of soft clay on the end. The stick was bent back and the ball of clay let fly. We became very accurate with these. Hits were really hits! One boy had an eye put out. But the game was not encouraged. Wet clay was not very suitable for carrying round in the pocket and the hits were severe." (Kaikohe). "One of our gang specialties was the fern fight. Two gangs stood off at about twenty yards and hit off the tops of the yellow shoots of the bracken fern with sticks. The fern

[15] See *New Zealand Physical Education Society Bulletin*, Vol. 2, No. 4, 1947.

tops whizzed around like spears." (Huirau). "We all used
to ride to school with our bows and arrows. We would have
bow and arrow gang fights on horseback. Some boys were
able to stand on their horses' backs and fire the bows."
(Horoera). "We had two teams at war with fern spears.
Each player had about ten spears and a shield of wood or
tin. Any player being hit must drop out. We also divided
up into teams for sword fights with *manuka* sticks."
(Ruatoki).

These Maori war party games may be simply a parallel
for the European children's cowboy and Indians. Both may
be stimulated also by the influence of the films and literature.
On the other hand this type of Maori play may be an
expression of something peculiar to Maori culture. The
Beagleholes, for example, have pointed out that the Maoris
tend to foster inter-tribal competitiveness as one of the
means of supporting the " basic character structure of Maori
culture."[16] If this is the case, the children's play would
naturally reflect this spirit of inter-group competitiveness,
particularly in the terms in which that competitiveness was
originally expressed, namely, in terms of war parties.

The above article has dealt almost entirely with the
effects of the European tradition of games upon the games of
Maori children. The meeting of cultures has not, however,
been entirely one-sided. There are occasional reports of
European children playing at Maori games such as humming
tops and team whip tops. And also many reports of
white children building *raupo* huts and sledging on cabbage
tree leaves. It can be assumed that the Maori games which
were the same as the European games would confirm the
European children in the play of those games.

In conclusion it can be said that in the new cultural
environment provided by the meeting of these two cultures,
there has been a tendency for the unique pastimes of the
submerged culture to be cancelled out, and for the pastimes
which both cultures shared to be strengthened. But this
tendency has been affected by yet another influence which
has been stronger than the re-emphasis given by each culture
to the analagous traits in the other. This other influence has

---

[16] Beaglehole, E. and P., *Some Modern Maoris*, p. 145.

been the influence of organized sport which has tended to cancel out all the minor games of both cultures irrespective of their nature.[17]

[17] The incompleteness of the material I have recorded above will be only too apparent to the experienced eye. It is my hope, however, that the documentation of this material will stimulate others to record the spontaneous play life of Maori children today and yesterday in more detail and with more accuracy. Further material could be sent to me c/o The Polynesian Society, Alexander Turnbull Library, Wellington.

PSYCHOLOGY OF CHILDLORE

The Triviality Barrier

Brian Sutton-Smith

Psychology of Childlore: The Triviality Barrier

BRIAN SUTTON-SMITH

THE STUDY OF CHILDLORE is an interdisciplinary subject matter which is of concern to both folklorists and social scientists. Some of the activities covered are those that are a part of children's own group traditions. Thus: games, riddles, rhymes, jokes, pranks, superstitions, magical practices, wit, lyrics, guile, epithets, nicknames, torments, parody, oral legislation, seasonal customs, tortures, obscenities, codes, gang lore, etc. Other activities are those that children indulge in individually, but which they have in common with other children and which have a thematic character. Thus: solitary play, daydreaming, fantasies, imaginary companions and heroes, collections, scrapbooks, model worlds, comic reading, mass media interests, dramatizations, stories, art, etc. In addition to these basic data, childlore may be considered also to include a variety of special theoretical and methodological concerns, such as: the historical changes in the nature of childlore, the changing conceptions of child nature, adult memory for child nature, the ontogeny of symbols, theories of child symbolism, and developmental explanations of the phenomena of childlore.

The activities listed above can be recognized as those which compose the supposedly nonserious areas of child life. The word *"lore"* seems to fit both the commonality, thematism, and the nonseriousness of these phenomena most adequately, though it is obviously not a perfect fit. The term *juvenile folklore* would not be quite so good because it would not include the second category of activities, which never constitute folklore but which do exhibit innumerable characteristics in common with it. In fact, it is probable that in the matching of the two, say, daydreams and games, lies the understanding of both—each being points on some continuum of imaginative life. On the other hand, the term *imaginative behavior* would not be adequate either because it would not do justice to the fact that so much of the data are indeed folk phenomena, which is to say they are

[1]

mainly transmitted orally, are a matter of group tradition, and deal with the nonserious things of life.

Of course the word *nonserious* is not very satisfactory as a definition of either folklore or childlore, and it is part of the burden of this paper to indicate why it is not. The term does, however, cover another human reality, important to our definition, which must be approached through it, so an excursus is in order at this point. In a sense, when it is said that play, games, and reverie are nonserious, most persons in Western culture know what is meant. When this class of activities is contrasted with eating, sex, and work, Western man feels fairly strongly that they are nonserious and that he knows what he is talking about. For whether we folklorists like it or not, our subject matter is felt usually to be something of an oddity, involving the inherently or historically trivial. One must suppose that the neglect of this cultural notion of essential triviality in the definition of their subject matter by some of the major folklorists is a form of self-respect.[1] It need only be noted that the archetypal Thoms put the matter more realistically when in his famous *Athenaeum* article he advocated the collection of this "mass of minute facts, many of which, when separately considered, appear trifling and insignificant." [2] He went on to say that they were dignified by the system into which Grimm had woven them. The important point for the moment is that he did indicate their essential triviality in terms of the cultural standards of his day. Naturally it is hard to incorporate this notion of triviality into a substantive definition, as it refers to attitudes toward the subject matter rather than a description of the subject matter's intrinsic dimensions. We must ask, therefore, what it is in the subject matter of childlore (and folklore) that permits such an attitude.

One answer lies in the view that the activities listed above are pursued by their protagonists because they are fun. Unfortunately, the view that fun is some sort of human ultimate[3] does not recommend itself to everyone, but as an ultimate it would have the virtue of explaining why a work-oriented civilization would, therefore, regard these activities as trivial. If one adopts the rather strenuous definition of adaptation to be found among most biologists and

---

[1] See, e.g., the definitions in Alan Dundes's *The Study of Folklore* (Englewood Cliffs, N. J., 1965), pp. 4–31.

[2] Ibid., p. 5.

[3] As is advocated by J. Huizinga, *Homo Ludens: A Study of the Play Element in Culture* (London, 1949).

psychologists[4] then it follows naturally that anything which is full of fun and has no obvious survival value can hardly be of critical importance.

Behind the notion of fun, however, lies the more important concept of expressive activities. Expressive activities in young babies (laughing, babbling, playing) have long been recognized, but like the expressive activities of older children (riddles, rhymes, etc.), they have been pretty much ignored. Most orthodox psychological attention to infants has concentrated on the ways in which the infants' immature response-systems are guided toward more "mature" forms of behavior. The developmental studies of language, for example, pay most attention to the establishment of communication—not to the expressive character of language activity itself. The arguments concerning the origins of symbolization usually have to do with the way in which this referring to others or to things is learned, whether, for example, as a function of reinforcement or as an organismic act on the part of the subject.[5] With some exceptions[6] relatively minor attention is given to the function of sound-making, symbolization, laughter, and play simply as expressive activities for the child though the presence of such activities is usually acknowledged. What this utilitarian emphasis implies is that these forms of infant behavior are being seen mainly from an adult point of view. The implicit question usually being asked is, How do these infant responses lead to some more useful adult type of adaptation? As the notion of what adult adaptation is has already been skewed in favor of a predetermined and pragmatic notion of "adaptation" or "survival," great heed is paid only that which in the infant's behavior is seen as a precursor to survival. Those of the infants' sounds which refer and those of their laughs which are social receive prior attention. Those which merely express feeling or meaning for their own sake or are autistic are relatively neglected (unless of course the children are really autistic). Those of the children's plays which contain representations of overwhelming conflict receive great attention because presumably they lead to neurosis, but those which are normal are relatively neglected.

---

[4] The criticism of the customary notions of "adaptation" has been developed by Louis Carini of Bennington College in a series of unpublished papers. It is also implicit in my own criticism of purely compensatory theories of play in "Piaget on Play: A Critique," *Psychological Review* 48 (1966): 111–121.

[5] C. E. Osgood, C. J. Succi, and P. H. Tannenbaum, *The Measurement of Meaning* (Urbana, Ill., 1961); H. Werner and B. Kaplan, *Symbol Formation* (New York, 1964).

[6] M. M. Lewis, *Language, Thought, and Personality* (New York, 1963).

If we suspend for a time our built-in biases about what is trivial
and what is not and look at those activities which are expressive and
full of fun for the child, then we are forced to acknowledge that there
is an inherent grammar in their development. Whether we talk of
humor, babbling and talking, or of play, each takes place in terms of
a developmental series of forms. The structures of infant play forms,
for example, have been described most adequately to date by Jean
Piaget.[7] Along with other observers, Piaget says that each behavioral
form or structure even in infancy has autotelic or self-sustaining moti-
vational properties.[8] The infant appears to babble for the joy of hear-
ing himself. The child plays for the fun of it. The adults return
addictively to their games for the enjoyments they find contained
within them.[9] We are saying, that is, that childlore deals not only
with a definite series of *expressive forms* that can be traced throughout human development, but that these forms are normally, in some
sense, self-motivating structures. Which is after all only what generations of humanists have been saying when they have claimed that
poetry, drama, and other forms of human expression have their own
intrinsic vocabulary and system of internal dynamics which must be
understood in their own right before it is possible to study how they
can be put to the service of this or that functional end.

It is true, then, that childlore deals with behavior that has tradi-
tionally been regarded as nonserious, but as this behavior appears to
be a systematic part of the human repertoire, to think, therefore, it is
unimportant might be a mistake.

The use of the term *psychology* in the title to this article suffers
less from semantic problems than from the fact that psychology has
had so little to offer. Psychology which takes the whole field of human
behavior for its subject matter can study childlore as well as anything
else if it wishes to do so, but it has by and large not wished to do so.
Probably most academic psychologists of the recent era would feel
that there was something slightly worthless in studying such a subject matter, being confined by their self-respect to "more important"
matters such as eating, sex, and work. As we can define childlore
partly in terms of its "triviality," it follows also that most serious

---

[7] *Play, Dreams, and Imitation in Childhood* (New York, 1963).
[8] O. K. Moore, "Some Puzzling Aspects of Social Interaction," *Review of Metaphysics*
55 (1962): 409-433.
[9] The notion of game addiction was developed in collaboration with John M. Roberts
and will be more fully reported in a forthcoming book: *Games: Models of Power*
(McGraw-Hill, in preparation).

persons will find it too trivial to study, that at this historical time there will be a "triviality barrier" against its serious pursuit.

The historical roots of this bias have to do with the character of this civilization, including its respect for work, rationality, and science and its disrespect for play, irrationality, and aesthetics—attitudes which, in turn, are said to have originated about the time of the Reformation, though their precise constituents have been a matter of debate among scholars throughout this century. But, still, to be gripped by the postpuritan enthusiasms of one's own era provides no good theoretical reason why psychologists should not study the occasions of expressive forms including what we have here termed childlore.[10] At least that is true if this article is to make any sense. Though again we can be very serious about the matter and point to two lines of emerging psychological research which presage the demise of "triviality" as an essential attitude toward the subject matter of childlore. First, there are those recent researches in playfulness which indicate that such "fun" is actually associated with manifestations of creativity.[11] The paradox emerges that those who are the most creative and talented and to whom an inventive civilization is beginning to turn for its answers may in the long run turn out to be those who were as children and still are as adults the most intellectually playful and funloving—those who perhaps spent a considerable proportion of their time in trivially divergent activities.

Secondly, the advent of Head Start and poverty programs has led to the discovery among many social workers and recreationists that there is no natural and universal language of lore for all children.[12] In fact, children from different socio-economic and ethnic groups have considerable difficulty in relating to each other through play; they have quite different expressive formal systems. Attempts are now under way to fathom the nature of the codes of these different systems in order to discover how to mediate among them. Given this trend we can predict that the phenomena of childlore will steadily become

---

[10] Not all expressive phenomena, e.g., babbling, are of equal interest in childlore; in effect, we confine ourselves to those expressive phenomena which develop a common thematic character, most particularly, to those that take on a group character.

[11] M. A. Wallach and N. Kogan, *Modes of Thinking in Young Children* (New York, 1965), and J. N. Lieberman, "Playfulness and Divergent Thinking: An Investigation of Their Relationship at the Kindergarten Level," *Journal of Genetic Psychology* 107 (1965): 219–224.

[12] "Rules and Freedom: Games as Mechanisms for Ego Development in Children and Adolescents" (paper delivered at the Annual Meeting of the American Orthopsychiatric Association, San Francisco, March 1966).

a more serious academic pursuit. We are perhaps on the verge of a revolution in folklore like that which has characterized the emergence of structural grammars in linguistics or the examination of parent–child relations in child psychology. In both cases a part of the functioning culture previously implicit is made explicit and, therefore, partly at least, subject to manipulation and control. The effect of such understandings on the normative character of the expressive phenomena itself is, of course, likely to be an affront to those who sustain their interest in child or folklore from nostalgic motives.

In sum, to this point I have argued that childlore is concerned with expressive forms, and that for this reason it has historically been regarded as a trivial subject matter, but that current trends in research would appear to foretell the end of this demeaning epithet.

The necessary conjoining of the two fields of psychology and folklore may be illustrated from my own work on Tick Tack Toe—the most trivial of all games of strategy—so trivial in fact that mathematically-minded players always force a draw, although children and the rest of us manage to win and lose in our own unwitting ways. My anthropological colleague, John M. Roberts, and I chose Tick Tack Toe because we were interested in the history and development of strategic competence and because Tick Tack Toe was the most elementary game of strategy and the only one universally played in this culture. In choosing it for serious study, of course, we had behind us the great prestige of game theory. By such a choice we avoided the endless taxonomic uncertainties that still lie ahead in this field. By defining a game as a recreational activity characterized by organized play, competition, two sides, rules, and criteria for determining a winner, we simply ignored most of the games of young children which have rules but are somewhat diffuse with respect to sides, competition, and winning (as, for example, Farmer in the Dell and Red Rover). I suspect that the road ahead in childlore lies in a series of such narrowly concentrated efforts from which there can be considerable yields of empirical data.

First with respect to games of strategy in general. Our cross-cultural studies had indicated at first that there were some cultures with no games and that such cultures and others with only games of physical skill were relatively simple cultures. But, by contrast, cultures which also had games of chance or games of strategy were much more complex. In fact, cultures possessing games of strategy were at a higher level of cultural complexity than any of the cultures without such games. They were characterized by larger settlements, more complicated subsistence patterns, higher technology, higher levels of political integration, jurisdiction, social stratification, occupational specialization, and many other traits also indicating that these cultures were complex.

Child socialization tended to be severe. There were briefer periods of nurturance, a high inferred transition anxiety, a high level of pain inflicted by the nurturant agent, a low degree of reduction of the infant's drives, low overall indulgence, and yet high responsibility, achievement, self-reliance, and obedience training. In these cultures with strategy games, then, the child had to be obedient and responsible but at the same time he had to be achieving and self-reliant, all of this within the context of a stratified and highly organized social system.[13]

The cultural correlates of these games were also impressive: there were complex political, judicial, economic, military, and religious organizations in which strategic skills and strategic decisions would obviously be rewarded. It was not hard to envisage that in contexts of this character games of strategy would be forms of social system learning. In a parallel study of folktales, furthermore, we established that folktales with strategic elements flourished in the same cultural environments as games of strategy.[14]

From these cross cultural studies we developed the thesis that games of strategy were buffered learning situations in which the child or adult was given safeguarded and sanctioned display of the elements required in strategic thinking. It was a natural next step, therefore, for us to attempt to prove this true. If it were true, we argued, it should follow that those who were particularly skilled at strategy games should be fundamentally different from those who were not. Earlier historical studies of children in this culture seem to have shown that there is more of such strategy gaming among children today than was formerly the case.[15] The game of Tick Tack Toe itself seems to have been of relatively recent origin, though it is a member of a historically much older class of games of alignment which includes Three Man's Morris. It may have been a child's adaptation to

---

[13] Brian Sutton-Smith and John M. Roberts, "The Cross-cultural and Psychological Study of Games," *International Review of Sport Sociology* (in press).

[14] John M. Roberts, Brian Sutton-Smith, and A. Kendon, "Strategy in Folktales and Games," *Journal of Social Psychology* 61 (1963): 185–199.

[15] Brian Sutton-Smith and B. G. Rosenberg, "Sixty Years of Historical Change in the Game Preferences of American Children," *JAF* 79 (1961): 17–46.

the fact that permanent alignments boards could not exist in the nine-teenth-century schoolroom under the master's vigilant eye, but that transitory forms involving only a slate or pencil could.

Our psychological study of Tick Tack Toe proceeded both by developing a Tick Tack Toe test within which a child marks a series of crosses on diagrams already partially filled and through the use of Tick Tack Toe tournaments. In both cases the results were essentially the same. The boys who were the winners on the test were the winners in the tournaments. They were perceived by their peers to be leaders because of their ideas; they were rapid decision makers and had a high concentration on intellectual pursuits as judged by obser-vations of their free play activity. The boys who played for a draw on the other hand, appeared to be high school-achievers, but mother-dependent boys. Girls who played for a draw were also high school-achievers but also feminine and cautious in their social behavior. They were good girls, and they played for a draw. As judged by the game, good girls play it safe. The winning girls were on the contrary hyperactive, aggressive, and masculine in their interests.[16]

What is implied in these studies is that where game involvement and competence is high, the game is a systematic part of the person-ality and culture patterns in which the player participates. Even this most trivial game of Tick Tack Toe reflects important cognitive and expressive characteristics in the players. What is on the surface trivial is as deeply grounded in psychological functioning as it is in historical roots. It follows, I believe, that the same will be found to be true whether we study Tick Tack Toe or riddles, rhymes, codes, gang lore, or collections. Each and every one is a part of orderly expressive se-quences with its own historical and developmental characteristics. The further understanding of the formal and functional nature of these phenomena is then the research focus of the psychology of childlore. A focus against which there may still be a triviality barrier but which, as the Tick Tack Toe case study suggests, is a focus which is not of trivial concern for human understanding.

Teachers College, Columbia University

---

[16] Brian Sutton-Smith, and John M. Roberts et al., "Studies of an Elementary Game of Strategy," *Genetic Psychology Monographs* 75 (1967): 3–42.

SOME CHILDREN'S GAMES FROM TANNA, NEW HEBRIDES

W. Watt

Melanesia : Social Anthropology.

Watt.

Some Children's Games from Tanna, New Hebrides. *By the late Rev. W. Watt, edited by* *A. Capell.*

The games described below came into the editor's hands in the following way : The late Rev. W. Watt was the Presbyterian missionary at Kwamera and Port Resolution, southern Tanna, New Hebrides, for many years, about the close of last century. At the same time the late Rev. Dr. Gunn was missionary on Futuna, in the same group. The latter was of a scholarly type, and sent a number of questionnaires round to his fellow workers at different times. Just before 1930 he passed on the bundles of MSS. to the present editor. These games here described were given by Mr. Watt in answer to one of Dr. Gunn's questions. They have been left just as Mr. Watt wrote them, with the one exception that Kwamera words have been spelled according to the system usual in *Oceania*. The only point necessary to note here is that ŋ is used to represent the sound of *ng* in *sing*. In Mr. Watt's MSS. as in the mission printings g is used alone, as the hard g does not occur in the dialect. A very few alterations in Mr. Watt's actual wording have also been made. The original document was written about 1893.

" Many games are played chiefly at certain seasons of the year, as was our own custom in Scotland. We have been astonished to see how many of the Tannese games resemble closely games played at home. We have not seen a native race, but in racing at our request they ran in Indian file, but there was no real trial of speed, because they had made up their minds to allow a certain one to get the prize.

" Have not seen and can learn nothing of any game like draughts. Some of the Tannese games are as follows :

" (1) The natives throw reeds, striking them on the ground, from which the reed glances off and flies to a distance. The aim is to see whose reed goes farthest. The Tannese name is *auini kwaniŋ*.

" (2) A similar game played on the water. A stone is thrown so as to glide along the top of the water, and the victor is the one who strikes the water most frequently. Often as a boy did I do this. The challenger says, *seim napuei keva ?* literally, how many coconuts have you ? Meaning, how often has your stone struck and rebounded off the water ?

" (3) *Merpatan*, a sham fight with reeds in imitation of spears. Two sides are formed, and they endeavour to strike each other as they did when fighting with spears in actual warfare.

" (4) *Merkwatan*, a sham fight with fruits, instead of reeds as above. In actual fighting stones would have been thrown. They apply the term to fighting with rifles, called by them foreign stones (*kapir itoŋa*).

" (5) *Nukwane manu* (the heads of fowls or birds). This game is generally, or rather always, played at the time when food is scarce, just before yams are ripe. They say it is an incentive to seek for food. There are two sides. Each does its best to outdo the other in the quantity, variety and rarity of the fishes, birds, etc., it gets. The exchange is made in the evening, and the following day land and sea are ransacked to procure like quantity, variety and rarity, which is given in return, and if possible other articles in addition, for which the other side must give an equally valuable return. They may go on for weeks and on no day may it be omitted. Those who keep the count satisfy the demands of custom by going to the place where the exchange is made and making a promise for the morrow.

" (6) *Tabasina* (hide and seek). One or more shut their eyes. The others pat them on the back as if putting them to sleep and repeat a rhyme, after which they slip away and hide. When hidden they whistle and then the seeker or seekers go and search for them, saying all the while *avarep* (whistle). Those hidden endeavour to get in without being touched.

" (7) *Kwanapit* (Scotch tig). Any number can play ; all are out except one or two, and those out try to catch those in without being touched in return. If one fails to touch in return the game is ended and has to be reconstructed.

" (8) *Kwanapit harre* (Scotch tig). Any number can play. It is the reverse of the foregoing ; one is ' in ' and all the rest are ' out.' The one ' in ' tries to touch one of those ' out.' The one touched becomes ' in ' instead of him.

" (9) *Mo kasēn* (a species of tig). Any number can play. Two, called father and son, occupy a central spot called a house. The others have each spots or houses of their own, but endeavour to get the spot of the father and son without being touched. They try to entice them away from the spot. Should they succeed and one or other reach the spot without being touched, all gather round the two vanquished and sing a song of victory. If the father or son touch one of the others while attempting to reach the spot, that one and a companion take the place of the father and son. They can only be touched off their own spot.

" (10) *Numai niŋ* (reed leaves). Any number can play. There are two sides. Each side has a post in the ground, called a house. The posts are a considerable distance apart. Two of each side are allotted to guard the posts. Each side as in *mo kasēn* tries to draw away the guards from their opponents' posts in order that one or more may get to the said post without being touched. If they are successful a piece of reed is put in the ground at the foot of each post to signify a victory. Having gained a victory or more, if in attempting it one is touched, the whole of his party gather round him at the post and one secretly pulls up the reed or reeds which had previously been put in. The other side are then called on to guess who pulled up the reeds.

" (11) *Taŋarua isumu* (the sea snake of Isumu).[1] Any number can play. One is called *nukwaren* (its head) and stands as a pivot round which the others wind themselves. They hold each other by the wrists, all facing in one direction. They try to keep the line as straight and taut as possible. Going forward they wind themselves round the pivot, and in unwinding all go backwards with the exception of the outer one.

" (12) *Tareŋa mas* (tug-of-war). Any number can play. Two sides are formed nearly equal ; instead of a rope they hold each other by the wrists and stand in a straight line. The two centre ones are the leaders and are generally the strongest. At a given signal the leaders join hands, each side endeavours to drag the opposite party on to their ground. If in so doing the line breaks, those broken off change sides.

" (13) *Tuavini irahame* (' they will cook each other '), a sitting tug-of-war. Any number can play. Two sides are formed, and sit near each other. Each side endeavours by fair means or foul to snatch one or more from the opposite side. Each side tries to retain its own, and so the snatched one is dragged back and forward till either rescued or taken captive. The captured one is supposed to be cooked and so is out of the game. Frequently one or more is lost on each side during the scuffle.

" (14) *Turaberaber ruuta* (' the reeds go up '). Any number can play. A large number of pieces of reed are got and distributed among the players, who, all except one, sit in a circle. The one excepted is outside. All in the circle hold up a piece of reed each, over their heads, and sing. The one outside has to hop round the circle and gather the reeds on the way. As each reed is taken another is held up in its place. The hopper goes round and round till exhausted, when he gives in. Another one becomes hopper and a new circle is formed. Each hopper strives to gather the greatest number of reeds.

" (15) *Napuei*. Any number can play. All except one form themselves into a circle holding each other by the wrists, and standing. All hold firmly except one, and that part is called *ikinan*. The circle is supposed to be a garden fence, and the *ikinan* is the weak part and at it all rubbish is thrown out. The person excepted occupies the centre of the ring and is called ' the thief.'

" (a) The thief goes round the circle and in so doing touches the feet of each individual and says opposite each, *Yakamütte kabasak eri sana, mapa sana*, ' I am working at this taro plant of mine, and passing by this one.' Having completed the circle and arrived at the *ikinan* he professes to throw out the weeds he has gathered.

---

[1] The first word of this name is undoubtedly the Polynesian Tangaroa, the name of the chief god of the western Polynesian pantheon. This is of interest, in that Tangaroa cults are found (albeit much degraded) in the Northern New Hebrides, but Maui-tikitiki is the chief figure of Polynesian mythology who has found his way into the knowledge of the southern tribes. See John Layard, *Stone Men of Malekula*, Vol. I, pp. 205 ff.

" (b) The thief goes round and touches the hair of each one's head and says, opposite each, *Yakatumi basak uwas sana, mapa sana,* ' I am plucking the leaves of this cabbage plant of mine, and passing by this.' Having completed the circle and arrived at the *ikinan* he professes to put the cabbage leaves outside.

" (c) The thief goes round touching the ears of each individual, and opposite each he says *Yakesi nakakararey sana, mapa sana,* ' I am pulling this mushroom my food and passing by this one.' At the completion he behaves as before.

" (d) The thief goes round and takes hold of the arms of each individual and bends them over his knee as if breaking sugarcane, and opposite each says, *Yakeipui suk aruk sana, mapa sana,* ' I am breaking this sugarcane of mine to drink and passing by this.' He completes as before.

" (e) The thief goes round taking hold of the legs of each individual, as if pulling taro out of the ground, and opposite each he says, *Yakeivi basak-eri sana, mapa sana,* ' I am pulling up this taro-plant of mine and passing by this.' He finishes as before.

" (f) The thief now stands in the centre of the circle and stamping with his feet on the ground imitates the thud of coconuts falling. Those forming the circle cry out, *Sin fa ramesi napuei ?* ' Who is that pulling coconuts ? ' He replies, *Iau, yakamesi napuei,* ' It is I, who am pulling coconuts.' They then ask, *Ik urkurau paku ?* ' Where did you get in at ? ' He then goes round and trying to break the circle at each link says, *Yakurkurau i,* ' I got in here.' At each link they reply *Ikinan, ikinan,*[2] ' Sacred, sacred.' When he arrives at the weak place he breaks the circle and all scatter, he giving chase and trying to worry them. The one he catches has to take his place.

" Such are a few of the games on Tanna. They have many more too numerous to mention."

W. WATT.

---

[2] I have kept Mr. Watt's translation, but " taboo " would be better. It rather means, " You mustn't."

STUDIES IN PLAY AND GAMES

An Arno Press Collection

Appleton, Lilla Estelle. **A Comparative Study of the Play Activities of Adult Savages and Civilized Children.** 1910

Barker, Roger, Tamara Dembo and Kurt Lewin. **Frustration and Regression: An Experiment With Young Children.** 1941

Brewster, Paul G., editor. **Children's Games and Rhymes.** 1952

Buytendijk, F[rederick] J[acobus] J[ohannes]. **Wesen und Sinn des Spiels.** 1933

Culin, Stewart. **Chess and Playing-Cards.** 1898

Daiken, Leslie. **Children's Games Throughout the Year.** 1949

[Froebel, Friedrich]. **Mother's Songs, Games and Stories.** 1914

Glassford, Robert Gerald. **Application of a Theory of Games to the Transitional Eskimo Culture.** 1976

Gomme, Alice B. and Cecil J. Sharp, editors. **Children's Singing Games.** 1909/1912

Groos, Karl. **The Play of Animals.** 1898

Groos, Karl. **The Play of Man.** 1901

Lehman, Harvey C. and Paul A. Witty. **The Psychology of Play Activities.** 1927

MacLagan, Robert Craig, compiler. **The Games and Diversions of Argyleshire.** 1901

Markey, Frances V. **Imaginative Behavior of Preschool Children.** 1935

Roth, Walter E[dmund]. **Games, Sports and Amusements.** 1902

Sutton-Smith, Brian, editor. **A Children's Games Anthology.** 1976

Sutton-Smith, Brian, editor. **The Games of the Americas, Parts I and II.** 1976

Sutton-Smith, Brian, editor. **The Psychology of Play.** 1976

Van Alstyne, Dorothy. **Play Behavior and Choice of Play Materials of Pre-School Children.** 1932

Wells, H[erbert] G[eorge]. **Floor Games.** 1912

Wolford, Leah Jackson. **The Play-Party in Indiana.** 1959

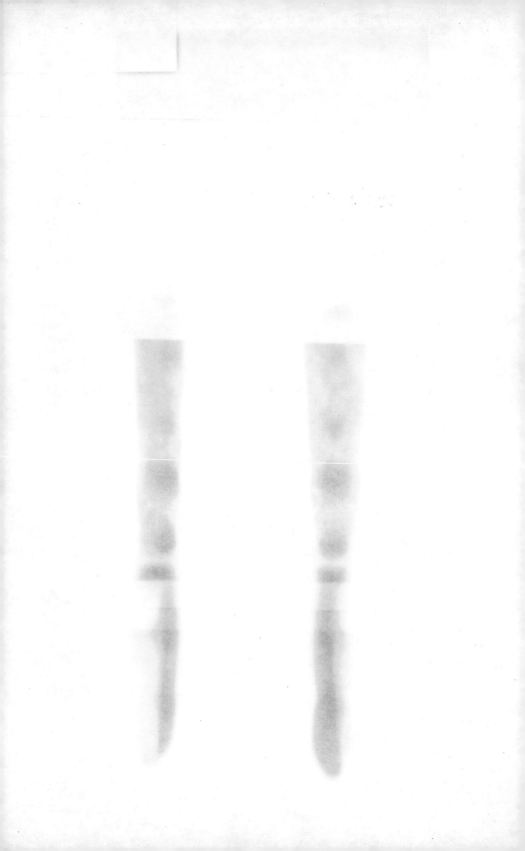